Designing the Editorial Experience

© 2014 Rockport Publishers

Text © 2014 Sue Apfelbaum and Juliette Cezzar

First published in the United States of America in 2014 by

Rockport Publishers, a member of
Quarto Publishing Group USA Inc.
100 Cummings Center
Suite 406-L
Beverly, Massachusetts 01915-6101
Telephone: (978) 282-9590
Fax: (978) 283-2742
www.rockpub.com

Visit RockPaperInk.com to share your opinions, creations, and
passion for design.

10 9 8 7 6 5 4 3 2

ISBN: 978-1-59253-895-9

Digital edition published in 2014

eISBN: 978-1-62788-049-7

Library of Congress Cataloging-in-Publication Data available

Design: Juliette Cezzar / e.a.d.
Cover illustration: Damien Correll

Designing the Editorial Experience

A Primer for Print, Web, and Mobile

Sue Apfelbaum   Juliette Cezzar

Rockport Publishers
100 Cummings Center, Suite 406L
Beverly, MA 01915

rockpub.com • rockpaperink.com

Contents

Case Studies & Interviews

The newsstand and the Newsstand

Preface

When we were first presented with the opportunity to create this book, it seemed perfectly obvious that it would be a collaboration between a designer and an editor. We first met in 2005, as an editor (Sue) and art director/designer (Juliette) for *RES* magazine, a publication that, over its decade of existence, moved from covering the world of digital filmmaking to a more general magazine that covered music, art, film, video, and new media. The magazine's edge was that it came packaged with a DVD, an idea that sounds impossibly quaint several years later. Despite having a unique niche, the magazine failed to realize its online potential and folded in late 2006 as YouTube was taking off.

Through all of this, we both learned an immeasurable amount and moved through many successive projects and roles. We also remained determined readers and enthusiasts for the new ways of reading and communicating that arose in the seven years since our time working together, meeting for many conversations about the changes that have come about for writers, editors, and designers. Putting this book together now has been an enormous challenge, partly because as a field, editorial design is in near-constant transition. In the time that we have been writing this book, a half-dozen or more well-known publications have gone through major redesigns or gone digital only; web type and mobile design have gone beyond beta status; readers and content producers have turned their time and resources toward longer-form story-telling; and the advertising and branding world has invested more in editorial and original content as a way to reach audiences in the current age.

This attention to content should not come as a surprise. As the divide between the digital and the physical narrows, it becomes apparent that our need for these forms of communication transcends technological limitations and economic forces. We need to share what we know and what we've seen with each other—in the present, the past, and in the future.

A note about this book

This book is written for the advanced design student, the editorial designer who would like to move beyond print, and the interaction designer who already has some expertise in creating branding, advertising, or product experiences online and would like to move toward shaping editorial content. The Elements chapter is mostly intended to bring design students or non-designers up to speed, while the Interviews, coming from many different viewpoints, seek to deepen the conversation and open up questions about where the discipline is headed and what it may require from a designer. In between are the Case Studies, presenting ways in which various publications do what they do well. And for all audiences, this book seeks to drive home the idea that making something of value transcends categories such as *digital* and *print*, *designer* and *author*, and is the result of empathy for a reader combined with the desire to create beautiful and moving experiences.

Introduction

What Is Editorial Design?

Editorial design is a discipline of communication design that specializes in publications of a serial, periodical nature, which are unified by a distinct editorial or creative vision, are produced at a predetermined frequency, and are made available by subscription and/or strategic distribution.

A more tangible way to define editorial design would be to say it is the design of magazines, newspapers, and journals. But what is a magazine, newspaper, or journal in an era where the form reading takes is not tied to a single medium such as paper? Is a magazine defined by its physical properties or by its content? Is a blog any different from an online magazine? And if we were to decide that a magazine or newspaper is something that exists in print only, what would we call the periodical reading experiences being created for the web or for devices such as smartphones and tablets?

After leaving his post as the director of digital design at *The New York Times*, Khoi Vinh wrote an entreaty on his blog called "Where Are All the Ed Ex Designers?" (Subtraction.com, October 27, 2011). He was referring to what he perceived to be a shortage of designers who can both "create a highly effective, truly immersive architecture around the way real users interact with software and . . . know how to enhance and even maximize an audience's understanding of published content . . . [and are] comfortable working with writers and editors to help shape what we read." At the same time, he recognized that there would be an increasing need for designers with abilities in both areas. Smartphones, for example, are used as much, if not more, for reading than for communicating. A designer who applies the rigorous thinking that comes from user experience to editorial experiences is a true "ed ex designer." In Vinh's formulation, ed ex designers have been weaned off of thinking of magazines and newspapers as print objects first, that are followed by

a digital offshoot. He writes: "You must understand users and their expectations, and you must also understand authors and their expectations, and somehow, by hook or by crook, you must reconcile these wildly divergent worldviews into a single, coherent whole that looks and feels effortless." All editorial designers would benefit from seeing themselves as designers of editorial experiences.

Just as the phrase itself is slippery to define, editorial design is not easy to do well. The good news is that, every time we publish—whether it's by the minute, hour, day, week, month, or season—we get a fresh opportunity to do it again and even better the next time. Still, periodicals are both of a moment and indefinite. The content could have a limited shelf life, or it could resonate with readers and last for the long haul. With constant competition for readers' attention spans, design cannot simply fill in a template with new words and images for each issue. Strong editorial design has always acknowledged its content, its context, and its readers, and is responsive to the ways that audiences engage with it. And as time goes on, designers have to consider the editorial experience of the contemporary, social reader, who has a new set of habits and patterns that move across platforms and across time.

In that spirit, we'll talk about what it means to design for the editorial experience, which goes far beyond arranging type, graphics, and images on a page. We'll talk to people on both the design and editorial fronts—and digital strategists, too—about what is constant and what is changing in the field, and show examples of the best editorial design being produced today, many of them across multiple platforms. We will explore who reads the content, how it takes shape, what forms the content takes on, and offer a primer on the elements of editorial design that result in rich, thoughtful, and rewarding editorial experiences.

Who Reads It?
The Reading Experience

Designing the editorial experience begins and ends with the reader. There are two somewhat contradictory thoughts to keep in mind when designing. First, the way that people read at the micro level is fundamentally the same as what it was 100 years ago. Readers' preferences and delights do not change according to the whims of designers or content producers, and they read in a similar way whether it's a paragraph in a novel, on a wall, or in a chat bubble.

Second, with the vast availability of meaningful content everywhere, at all times, reading habits have changed. Many people are alarmed that the tablet or mobile phone will replace the printed page, but really what has happened is more complicated than that. Readers have not maintained their old habits, simply switching out their paper magazines and newspapers for iPads. Instead, everything from how they discover content, to how they sort, save, and consume it, has changed. Most of all, their expectations have changed. If you can discover an article on a desktop computer, tablet, or phone, you fully expect to also be able to read it right there, without any friction. You may also start reading on one device and expect to continue on another. You may want more information about how far along you are in the content and how it relates to other things. These are really important cues that a sensitive designer responds to.

For an avid reader, the present moment brings an embarrassment of riches. Good, thoughtful written and visual content is abundant and often free. There are also a number of platforms that have been developed that help readers find, prioritize, and consume content. Flipboard, Feedly, and Byline are some of the current tools that allow readers to subscribe via RSS (Rich Site Summary, though also called Really Simple Syndication), a standardized XML format that many sites use to export their content. Many articles or essays make their way to readers through feeds and social sharing through Twitter and Facebook, platforms that are developing their own news readers as well. While the reader is often presented as a hunter looking for good material, it may be more accurate to think of the reader as a giant whale with its baleen spread wide, filtering through a rich stream of thoughts and images.

So where does this leave print? While many print publications have closed down or gone digital only, there's been a wave of new print publications that are more beautiful and thoughtful than ever. That ocean of online content has changed what readers expect from a print magazine. Frequency, affordability, and immediacy have given way to careful curation, higher print quality, and more book-like experiences. Readers approach printed publications (and, to some extent, tablet magazines) differently, hoping instead for an uninterrupted immersion in the ideas and images laid out within.

Who Makes It?
Staff and Workflow

Publishing has always been something that could be accomplished by a single person or a coordinated army of hundreds, with visibly different results. While many traditional publications, in the name of efficiency, still quarantine design as a last-step dressing before production, they are not the publications that will survive well into this century. Thriving and influential publications at every scale integrate designers into every step of the process, and encourage communication and rapport between the creation of content and form-giving. This is, of course, not new—designers have often sat alongside editors, and the quality of the final production has always mapped itself to the quality of that relationship. But now, more than ever, roles themselves will blur, especially since publications have faced ever-tighter budgets. Many publications are made by people wearing multiple hats, and designers that are limited in the scope of what they do may find themselves shut out of all but the largest, most traditional contexts.

The same generalization is also starting to happen in the making of publications across multiple platforms. When the iPad first came out, for example, publishers made their initial tests by temporarily hiring people from outside, with money set aside for research and development. As publishing on these platforms is becoming the norm, continually using specially earmarked resources is not sustainable. For people just starting to publish, learning or hiring this expertise is usually out of reach. Increasingly, the same number of people with the same amount of time and financial resources has to sort and publish the content across as many platforms as they can with what they have.

Any publication created, modified, and edited by multiple people has always had a system for managing and tracking content, whether using a paper system, shared drives, or enterprise software. In the mid-2000s, bloggers popularized the use of web content management systems, especially WordPress. For any publication seeking a content management system (CMS), there are dozens to choose from, though all have their strengths and idiosyncrasies, and often any publishing operation finds itself duplicating work across several different systems and software.

These days, you're likely to find an editor or writer using Microsoft Word, a print designer using Adobe InDesign, and a web producer or interaction designer using a CMS for web and mobile. As these distinctions between roles fall away, these multiple systems will fall away as well. New editorial products such as Editorially (see our interview with Mandy Brown, page 126) promise to break the divide between writing and editing and marking up copy with HTML tags. Adobe has been making efforts to bring editors, writers, and digital designers into InDesign through products such as InCopy, while expanding designers' abilities to export to multiple digital formats through XML

export and its Digital Publishing Suite. Enterprising writers and programmers are using versioning systems such as GitHub for documentation and revision. Large organizations such as newspapers tend to use custom enterprise software for both the editing and publishing process, though these are notoriously difficult to change and usually not very user friendly. At the time of this writing, we are a long way from a coherent system that can move content from a writer's mind to printed and digital pages without cutting, pasting, and importing. Each publication—depending on its size, its habits, and the programming mettle of its staff—is forced to create and re-create its publishing systems on a continual basis, using and learning what they can to best serve the reader.

Roles and responsibilities

There are as many different scenarios as there are publications. Following are some common roles found in medium- to large-scale publications. In smaller publications, multiple roles will fall on a single individual, while in others, multiple people may share the same title.

The **editor in chief** is responsible for overseeing the quality of the publication as a whole and often serves as its public face.

The **managing editor** oversees the publication internally and is responsible for staffing, scheduling, and resourcing.

An **editor** assigns and oversees writing from staff or freelance contributors. An editor's scope may be narrow or broad, depending on the size of the editorial staff, and could be specialized by subject (e.g., sports, arts, music) or length (features, front of book).

A **copy editor** is attentive to the mechanics of grammar and punctuation and ensures consistency of style and voice.

A **fact checker** or research editor verifies facts that appear in the text.

A **photo editor** sources and chooses photographs to be used with stories.

A **creative director** is responsible for the quality of the design as a whole and is often part of the team that makes major decisions for the publication.

A **design director** often oversees a specific area of design. For example, some publications still have separate design directors for print and digital.

An **art director** makes day-to-day design decisions, sources and manages illustration and photography, and is often the contact point for the editorial team.

A **graphics editor** is responsible for the production of informational graphics and illustrations.

A **print designer** designs the print publication to the content, often using preexisting guidelines.

A **typesetter** or paginator adapts the design for production in cases where a publication has a proprietary content management system.

A **web producer** adapts and inputs written and visual content for the web.

An **information architect** spatially maps content to web and mobile pages.

A **content strategist** works with editors to plan how content is published, structured, and consumed over time.

A **user experience (UX) designer** is responsible for how a reader navigates and consumes online content.

A **front-end developer** writes code for pages, features, and products that determine what a user sees and how they interact with it in real time.

A **back-end developer** writes code for underlying systems used for content management and delivery to users.

A **publisher** oversees the publication as a business, ensuring that resources are in place for everything from staffing to fulfillment.

Elements of Editorial Design

Formats

Successful editorial design begins with understanding and selecting the most appropriate format (or formats) for publishing your content. Before the twenty-first century, most periodicals existed in a single medium—content was either printed or published digitally on a blog, as a PDF, or in an email newsletter. Today, it's just as likely for a publication's material to appear simultaneously in print, on a smartphone, on a tablet, and on a website sized for a desktop monitor. The type of content, publication frequency, and expectations of readers all greatly influence what, where, and how we publish. Just as there isn't simply one way to print, screens are not one size fits all. While technically infinite in variety, print formats communicate an array of content and often respond to the limitations of printing, distribution, and display. And while screens may become more standardized, differences in physical size, ratio, and screen resolution (pixels per inch) present dozens of possible impressions.

From the earliest to the latest innovations in publishing, here are some of the more popular types and formats for distributing editorial information.

Broadsheet

29.5 × 23.5 in. (749 x 597 mm)

The first broadsheet newspaper, *Courante uyt Italien, Duytslandt, &c.*, was published in Amsterdam in 1618. Prior to this, news was usually relayed in quarto size, similar to today's magazines, and the broadsheet format was used for official government notices. The broadsheet retained its importance and gained popularity after a 1712 British newspaper tax that was levied by the page. It is now the most popular format for disseminating printed news.

Berliner/Midi

12.4 × 18.5 in. (315 × 470 mm)

The Berliner format is narrower and shorter than the broadsheet but shorter and slightly wider than the tabloid format. It is more popular in Europe and Asia than in North America. *Le Monde*, *El Pais*, and *The Guardian* are all printed at the Berliner size.

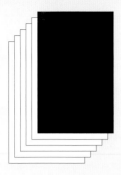

Tabloid/Compact

16.9 × 11 in. (430 × 280 mm)

Long favored by alternative and sensational newspapers, the tabloid adopted its name from a pharmaceutical innovation that compressed messy powders into tablet form. "Compact" generally refers to a broadsheet-quality newspaper printed in a tabloid size. Many magazines, such as early *Interview* and *Rolling Stone*, have published in a tabloid format. Fashion and luxury magazines such as *V* benefit from the maximized effect of the oversized glossy.

Magazine

8.38 × 10.88 in. (213 × 276 mm)

Many large-circulation and hobby magazines have settled on this "standard" magazine size in order to minimize printing and mailing costs, as well as to fit on newsstands. Subtle variations, such as going slightly bigger or smaller than the norm, can help these publications stand out. Consider *National Geographic*, with its signature 7.13 × 10.25-inch (180 × 260 mm) trim size.

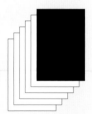

Journal

6 × 9 in. (152 × 229 mm)

Usually a clear marker of a literary journal or scientific publication, the journal size lends itself to easy readability for text-heavy content. Quarterlies also tend toward the smaller journal format, differentiating themselves from monthly and weekly periodicals.

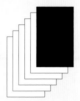

Digest

5.38 × 8.38 in. (137 × 213 mm)

In the twentieth century, *Reader's Digest*, *TV Guide*, and *Jet* made the digest size a very popular format. In the days before digital cable provided on-screen program listings, *TV Guide* once had 20 million subscribers. It was also used for science-fiction periodicals and comics. *Reader's Digest* is currently the largest paid circulation magazine in the world.

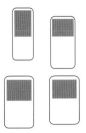

Basic feature phone

Internet-enabled mobile phones, also called "basic feature phones," are the only connection to the internet for millions of people around the world. Because they have a longer battery life, they are more functional in areas that don't have consistent access to wired electricity.

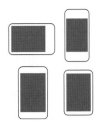

Smartphone

The vast majority of mobile phone subscribers in the United States use smartphones. At the time of this writing, about half of these phones operate on the Android operating system, a third are iPhones, and 15 percent use another operating system. Higher-resolution screens made by Apple and Samsung in 2010 made the smartphone a comfortable device for reading.

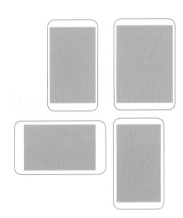

Mini-tablet

When Amazon's Kindle Fire was released in late 2011 with a 6 × 3.5 inch (152 × 89 mm) screen, it became immediately obvious that both the smartphone and the tablet weren't ideal reading devices for long-form text. Google, Samsung, and Apple quickly followed with their own versions of the 7-inch tablet, which allows for easy reading of larger text while holding the device with one hand, much as one would hold a paperback.

Tablet

Before Apple's iPad was released in April 2010, tablet computers had mostly been failures. Initially, Apple was widely ridiculed for introducing what many people thought was an unnecessary device. Within two years, 100 million iPads had been sold, followed by Kindle Fire with 7 million, Samsung's tablets with 5.1 million, and Barnes and Noble's Nook with 5 million. The iPad distinguished itself as a device for the consumption of content and benefited enormously from the iOS apps and infrastructure developed for the iPhone since 2007.

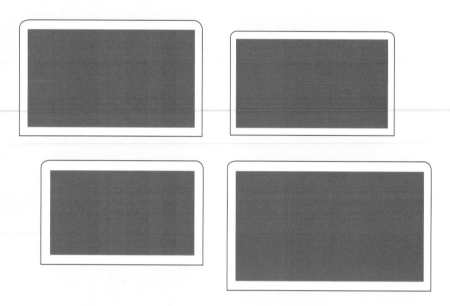

Laptop

As of January 2013, more people access the internet through laptops than through any other device, as evidenced by screen-size statistics gathered by Google and other organizations. (Display resolutions of 1366 × 768 surpassed 1024 × 768 as the most common screen size in mid-2012.) This ubiquity, combined with the additional screen space, makes it one of the most important formats for both browsing and reading.

Desktop

While both the industry and consumers in the last few years have been focused on tablets as the new medium for reading, surveys have shown that the majority of people who read books on screens read them on laptops and desktops, and usually while at work. The additional screen space also allows for many different types of content to appear at once and to have a greater hierarchy between design elements—a luxury not afforded to smaller screen formats.

Time

Time is everything for a periodical publication. Publishing frequency dictates how much time goes into designing and editing each issue and also reflects how readers will ultimately digest it. Newspaper sections and website verticals communicate through their design whether an article is fresh and of the moment (i.e., short and quick to read, produced within the day or week) or broader in scope (i.e., longer form, more substantial in text and imagery, created well in advance). Pick up a newspaper from today or twenty years ago, and you will find within it articles that were put together over weeks or months alongside smaller pieces that came in just before deadline, and sections that build from week to week. Along with the proliferation of web publishing and social media has emerged the idea that the same publication can publish in different increments simultaneously, turning what were weekly or monthly periodicals also into daily or hourly publishers for bite-size, more timely content. At the same time, continuously publishing sites are starting to anthologize, offering weekly, monthly, and yearly roundups of their best material, even spinning off into tablet apps and print.

Design communicates intent in two important ways: through content strategy and identity. Content strategy is the continuous design of the system by which content is distributed over time. Or, to put it more simply, content strategy dictates what's going to appear when, and according to what criteria. Print publications have always strategized content, holding articles for future publications and prioritizing the ones that will be published. On screen, there are other questions to be answered: How many blog posts will be published each day? Will they be posted when available or at specific times? Is the time that something is published the only consideration for its visual hierarchy? How frequently will content appear in a Twitter stream or a push notification from a mobile app? And, for many publications, how will breaking news affect the rhythm that has been set in place?

Identity becomes critical when a publication is a collection of transmissions that do not appear together in the same place and the same time. What will always travel with the content? Does the content have a specific editorial voice that is distinguishable from content coming from other publications? And when content with different time schedules appears in the same place, how does it visually identify its character? Here are the most common frequencies and their design implications.

One minute

When publications started to make their first forays onto the internet in the 1990s and 2000s, it was not immediately apparent what their websites would be for. Most used the web to advertise their publications or offer samples of content, a model that is still functional today. Meanwhile, larger publications began to think of how the web could eventually be the primary format for delivering both content and paid advertising without involving the printed publication at all. For these publications, short-form, frequently updated content meant more frequent visits and, more generally, timeliness: the opportunity to be the first to report on or review a recent event or development.

When the social networking service Twitter became popular in 2007, it was met with both enthusiasm and derision. Those who saw it as a service disconnected from other outlets were incredulous that users would use the 140 available characters to announce what they were eating for breakfast to their followers and that anyone would care about these little bits of information. Savvy publications and news outlets, however, quickly saw its potential to take the short-form content they were already writing and give it another distribution channel that builds community, cements identity, and drives traffic to websites.

In 2010, Twitter went through a redesign that allowed a single tweet to carry almost a dozen different elements. Already the visual identity of the publication was carried through its icon, its name was prominently featured, and short copy could precede a link. After the redesign, the actual headline of an article, teaser copy, a small image, the identity and title of a sub-brand, and a summary of social interaction with that content (sharing, comments) were bundled with the tweet, posing new design considerations for each of these components, and distinguishing self-containing tweets from links to articles.

Many publications post longer-form content several times a day, depending on the number of writers and a predetermined schedule, if there is one. The article post is by any measure the unit online, and the article page the most visited, since it's where a user lands after clicking on a link elsewhere.

An expanded tweet for a *Huffington Post* article gives Twitter readers a preview, pulling in the title, thumbnail, summary, and attribution from the webpage's embedded metadata.

Article-post pages offer several design challenges. First, two posts might not share the same elements. One might have only a headline, byline, date stamp, and article copy, while others may include (or not) comments, videos, sharing prompts, images, slideshows, subtitles, pull quotes, information graphics, tags, credits, and captions. Second, because they tend to be the landing page for a new reader, they also need to point the reader toward other content and give the reader some sense of location. Third, all of these elements need to be visually considered in a way that makes the page identifiable. With so many elements pushed into a small space, one post page can easily look like another. Finally, the sheer number of elements on a page can crowd the reading experience by shrinking the space allotted for the article itself.

Front pages of daily print newspapers *USA TODAY, The New York Times,* and *the Guardian*

One day

The daily newspaper is by far the most familiar and thoughtful example of the transmission of daily content. Despite their decline over the past decade, there are still thousands of daily papers printed that sell hundreds of millions of copies every day. Daily papers are almost always printed on broadsheet, Berliner, or tabloid-size paper, and the primary design consideration is usually the relationship of articles to one another rather than the appearance of any one article. A glance at the front page of a newspaper will inform the reader not only of what has happened the day before, but the relative importance of each event both to other current events as well as past events.

When *The New York Times* website started getting traction in 1996, it would update the content once daily at midnight, reflecting what would be printed in the next day's newspaper. Over the next decade, however, this daily rhythm was gradually broken. Continuous news items started to appear, and in 2005, the newspaper started publishing blogs as well, with some of the content spilling over into the physical paper.

Still, for many daily publications, there is a sense of responsibility to display the "news of the day" on screen as it has been represented in print for more than 100 years, even if it is more loosely interpreted as the "news of the moment." At the same time, a daily newspaper, both on paper and online, is always aware of its responsibility to record history as much as its responsibility to broadcast the present. With news breaking down into smaller and smaller increments, many of which will disappear when no longer linked to, the design of a home page or front page becomes an even more meaningful artifact.

One week

The weekly magazine used to be the only way to publish timely visual content, and high-circulation mainstays such as *People* and *US Weekly* reflect that history. Paradoxically, the week is also a good time span for text-heavy reflection on current or ongoing events, as evidenced in the popularity of publications such as the *Economist* and the *New Yorker*. And in between, the week is a favorite time span for industry news (*Advertising Age*, *Publishers Weekly*, *Billboard*). Many newspapers also publish weekly magazines on Sundays in conjunction with their daily content, including *The New York Times Magazine*, *WSJ* magazine, and *Parade*, which is distributed by more than 600 daily newspapers, including the *Boston Globe*, the *San Francisco Chronicle*, and the *Washington Post*.

A successful weekly publication, like a successful daily publication, works within a relatively rigid design and content grid, but unlike the daily publication, has no implied mandate to represent the week itself. The result is a design that is more strictly defined and more recognizable than most monthly magazines. Still, this does not mean that all issues of a weekly magazine look the same; the variations are just concentrated within the photography or illustrations rather than the overall design, leading to striking covers and commissioned art within the pages of the issue.

One month

The first general-interest magazine, *The Gentleman's Magazine*, was published on a monthly basis from 1731 until 1922. It derived its name from the French word for "storehouse," which was in turn derived from the Arabic *makhazin*, which meant "treasuries." The vast majority of consumer periodicals still publish on a monthly basis, maintaining both reader and advertiser interest alongside a sustainable work schedule for writing, design, and production.

Two months

A monthly magazine has its limitations. The cost per issue must remain low in order to remain affordable to readers, limiting the budget for size, design, and commissioned artwork and photography. A handful of magazines, such as *Brides*, have moved to a bimonthly format in the past few years. These moves have been accompanied by a more prominent online presence, making the printed publication more of an experience and less a vehicle for all of the brand's content. Many high-production magazines, such as *V*, *Cook's Illustrated*, and *Frieze*, have always been published bimonthly.

Three months

A wide variety of publications choose to print on a quarterly basis, from literary collections such as *Lapham's Quarterly* to *Eye*, a London–based graphic design magazine, to *Make*, for the technically crafty. The period lends itself to publications from organizations that do more than produce the magazine, so production values vary widely. Most quarterlies have a smaller trim size.

Six months

Biannual publications can take on either the high production value of bimonthly magazines, the minimal outlay of quarterly magazines and journals, or both. Biannual publications tend toward the greatest degree of specialty, and generally aim for a small and specific audience. The long lead time produces some of the best and most experimental publication design for periodicals, and publishing biannually doesn't make a high cover price restrictive for a dedicated reader. A large number of journals also publish biannually.

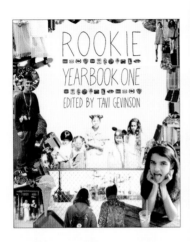  

One year

Annual magazines are now rare, but still serve an
important function, whether to summarize a year's
activities for an organization (such as the *American
Alpine Journal*) or to host a collective making by students (such as the Finnish *Kevätpörriäinen*). An annual
publication both attempts to encapsulate the year at
the same time that it takes on many of the characteris-
tics of a book, despite being a periodical publication.

Identity

A periodical is really a strange kind of container. A reader leafs through an issue, and upon receiving the next issue, refers to it as being alike, even though the content is *100 percent different*. The aspect of design that makes this possible is identity, which is tied into every aspect of the design, from typography to layout to the selection of art, and first asserts its presence in the writing.

Identity is a little easier to put into context when you consider that the first newspapers were really handwritten letters. You knew from both the handwriting and the syntax whether or not the writer was to be trusted. The visual identity of a publication, combined with its writing style, determines the credibility and authority of the work. This is easiest when there is only one person designing and one person writing, since the hand of each will always be consistent. Most publications, however, are designed by several people on an ongoing basis and include the voices of many writers. Both a style guide and an identity system are needed if the visual expression and the textual voice are to be identifiable as being from a particular publication.

It may be useful here to zoom out and talk about what identity means in general and what it aims to do. Identity design is often seen as synonymous with logo-making. A mark, however, is only one part of an identity system, and to conflate the two would be the same as mistaking a pair of shoes for a sense of style. While an identity system is increasingly difficult to execute well, its purpose is easy to define: marking something as being part of a group, and differentiating that thing from the other members of the group. A quick look at style in other contexts gives us some clues. You listen to some music, and you say *aha, that is jazz.* You listen a little closer, and if you know about jazz music, you might say *that's Wynton Marsalis.* The rhythms and arrangement suggest jazz; the differences between that piece and other jazz pieces identifies a specific musician.

The same is true for any kind of publication, and it is difficult to do on every platform and in every iteration. The loosening of restrictions on the web with the introduction of web fonts, larger screens, and dynamic web interfaces were met with a sigh of relief, only to be followed by the gaining importance of the mobile web, with its tiny screens and intolerance for large file sizes. Maintaining identity—where a publication is recognizable at a glance—is easy on a large surface, but increasingly difficult when similar decisions have to be made in response to the common design problems. Following are the ways that a publication maintains its identity.

- Structural
- Graphic
- Informational
- Flexible
- Dynamic

Dwell magazine's identity redesign proposal by Rational Beauty/Jeanette Abbink, 2013.

Style and Voice

Writing style is possibly the most important element for maintaining the identity of a publication. Writing is often pulled away from its official source into RSS feeds, email in-boxes, and personal aggregators such as the Flipboard app. The writing style of one person, or even a tightly coordinated group, may be identifiable, but bringing the writing of many people toward a similar voice requires planning and a certain degree of design, collated into a set of standards called a house style. Some style guides, such as the *Chicago Manual of Style*, the *MLA Handbook*, or the *AP Stylebook*, serve as a basis for many publications and publishing houses, but are then modified to suit their individual preferences. Many large publications have their own stylebook that they update on a regular basis. Some are private, some are published in written form, and some, such as that of the *Guardian*, are public and maintained online.

Stylebooks are usually extensive and inseparable from the editorial work done at a publication. The more idiosyncratic the style choices, the more similar articles within a publication feel when placed together. Newer words such as *email* and *website* will also vary according to a preestablished style and are usually good indicators of editorial consistency.

Typography

Typography does not conform to various screens as easily as writing does, but it does express itself at every scale and can appear in all of the platforms directly governed by the publication. It's the most important characteristic, after writing style, to establish identity. Choosing distinctive type puts less pressure on writing style, art, and layout to carry out the identity. While choosing type that could be described as "quirky" would quickly tire your reader, choosing type that is ubiquitous means the reader soon forgets where he is reading an article.

In larger formats, such as printed magazines, playfulness with type for titles, headers, and pull quotes can also be a way to establish a unique identity. More reliable, however, is setting and clearly communicating guidelines for proportioning this type. A custom type treatment may not travel to a smaller device, but a simple proportion and spacing can always be kept consistent, regardless of platform.

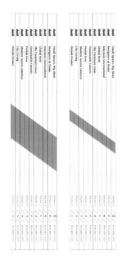

Art

A consistent eye in directing and selecting illustrations and photographs goes further than any rearrangement of type to set the character and attitude of an article or publication. Photography, in particular, holds the power to connect with a particular audience in ways that can't be achieved through writing and typography alone. It also is the most flexible: An issue of a periodical with a particular theme can, through its images, create a completely different environment for reading while still maintaining the structural integrity of the identity.

Art also travels with written content, but on mobile devices, it is often overwhelmed by the writing or quickly pushed upward or aside by the reader. Large images also can take much longer to download on a mobile device with a slow connection, so a responsive design is likely to do away with all but the most necessary images. Still, the fewer the images, the more important the direction and selection becomes, and the more quickly art needs to make an impression.

Layout

Of all the different ways to express and enforce identity, one-off custom layouts are probably the weakest. But a consistently applied grid, especially in print, goes a long way in affirming the character of the publication. The use of space can also be a differentiator. Text-heavy publications, such as *The Economist* tend toward packed columns on every page, while more image-heavy publications will have both more white space and a less perceptible grid.

Whether text heavy or not, the structure of the design directs the habits of the reader, who becomes accustomed to a particular rhythm when interacting with the publication. That rhythm of reading is an essential part of its identity and is impacted by both content choices (how long or short pieces are, the authorial voice) as well as how the writing is arranged and broken up. Reading in multiple columns feels very different from reading in one column, because reading short lines creates a different rhythm than reading long lines. This experience is a critical part of the identity of a publication.

Anatomy

A positive editorial experience is built on the consistent practice of naming and handling elements within a design. If elements are sufficiently distinct, a reader learns quickly to find and identify the information to guide what is being read and how it relates to other content from the same publication, whether in the same issue or over time.

A study of the anatomy of editorial design across platforms reveals why and how interactive and mobile platforms are challenging. The total number of potential elements more than doubles, while space shrinks. It is far easier to distinguish six elements rather than twelve, and twelve different things, presented slightly differently, are guaranteed to make a layout look cluttered and hopeless. At the same time, strong decision making about the appearance and behavior of each element strengthens the identity of the publication.

Here we will start with descriptions of elements that are present in both static and interactive editorial designs and move toward additional elements found only in interactive work. Some of the elements here are paired with the lingo that is often used when working on layouts. The lingo is deliberately misspelled, which is useful to attract the attention of proofreaders or when searching through documents, as they are often put in as placeholders as copy is being written or finalized.

1 Opening Remarks

When Animal Spirits Attack

Despite one meltdown after another, the denizens of high finance continue to make reckless bets. Is biology to blame? By Drake Bennett

Traders are encouraged to take on more risk even as their hormones push them toward recklessness

Spread from *Bloomberg Businessweek*, June 6–10, 2012

1. Kicker

A kicker is a short tag that helps the reader understand the context of what will follow. It usually indicates either a subject category (such as "arts" or "music") or type of writing (such as "opinion" or "essay"). For a habitual reader, kickers also link articles that would otherwise have no obvious connection through either headlines or photographs.

2. Headline or Hed

The headline is almost always the largest element presented on an article page. For print publications, headlines are often written to predetermined lengths dictated by the design, while online, headlines are carefully crafted so that they can be found when readers search for particular content. Headlines also get removed from their accompanying layouts and images, so a headline that could be a clever pun when combined with an image can completely fall flat when decontextualized to a search listing. For publications that publish on multiple platforms, this dilemma often results in publishing the same article with different headlines.

3. Subhead or Dek

A subhead can be a phrase below a headline, a few sentences, or even a question. Its purpose is to clarify and contextualize the headline so that the reader knows whether to invest in the body of the article or move on. Subheads are usually less prominent than headlines but significantly prioritized over body copy. Some publications, such as *The New York Times*, rarely use subheads in print and almost never use them online. The *Economist*, however, uses a long subhead combined with a short headline for almost every article, and the combination is an important part of its editorial and visual identity.

4. Lead-in or Lede

The lead-in or lede introduces a story to further entice the reader to commit to reading the article. While strong writing is the best way to distinguish a lede, a visual boost is helpful, in part because short sets of sentences are often read without implied commitment. The lede is part of the body text and should be obvious as such. If it ends up looking like another subhead, a reader may skip it and be puzzled by an article that seems to start in the middle of a thought.

5. Byline

The byline indicates who wrote the story, and where photographs are significant, it will indicate the photographer as well. For some publications, columns, or articles, the authors or photographers are a bigger draw than the subject, which may not be very distinct. In other cases, the authorship is secondary, and may not even be listed, or it may be shared. Whatever the relationship, the design has a responsibility to present it in a way that best fits the publication and the piece.

Spread from *Vanity Fair Italia*, May 15, 2013

6. Body

Body copy is the candy in the wrapper. Once reading is under way, the task of the designer is to make reading as comfortable as possible, stopping and punctuating at appropriate points. The challenge is that once these conditions have been fulfilled, it's difficult to be distinctive, especially for publications that do not have the luxury of commissioning custom typography.

7. Pull quote

Not all publications use pull quotes, but when done well, they can be a very useful tool to both draw a reader into an article and punctuate the reader's rhythm, highlighting key points. Pull quotes are often several times larger than body copy, offering visual hierarchy on continuing pages or scrolls without titles and subheads. When overused, however, they can clutter or disjoint the reading experience.

10. Credit

Every image must be paired with a credit that indicates where the image came from. These are usually the smallest elements on a page, and are often set in all caps or even sideways (alongside the image or in the gutter) to distinguish from other short pieces of text. In some cases, it makes more sense visually for the credit to follow the caption instead of creating an additional style.

11. Folio

A folio is a printed page number, and may be accompanied by the name of the publication, its date, a kicker, section name, article name, or author name. The purpose of a folio is to allow a reader to find an article referenced in a table of contents or a citation in another publication. Folios do not need to appear on every page—always avoid placing them over art or advertising.

8. Art

"Art" is a term generally used to refer to commissioned illustration and photography. In some cases, as with a photo essay or information graphic, the art is the content. In all other cases, the art serves one of two purposes: enticing the reader to engage with the content, or demonstrating something in the content that the reader would like to see. For more, see "Elements: Art" on page 38.

9. Caption

Not all art needs to be captioned, but where captions are used well, they either illuminate something not obvious in the image or present commentary that echoes sentiments in the article body. Captions need to be clearly connected to the images they are associated with, which can be a challenge to differentiate with other short pieces of copy, such as credits or similarly sized pull quotes.

12. Publication time and/or date

While printed material is bundled according to date, online content is often divorced from context, and a publication date is essential to determine its recency. Breaking news is particularly time sensitive, because readers often look for the latest update for an unfolding situation. While most articles on the web find a date stamp or date and time stamp sufficient, relative descriptions of time are sometimes called for.

13. Share tools

For content on the open web, most readers arrive through links shared by friends, family, or the publications themselves. While the specific tools change continuously, share tools are critical to retaining and increasing readership, especially on mobile platforms where copying and pasting a link is more difficult than on a desktop or laptop computer. Share tools are a useful measure of interest, too. The analytics provide the publisher with data about which articles are shared, along with how and when.

An article page for *The New York Times* Well blog

14. Subscription tools

Dedicated readers of multiple publications often subscribe to them through electronic feeds. A feed reader works much like email: bringing in content from multiple sources and showing whether they have been read or not. Subscribing can be especially helpful to readers who want to stay informed, regardless of whether your publication posts often or sporadically. Not having the tools visible doesn't prevent someone from adding the link to their feed reader, but having them there does encourage subscription.

15. Links for previous and next articles

Previous and next links can help a reader avoid returning to an index page and keep them with the publication. These links can be as minimal as arrows or as elaborate as full titles and subtitles, and are expected to lead to content immediately published before or after. On mobile platforms, a left or right swipe often stands in for the same function, though the button may still be present.

16. Tags

Tags, metadata, and keywords are almost always present behind the scenes of a properly coded site, because they help with both search and accessibility. Tags were undeniably popular in the Web 2.0 era, rightfully lauded for their ability to categorize and connect content under multiple categories. Over the years, however, analytics have shown that social media is the champion referrer and the overt presence of tags (such as tag clouds) has mostly gone away.

17. Navigation and taxonomy

It's important to provide readers with navigation, not just to help them find their way but to also show what's discoverable. Until recently, almost all complex websites placed their navigation and taxonomy in a fixed order at the top of a page, with drop-downs menus for each category. As with tags, analytics have repeatedly shown that these navigational links are not used as often as expected, and links at the top of a page are awkward for mobile users. More contemporary layouts now tuck these indexes into a drawer to the left or right, or drop them down from a single link.

18. Related links

Related links are second only to social media in driving traffic, but their number and location determine when and how they are effective. For some publications, especially news publications, links that refer to previous content on the same subject is the most successful, while for others, readers look for the most emailed, most clicked on, or most currently engaged content.

19. Comments

When well executed and moderated, comments can encourage debate and discussion among a community of readers. Each comment usually includes identifying information about the commenter, their comment, a date and time stamp, and reader actions, such as recommending or flagging a comment. Comments can also include sharing tools. Threaded comments allow readers to respond directly to other readers. A unique style might be used for editorially selected comments or comments from the author. Some editorial sites have dropped commenting because of the difficulties of moderating it well or the lack of activity, as discussions happen more often on social media platforms.

Art

Just as written content for a publication must be chosen, commissioned, and edited, visual content for a publication also needs to be chosen, commissioned, and edited. For a large publication, an art director would be responsible for this work, overseen by a creative director. For smaller publications, it is just as likely to be shared between designers and editors. For designers, art direction requires an additional skill set that is also built through practice: spotting, engaging, and directing creative work, and maintaining relationships over time.

Art direction begins with a collection of possible sources and inspirational material. Sometimes, the visual style for illustration and photography within a publication is predetermined through identity research, but often it develops organically in relationship to similar periodicals. Illustration and photography are routinely credited, making it easier to source and collect. The ready availability of online portfolios for creative work, as well as agencies that broker commissions, makes the job of art direction much easier, especially when under time pressure.

Sourcing

The first and ongoing task of art direction is to build and maintain diverse lists of possible sources, adding and pruning contacts as time goes on and the identity of the publication evolves. Depending on the publication, you may need individuals who work in different places, on different topics, or with different media. Some may require more direction than you have time to provide, while others may require a fee beyond your budget, or may be difficult to schedule. Time and experience will build relationships that produce good work without much back and forth communication.

Time and experience also bring a stronger sense of identity for the publication. It's important to continually be looking critically at the photography and illustration choices being made in the field. Is the publication so different from its peers that it's not recognizable as being part of a genre? Is it too much the same, and hard to tell apart from the others in a crowded field? Especially in the second scenario, art is the most powerful tool for differentiation. To breathe new life into a genre, inspiration can be found by going outside of that genre, or even going outside of design and into contemporary art.

Scheduling

The second part is scheduling the material and deciding what you need. Is it more appropriate to include an illustration or a photograph? Illustrations can unify repeating content, such as a regular column or essay, to signal continuity from the previous issue along with an indication of a new subject. In other words, an illustration can say "Hey, I'm the same type of thing you read last week, but on a different topic or by a different author." Illustrations are also more appropriate for more abstract content, where subjects cannot be photographed and meaningfully connected to the written work.

Photography is what we are most familiar with in terms of commissioned editorial art and can play a very important role in reading. For long-form written content, there are really only two reasons to include an image with written copy. Either the image should draw the reader in, compelling her to read what has been written, or the image should be something the reader is looking for while reading the article. An article about a scientist, for example, could open with a large image of the scientist at work, while an interior image could show the work being described. This allows the reader to identify with the subject of the article and when she wants to see what she is reading about, she can see it.

Illuminating written work, however, is only one use for commissioned photography and illustration. There are many situations where the piece itself is the content, such as with an information graphic or a photo essay. Both of these forms may require a writer and a creative practitioner to work on iterations of the piece or series. An ambitious photo essay may also require a stylist, whether for food, fashion, or sports, with the editors and designers weighing in on content and fit. For pieces where the art is the content, the work has that responsibility to communicate while fitting within the identity of the publication as a whole. The iterations will come from questioning both aspects.

Communicating and gathering

The third task, if work is to be commissioned, is to communicate a brief description of what is needed to the photographer or illustrator, along with the time and budget constraints of the project. This is especially important if you can't be on site and when there is only one chance to set up a photo shoot. The best work comes from communicating clearly to a talented practitioner what the piece should communicate to its audience, not from dictating what the image should look like. If there are specific aesthetic requests emerging from the design concept of an issue, explain them at the outset. For example, if multiple photographers are shooting subjects for a single piece, it could be requested that they all be shot against a common background, so that the images all relate when placed next to one another.

If the work is not commissioned, available photographs must be sourced and assessed. Any news publication relies heavily on image wires such as Reuters, Getty, and the Associated Press, even those that are fortunate enough to have their own photographers to cover events. A more esoteric journal may reproduce images of artwork or art photography to accompany its text, while a more utilitarian publication may rely heavily on stock photography to get its message across.

Selecting

At some point, sketches come in from the illustrator, and images from the photographer, or an initial round of selections are made from external sources. For an illustration, often there is a chance at a second round before the final, so this is the time to ask: Does it communicate what it needs to communicate? How does it relate to the other illustrations and photographs in the publication? Is it too heavy or too light? If there is an idea, is it legible at this scale? For the photographs, often there are many to choose from, and the original brief becomes useful: Will this image compel someone to read this article? Does this image explain what's being talked about? Does this set of images feel at home with the ones commissioned for other articles? Are there unintended, distracting similarities between unrelated images that should be avoided? Should the content, in consultation with the editor, be reordered?

The more varied the content, the more difficult it is to make the images feel like they belong together in the same publication, putting more responsibility on the typography to provide assertiveness and continuity. Similar content, however, can provide its own challenges. If, for example, a food magazine tends toward gauzy, soft images of plated food, a starkly shot series will draw attention to itself, making it difficult to tell the difference between the other sets. This balancing act determines the difference between a publication that is beautifully art directed and one that is not.

Following up

Once the images are in the layout, final touches might need to be made, some of them either from or in consultation with the artist or photographer. The scale or location of the art might have changed, or there might be some production work necessary to fit the piece among others that have been commissioned. Bring the artist or photographer into the process when checking proofs, if possible. While that piece could be one of dozens in your publication, it might be a significant work for the artist, who might spot an error that you have missed or make a suggestion that makes the publication better as a whole.

If work is commissioned, this is also a good time to reflect on that relationship and show appreciation and courtesy for work well done. For commissioned work, building communication and rapport with photographers and illustrators is the best way to ensure the future quality of art in the publication.

Typography

Typography, like writing, is a practice. While good typography is fundamental to any work of design, professional editorial design communicates hierarchy and structure in addition to identity. A strong editorial designer grasps the relationship between words, sentences, paragraphs, titles, captions, and images, and conveys them through systems of scale, position, form, density, and color. Similar to writers, the best editorial designers read voraciously and practice, practice, practice.

Typography is also a broad field without a single definition and difficult to separate from both layout and identity. In these pages, we'll focus more on the aspects of typography that frequently come into play in editorial or systems-based design, and less on the qualities that would be more important in persuasion-heavy work such as advertisements, book covers, or film titles. While editorial publications (and especially print publications) also have covers and opening pages that are designed for impact, the primary function of typography in editorial design is informational rather than persuasive. We'll also avoid the specialized language of typography as much as possible: For anyone who would like to be thoroughly initiated into the world of typography, there is no better recommendation than to read *Book Typography: A Designer's Manual* by Michael Mitchell and Susan Wightman from cover to cover.

Creative Types On The Silver Screen — How Hollywood Reflects Our Industries

VORRESTE un uomo COME ME?

«Non sono l'ideale per una relazione stabile», ammette l'attore-sex symbol americano. E dà la colpa a una vita

...lace wave — the Rossby wave — it will focus on ...e properties of balance, movement, dynamism ...d unrivaled stamina. If I have done my job well ...ding this will remind you of the closeness of far ...art things, the doggedness of time and the ever ...ding mysteries of nature. It might also remind ...n of why so many children aspire to be astronauts ...marine biologists, two disciplines that present ...e unique possibility of waging adventure into an ...charted void. Though most of them will take on

By EDWARD WONG and NICOLA CLARK

BEIJING — From the moment Turkey announced plans two years ago to acquire a long-range missile defense system, the multibillion-dollar contract from a key NATO member appeared to be an American company's to lose.

For years, Turkey's military had relied on NATO-supplied Patriot missiles, built by the American companies Raytheon and Lockheed Martin, to defend its skies, and the system was fully compatible with the air-defense platforms operated by other members of the alliance.

There were other contenders for the deal, of course. Rival man-

— but not in favor of the American companies. Its selection last month of a little-known Chinese defense company, China Precision Machinery Export-Import Corporation, stunned the military-industrial establishment in Washington and Brussels.

The sale was especially unusual because the Chinese missile defense system, known as the HQ-9, would be difficult to integrate with existing NATO equipment. China Precision is also subject to sanctions from the United States for selling technologies that the United States says could help Iran, Syria and North Korea develop unconventional weapons. A State Department spokeswoman said this

government "serious c about the deal, which ha been signed.

Industry executives a sales analysts say the probably beat out their tablished rivals by sig undercutting them on fering their system at $ Nonetheless, Turkey's of a Chinese state-owne facturer is a breakthr China, a nation that ha sights on moving up t chain in arms technolog tablishing itself as a competitor in the global market.

"This is a remarkabl the Chinese arms indus

Continued on Page

Clockwise from top left: Type choices in *Printed Pages, WAX, The New York Times,* and *Vanity Fair Italia* all reflect their content and audiences.

1. Choose appropriate type.

For beginning designers, the most stressful question always seems to be the meaningful choice of a typeface or font. After all, we are coming out of hundreds of years where form has always communicated meaning in a more or less reliable way. Now, we are well into an age where a couple of decades of pastiche, nostalgia, and the remix, assisted by digital production, have scrambled and diluted the ability to convey meaning through form alone.

What is appropriate changes over time, so be sure to pay attention instead to where and how type is being used in the present. Using the same typeface as something else (especially if it is done in a similar manner) will immediately create an association. If similar publications use a specific typeface or type treatment—such as the ongoing love fashion magazines have for Bodoni or

Didot Italic—the type forms begin to carry the aura of that specific content. Of course, a type treatment that is overused for a particular genre will also make it impossible to stand out within that genre.

So what then? Choose type that will allow you to maintain identity across print, web, and mobile, preferably a typeface that has been digitized in the past ten years, preferably from a reputable foundry. Commercial Type, Hoefler & Frere-Jones, Font Bureau, DTL, and LineTo are all favorites, though there are many more. Many popular typefaces were digitized in the 1980s or 1990s, and so were not tested with contemporary software. Their forms are often wonderful and classic, but their spacing is usually so poor that they require expert finessing in order to look professional, and they are often unavailable for use on the web.

captions, and images and conveys them through systems of scale, position, form, density, and color. And like writers, the best editorial designers read voraciously, and practice, practice, practice.

Typography

Typography is also a broad field without a single definition, and difficult to separate from both layout and identity. In these pages, we'll focus more on the aspects of typography that more frequently come into play in editorial or systems-based de-

Typography, like writing, is a practice. While good typography is fundamental to any work of design, professional editorial design communicates hierarchy and structure in addition to identity.

captions, and images and conveys them through systems of scale, position, form, density, and color. And like writers, the best editorial designers read voraciously, and practice, practice, practice.

Typography

Typography is also a broad field without a single definition, and difficult to separate from both layout and identity. In these pages, we'll focus more on the aspects of typography that more frequently come into play in editorial or systems-based de-

Typography, like writing, is a practice. While good typography is fundamental to any work of design, professional editorial design communicates hierarchy and structure in addition to identity.

Top row: The relationship between the header and the paragraphs before and after is ambiguous at left and clear at right. **Bottom row:** Spaces between words are greater than the space between lines, causing the eye to step down while reading. Reducing the space between words and increasing the space between lines gives the reader clear instruction on where to go next.

2. Things that go together should be closer to each other than they are to other things.

Good typography is really about signaling relationships. By using the space around letters, words, and content blocks such as titles and paragraphs, you draw a map of the content for the reader. Good typography acts as a guide that leads the reader through the content, using space to say, *this goes with this* or *we're going to take a break here* or *this is something new*. This is true at every level: paragraphs, lines, words, and letters. So a word should be closer to the word that follows it than to the word below it, a word in another column, or the edge of the page or device.

When a series of things goes together—such as letters in a word, words in a line, paragraphs in a column—a letter, word, or paragraph should not pick a favorite.

Adjust the spacing around letters or words when they are visibly closer to one side or the other.

This rule applies also for disparate elements that work together. A header should be closer to the paragraph it introduces than the one that comes before the header. Two paragraphs of a quote should be closer to each other than they are to the paragraphs before and after. A byline should be closer to a title—the thing that represents the article—than it is to the first paragraph. While subtle, this spatial organization will do more than anything else to reduce ambiguity in the mind of the reader.

Typography is also a broad field without a single definition, and difficult to separate from both layout and identity. In these pages, we'll focus more on the aspects of typography that more frequently come into play in editorial or systems-based design, and less on the qualities that would be more important in more persuasion-heavy work such as advertisements, book covers, or film titles.

out a single definition, and difficult to separate from both layout and identity. In these pages, we'll focus more on the aspects of typography that more frequently come into play in editorial or systems-based design, and less on the qualities that would be more important in more persuasion-heavy work such as advertisements, book covers, or film titles.

a broad field without a single definition, and difficult to separate from both layout and identity. In these pages, we'll focus more on the aspects of typography that more frequently come into play in editorial or systems-based design, and less on the

work such as advertisements, book.

Typography is also a broad field without a single definition, and difficult to separate from both layout and identity. In these pages, we'll focus more on the aspects of typography that more frequently come into play in editorial or systems-based design, and less on the

Typography, like writing, is a practice. While good typography is fundamental to any work of design, professional editorial design communicates hierarchy and structure in addition to identity. In 1919 the AIGA would state that even if the structure of an impend-

Clockwise from top left: A lonely word at the end of a paragraph; a short word ("In") sticking out from the right side of a paragraph; a line by itself at the top of a page; aligning numerals and an acronym distracting from the smooth reading of a paragraph.

3. No lonely things, and no misfits.

Nothing should stand out in a block of type. A quick scan will reveal words dangling by themselves, either precariously at the end of a line or tucked under a paragraph. A line floating by itself also attracts attention and pity, having no neighbors. An acronym in all caps or a date written with aligning (uppercase) numbers will also pull the eye away from reading, but using non-aligning numerals and small caps will allow them to blend into the paragraph. Heavy capital letters in poorly chosen type, or a single paragraph where the letters are set closer to one another than they are in other paragraphs will also distract the reader.

In other words, things that are the same should look like they are the same. A reader with a novel in hand is likely to move through it one word after another, but a reader moving through a periodical is likely to scan before committing to read any portion of the work. Unintended misfits neuter the power of things that are intended to stand out, such as headers and pull quotes, to capture the reader's attention.

Typography is also a broad field without a single definition, and difficult to separate from both layout and identity. In these pages, we'll focus more on the aspects of typography that more frequently come into play in editorial or systems-based design, and less on the qualities

Typography is also a broad field without a single definition, and difficult to separate from both layout and identity. In these pages, we'll focus more on the aspects of typography that more frequently come into play in editorial or systems-based design, and less on the qualities that would be more

Typography is also a broad field without a single definition, and difficult to separate from both layout and identity. In these pages, we'll focus more on the aspects of typography that more frequently come into play in editorial or systems-based design, and less on the qualities that would be more important in more persuasion-

Typography is also a broad field without a single definition, and difficult to separate from both layout and identity. In these pages, we'll focus more on the aspects of typography that more frequently come into play in editorial or systems-based design, and less on the qualities that would be

Typography is also a broad field without a single definition, and difficult to separate from both layout and identity. In these pages, we'll focus more on the aspects of typography that more frequently come into play in editorial or systems-based

Typography is also a broad field without a single definition, and difficult to separate from both layout and identity. In these pages, we'll focus more on the aspects of typography that more frequently come into play in editorial or systems-based design, and less on the qualities that would be

All of the fonts above are set in the same point size but their formal aspects make them look as if they are all different sizes.

4. Don't make the smallest text too small to read.

This may seem subjective, since some people have 20/20 vision and others do not. But even if you have good vision, there is a simple test that will bring you an answer: If, when you hold the piece with your arm fully extended, you squint or strain, the type is too small. "Smallness" is not just affected by point size, either. Type that is thin, hard to distinguish, compressed, or with really short lowercase letters will also be harder to read. Two 12-point fonts rendered side by side, for example, might seem to be completely different sizes.

As more people read on desktop and laptop screens, and the screens themselves have more pixels, the expected size of paragraph type on the web has increased. In the early days of the web, the desire to pack two or three columns of content in 800–900 pixels shrank text sizes to unreadable dimensions. While the text was legible, it was exhausting to read more than a paragraph or two. In part, this was because the screen was trying to mimic what appears on paper, without considering that a desktop or laptop screen is almost always at arm's length and so a comfortable size for text on paper won't be comfortable to read on screen. Similarly, text size for a handheld device, such as a phone, can be slightly smaller than on paper since it is likely to be held closer.

Typography

Typography is also a broad field without a single definition, and difficult to separate from both layout and identity.

In these pages, we'll focus more on the aspects of typography that more frequently come into play in editorial or systems-based design, and less on the qualities that would be more important in more persuasion-heavy work such as advertisements, book covers, or film titles.

While editorial publications (and especially print publications) also have covers and opening pages that are designed for impact, the primary function

Typography

Typography is also a broad field without a single definition, and difficult to separate from both layout and identity.

In these pages, we'll focus more on the aspects of typography that more frequently come into play in editorial or systems-based design, and less on the qualities that would be more important in more persuasion-heavy work such as advertisements, book covers, or film titles.

While editorial publications (and especially print publications) also have covers and opening pages that are designed for impact, the primary function of typography in editorial design is informational rather than persuasive. We'll also avoid the spe-

At left: A clear hierarchy between a header, lede and paragraph text. *At right:* Small differences make the reader question the relationship between the assembled elements.

5. More important things should be bigger than less important things.

A headline or paragraph heading should be bigger than text in a paragraph, and text in a paragraph should be bigger than that specified for a page number. If they are only slightly different, the ambiguity makes the reader pause and drag, attempting to sort out where something lies in the hierarchy, sometimes flipping back to another page or section to compare.

When presented with a wide canvas, such as a broadsheet newspaper, hierarchy is both easier and more complex. Large elements, such as headlines, can be many times the size of body text, and there is room for several layers of hierarchy in between, as well as hierarchy over time (as when a headline for an important event is twice the size of a less important event the day before). Comparatively, working in a small space such as a mobile phone can be challenging to the point of frustration. The small space of a phone screen defaults the content to a list, with a headline slightly bigger than body text. Making one item feel more important than another through size becomes difficult if the smallest text is still to be legible.

Typography

Typography is also a broad field without a single definition, and difficult to separate from both layout and identity.

In these pages, we'll focus more on the aspects of typography that more frequently

Typography

Typography is also a broad field without a single definition, and difficult to separate from both layout and identity.

In these pages, we'll focus more on the aspects of typography that more frequently

Typography

Typography is also a broad field without a single definition, and difficult to separate from both layout and identity.

In these pages, we'll focus more on the aspects of typography that more frequently

Typography

Typography is also a broad field without a single definition, and difficult to separate from both layout and identity.

In these pages, we'll focus more on the aspects of typography that more fre-

Clockwise from top left: Hierarchy is emphasized through changing value, changing color, placing more space around an element, and changing shape.

6. "Bigness" is not always negotiated with size.

An element can also be made bigger through changing value or contrast, color, position or shape, or by placing more space around an element. Using more than size and space to indicate hierarchy is a good way to establish and reinforce the identity of the publication. However, use only one means of making things bigger: If an element is heavier in weight, it likely doesn't need to be bigger in size, set in italics, or underlined. If you are wearing a belt, you do not also need suspenders.

Larger-proportioned items also need to be with each other. The reader is not always reading in a line, and is often scanning the publication, deciding what to read and in what order. Keeping pull quotes and subheadings consistent is a way to mark for the reader which parts go together and which ones don't. Changing these elements in the interest of variety in each instance is a sure way to lose the reader.

Typography is also a broad field without a single definition, and difficult to separate from both layout and identity.

In these pages, we'll focus more on the aspects of typography that more frequently come into play in editorial or systems-based design, and less on the qualities that would be more important in more persuasion-heavy work such as advertisements, book covers, or film titles.

While editorial publications (and especially print publications) also have covers and opening pages that are designed for impact, the primary function of typography in editorial design is informational

Typography is also a broad field without a single definition, and difficult to separate from both layout and identity.

In these pages, we'll focus more on the aspects of

Typography is also a broad field without a single definition, and difficult to separate from both layout and identity.

In these pages, we'll focus more on the aspects of typography that more frequently come into play in editorial or systems-based design, and less on the qualities that would be more important in more persuasion-heavy work such as advertisements, book covers, or film titles.

Top: Lines that are too long are tiring to read and create an unpleasant variation in line lengths. **Bottom left:** Lines that are too short can be exhausting as well, as the eye seeks out each next line. **Bottom right:** 8–12 words at a line comfortably break the text into manageable sections and pauses.

7. Respect the reader's rhythm and pace.

In his book *Stop Stealing Sheep,* Erik Spiekermann expressed this best when he said that lines of text are like flights of stairs: If each flight is too long, it's exhausting; if each flight is too short, it's annoying. Eight to twelve words in a line are most comfortable for reading body copy. Smaller items that consist of fewer than 100 words, such as captions or pull quotes, can break this convention, and justified text is sometimes more legible with twelve to fifteen words in a line. Readers do not read letters, or even whole words, but rather groups of phrases as they move through the text, Giving appropriate pauses allows the reader to take in the content at a natural pace.

Providing a comfortable line length while covering most of a printed page or tablet screen often requires breaking up the text into columns. On a desktop screen, however, columns can be awkward; the primary behavior of the reader will be to scroll rather than scan to a different part of the screen. Whatever the device, remember to respect the reader's expectations and habits. Even if a behavior doesn't seem to be the most logical way to move through content, disrupting it means breaking the relationship between the content and the reader.

Layout

Aside from organizing content across time, the designer also arranges it in space. The spatial arrangement of items on a page or field is most commonly called *layout*. The most fundamental layout principles are timeworn and apply regardless of medium: hierarchy, rhythm, flow, scanability, and affiliation. When moving beyond print, these principles still apply, but often under conditions with less control. The layout may flow differently, depending on the device and its orientation, or may be responsive to user input regarding type and window size. Whether the layout is fixed or fluid, well-designed layouts suggest multiple content experiences for the reader.

No matter what, any layout strategy should begin first with the content. Visual identity elements will of course be constant, but if done well, they will act in the background. The content is what your reader has come to experience, and anything that makes accessing it difficult, cluttered, or less pleasurable will drive your reader to put that content aside in favor of something else. If you're working on a publication that has a life outside of print, designing first for mobile or for platforms such as Readability that strip designs down to readable text is a great way to start thinking about giving form to that content. Even if the publication is print-only, it's useful to focus initially on a few paragraphs of type coupled with a headline and an image.

Content and Hierarchy

The benefit of starting this way is that you can think about basic formal elements such as the form of the type, the degree of hierarchy, and the relationship of image to text in an atomic fashion, then build on the decisions you've made across grids and the opportunities presented by larger formats. Hierarchy, simply put, is making sure that different text or image elements are scaled according to importance so that a headline isn't confused with a subhead, a subhead isn't confused with a pull quote, and body copy isn't confused with a footnote. Hierarchy is the most difficult to master on small handheld devices. Once the body copy itself is legible, making other elements such as headlines visibly larger may test the limits of the viewing area. If there are several levels of hierarchy, the differences between them can be minimal, negating their ability to communicate different levels of importance. While it is sometimes difficult to make elements clearly different from each other, this contrast will make the copy readable and scannable. Similarly-sized elements often result in an undifferentiated, decorated mess.

Rhythm and Flow

Once the visual and hierarchical elements of an editorial design begin to take shape, it is time to think about rhythm and flow. Rhythm is the pattern by which someone reads. Depending on the length, some copy is better read in small bursts with few characters to a line, while other kinds of content are more suited to containing full thoughts before breaking to the next line. Rhythm is almost impossible to achieve if it's not backed by a system of column grids that begin with testing body copy at different sizes and widths. A broadsheet newspaper page can have up to eight columns; a magazine usually has two or three depending on the page; a tablet may have two or three when held horizontally and one or two when vertical; and a phone will almost always have only one. Where there are multiple options for column grids, there is more variety in layout: Images and text can span multiple columns, or different grids saved as master pages can be used for a variety of content. If you have not worked with grids before, it may be useful to scan some pages of publications to reveal their underlying grids and see where designers will also break them for emphasis or variety.

Flow happens as a result of well-structured hierarchy and good rhythm. The reader needs to know where an article, section, or aside starts and stops, and should get a sense when reading a paragraph of text whether it is a continuation of content, new content but the same kind of topic, or a different kind of content entirely. All of this signaling is what editorial design is for, and if done correctly, this visual annotation will be read seamlessly and invisibly. There is no flow, however, when there are few visible markers, or when there are so many styles that it's difficult to see what actually does belong together and what does not.

Scanability

It's almost guaranteed that the reader will not move through the publication from the first word to the last. It's a common habit to scan instead for material of interest, and then to read in the order of interest. Scanability follows from flow in that distinguished elements such as headlines can be read quickly, independently of their body copy. Headlines are not the only bits that can be mobilized, however—pull quotes, captions, and first paragraphs are all pieces that can be quickly read or scanned, as long as they are kept to fewer than 150 words, which most will read without commitment. If there are too many small chunks of text, it can defeat the purpose of having scannable text, mostly because that copy itself will look like it requires commitment to read on its own, and in the worst cases, it will distract from the already committed reader's experience.

Affiliation

Affiliation is making sure that the design indicates unambiguously what goes with what. Is the headline affiliated with the paragraph that follows it or does it seem more affectionate toward the one that came before it? Does a paragraph end on the last line of a page, temporarily making the reader wonder if that's the end of the article? Is an image clearly connected to the text that it describes and the caption that describes it? Is it clear where the first paragraph of an article even starts? These are all questions that need to be asked when evaluating a layout. No amount of fancy footwork with type treatments or illustration will save a layout that doesn't accurately describe the relationships between unique elements on a page.

The benefit of this approach—paying closer attention to content relationships than formal relationships—is that it will not be broken apart once a layout is fluid instead of fixed. What looks like a perfect formal composition on a spread will lose its perfection once columns are rearranged and images are resized. Formal composition is always a part of the design of a page and should be striking in every format, but shoehorning a design into a medium it wasn't designed for purely to preserve formal composition is a terrible mistake. If you approach the design first from the content and develop it with respect to the relationships within that content, you will find that it will take on a distinct beautiful form in each medium.

newyorker.com

Horse_ebooks Is Human After All

by Susan Orlean • September 24, 2013

The Internet is full of mysteries. Two of the more intriguing ones have been a Twitter account, @Horse_ebooks, and a YouTube channel, Pronunciation Book, which have been running for the past several years. Both have the hallmarks of automation, chugging along anonymously and churning out disjointed bits of text in a very spam-like fashion. At the same time, their output has seemed strangely knowing and even portentous. Horse_ebooks, in particular, has inspired fan fiction, Tumblr accounts, T-shirts, and tattoos with its weird Zen-like sentence fragments, such as "Who Else Wants To Become A Golf Ball," or "For The Highest Price Possible, No Matter How Much Time You Have Had To Prepare!," or "Everything happens so much." Both accounts have spawned speculation among the hundreds of thousands of people who have viewed them. Were they really spambots? Were they some slowly unfolding promotion for, say, a new phone or movie? Were they machines testing out a new

A *New Yorker* article in the Readability app.

Prototyping

Making models is an important part of the design process, because the best way to make design decisions is to give form to your ideas and talk about them. A prototype is something that you make that's not the thing, but that gives you the information you need to make the thing by asking and evoking questions. Sometimes, a prototype is very similar to the final product, closer to a proof. Usually it's something that can be quickly made, tested, revised, and retested through several iterations. Sometimes, it is a version of the thing itself, before it is produced or released at scale.

Prototyping for print may seem unnecessary, since what is on the screen looks a lot like the printed product, but a full-scale mockup is absolutely critical for testing scale and proportion at the distance that someone is likely to hold the publication.

Print prototypes also help to visualize rhythm and proportion in a way that is never adequately communicated on a screen. A printed publication reads as a three-dimensional object with concrete physical relationships, while a digital manifestation of the same content often is accessed as a single sequenced line. Delineation and differentiation of sections, punctuation of stops and starts, and balance of text and image or original content and advertising are far easier to scrutinize in printed form, especially when printed at a smaller scale.

When you are looking at the screen, it's the equivalent of shrinking your publication and holding it at arm's length. Things that appear to be the correct size will seem too large when printed. It's important, too, to prototype at full scale to test the allowance made for the gutter, which is the distance between the last printed portion and the spine of the book or publication. Since a spread on the screen doesn't show the margin at an angle to the spine, a gutter that appears to be the right size on screen will look too small when printed, especially if there are many pages and it's bound with glue (perfect bound) instead of stapled (saddle-stitched). Another way to test the gutter is to print out a spread, fold it, and place it in the center of a publication that is about the same size.

Prototyping for web and mobile can be complicated, because behaviors are often as important as the layout, especially if the final website relies heavily on dynamic or responsive interfaces. There are dozens of prototyping tools available, some of which also offer tools for collaborating with developers and clients. Omnigraffle and Axure are two popular, longstanding applications, for creating wireframes that will let you experience and evaluate the flow through a multipage site. Newer applications such as Flinto, Invision, iPlotz, ProtoShare, Moqups, Proto.io, Balsamiq, Mockflow, HotGloo, and Justinmind offer different features or time-saving workflows that may be a priority depending on the project, especially for mocking up mobile apps.

You don't need a prototyping tool, though, to make a prototype. Many designers swear by Apple's Keynote for being able to work quickly at high resolution. The interface itself is well thought out with snaps, custom styles, and well-designed animation tools. As a bonus, the animations that are available in Keynote look and feel like those in iOS, making it easy to create a convincing prototype for evaluation.

Paper prototyping is often a good precursor to making mockups with software. Prototyping with paper is both low cost and inclusive, meaning that members of a team or audience who are not technically savvy can take part in the design process. A paper prototype is also furthest away from the experience of the final product, so there is little confusion—it is obviously not the thing itself, and a user may find it easier to ignore the elements that are not under discussion, such as

color or scale. Finally, paper prototypes are easier to document, because attempted actions can be marked, and feedback can be written directly on the areas that are being referenced. High-fidelity interactive prototypes often impress, but the wow factor itself can hinder criticism and feedback that would serve to make the product better.

There are also situations in which distance from the final isn't necessary or desired. If a prototype doesn't save time during the design process or produce feedback that a first-draft iteration would provide, it isn't doing its job. In situations where a project has a short schedule or isn't being created by multiple people, where the designer will also code or produce the work, it can often be more efficient to just make the thing and get feedback at critical points before the design is finished. One downside of this approach is that anyone looking at it is always looking at something that is unfinished or broken, and that doesn't announce itself as a model for review; another is that time invested in building can lead to attachment to ideas or components that should be discarded. The upside is that it can be reused and iterations can happen much faster, with the project slowly being brought into resolution.

No matter how a designer approaches making prototypes, they are an essential component of the design process. The conversations they generate improve the quality of the work, the designer, and the discipline. Making things that are specifically designed for critique can also be freeing, allowing for greater creativity while helping to prioritize design decisions and forging relationships between designers and other participants in the design process.

Production

While design is often confused with craft, most design is not craft. Most design is communication to other people who make the things that are designed. However, this does not relieve the designer from the responsibility of knowing how things are made, and the best way to know how they are made is to make them. Only a designer who truly understands the craft of what is being designed can truly be a key communicator and collaborator in the production process.

Production varies greatly in editorial design depending on the product, and new forms continuously require new knowledge and new tools. At present, there are no fewer than ten popular ways to deliver written and visual content, and new ones will appear as technology progresses. As each new medium emerges or is considered, designers, editors, and writers have to decide whether or not they have the time, budget, and vision to deliver the same quality of form and content on each new platform. At the same time, as each new method of delivery becomes popular, the new is proclaimed to be a replacement for the old, a common reaction that is not based on historical fact. Of all communication technologies in the past 200 years, only the telegram has fallen out of ordinary use.

When considering different media for distribution, the level of customization is a key factor. It is possible to publish in every medium in templated form, and new content management platforms, such as Readymag .com, Periodical.co, Typeengine.net, and Packa.gr make it easier to produce periodical content across phones, tablets, e-readers, and desktop screens. Several quality templates designed for editorial content are also available on content management systems such as Word-Press, Tumblr, Drupal, and Joomla, and most allow for a surprising degree of customization. Startups such as 29th Street Publishing offer more customized software for publishers that bridge websites and subscription-only tablet or mobile magazine apps.

Below is a brief introduction to production considerations for each of the media used for publishing today.

Print

There is an almost 1:1 correlation between the beauty of a print publication and the collective expertise of the people making it. Print production is not a moving target: The scale and orientation of the final publication is fixed, nothing moves around or changes size on a cover, page, or spread, and every reader approaches it in the same way. The challenge, however, is that the higher the quality of print production, the more difficult it is to prototype accurately. Until something is printed with the ink and paper that will be used, anything to demonstrate what it will look like is an approximation, especially when it comes to color. The experience of designer, printer, and print producer (if there is one) will determine the quality of the finished product, as only experience can accurately predict what something on a screen or an inkjet printout will actually look like.

Almost all commercially available printed publications are printed on offset presses, and a few smaller-run publications are produced on digital presses. "Offset" refers to how an image is transferred to the paper: A cylindrical plate transfers the image to a rubber sheet called a blanket, and then the blanket transfers the ink to the paper. The ink is laid down on the paper one color at a time. For standard four-color offset printing, cyan is printed first, then magenta, then yellow, and finally black. A large-circulation newspaper or magazine is likely printed on a web press, which pulls in paper from giant rolls and can be as large as a building. Most high-end books and magazines are printed on sheet-fed presses. A sheet-fed press is smaller, allows for better control of registration and color, and offers a wider range of paper choices. Offset printing is still the least expensive way to print quality images and text at high volume.

Producing plates and setting up the printing press is expensive, so very small-run or on-demand publications turn to digital laser printing instead. Digital laser printers use a laser beam to charge the surface of the paper, which then electrostatically picks up particles of cyan, magenta, yellow, and black powdered toner. A fuser later uses heat to adhere the toner to the paper. The use of heat both slows the printing process and changes in temperature during a long print run makes the printing inconsistent, and powder toner always sits on the surface of paper rather than sinking into it. Recent developments in digital printing have led to smaller and smaller electrostatic toner particles suspended in oil, or "liquid toner," most commonly used in HP Indigo presses. The smaller the particle, the more it conforms to the surface of the paper, making it more and more difficult to distinguish from offset printing with liquid ink. With a digital press, there is no minimum number of prints necessary to make it cost-effective, and a proof shows exactly what the finished product will look like.

Whether a designer is setting up a document for offset or digital, it's necessary to have a sense of the mechanical and physical processes that make the finished publication, especially when it comes to understanding the limitations of the machinery or processes at hand. While printing machines are surprisingly precise, it's impossible to move thousands of pieces of paper through a process without some give in trimming, folding, and registration. If a document doesn't allow at least ¼ inch (6 mm) of bleed for images that go to the edge, some pieces will come back with a sliver of white while others will not. Similarly, if at least ¼ inch (6 mm) of border around text and images is not built into the design, some text and images will jut up against the edge of a page, while others will appear to have too much space. Unpredictability does not make for a great printed product, and building in these allowances helps ensure the uniform quality of what is being printed, especially if it is being printed at high volume or low cost.

For text and solid areas, consulting a color guide (either a Pantone Process guide or a color guide that came with the laser printer) is the only way to accurately predict what color will look like printed. No amount of calibration on a backlit monitor will be accurate because print is a reflective medium. Color should always be set up as CMYK swatches with the corresponding numbers typed in. To allow for greater control over proportioning densities of color.

Except in very large-circulation publications, the designer is often responsible for color quality. This is particularly challenging when images and illustrations are coming from multiple sources, or from sources where heavy digital manipulation has already taken place. In the past, almost all photographs would come in as raw transparencies, prints, or negatives, leaving little chance of a poor image being chosen to begin with and a lot of room for preproduction correction after scanning. Almost all images now begin as digital images, so the image is likely to come in manipulated, but without regard to context or final output.

This matters because the first law of digital image manipulation is that you can take information away, but you cannot add more. The best results for offset or digitally printed images start with well-crafted, information-rich raster files. A raster file by definition is made up of tiny little boxes, or pixels, with color information stored as numbers for each box. The greater the number of boxes, and the greater the variety of color for each box, the higher the image quality. Every manipulation of the file from there is just an application of an algorithm to an army of boxes. To lighten a CMYK image, for example, the "lighten" algorithm may uniformly reduce the percentage of black in each pixel, or the percentage of all colors. For color correction, it's helpful to think in opposites. Removing cyan and yellow will make an image more red, while reducing cyan and magenta will make it more yellow. It's useful to sample neutral areas as well: A neutral gray will appear neutral if its proportions are 4 : 3 : 3 for cyan : yellow : magenta. The human eye is really flexible about color except when it comes to skin tone or food, so be vigilant about these things first. If a sub-

ject's skin color seems normal, a tree or a chair being the "wrong" color won't matter to your reader.

Finally, watch your blacks and whites. One hundred percent black appears as charcoal gray, while 100 percent of all four colors is a muddy mess. For large areas of black, 40 percent cyan, 30 percent magenta, 30 percent yellow, and 100 percent black will produce a rich black. Beware of lines or type that sneak in as mixes of colors instead of 100 percent black only. Since the plates never perfectly align, they will appear fuzzy or ghosted. White or "blown out" areas present another problem: stepping between, say, 66 percent and 65 percent of an ink color is mostly imperceptible, but stepping between 4 percent and 3 percent will produce a visible line or band, and between 1 percent and 0 percent, a line is very visible. In these cases, it's often necessary to mask the banding by adding tone to the image, defying the cardinal rule, above.

The work is not yet done even once everything is in place and images are color corrected. There is a difference between creating or using a document that only you will see or modify and one that is a set of instructions for another person. Go through and remove unused swatches and fonts and name everything that can be named appropriately: layers, swatches, type styles, and the files themselves. Swatches should be named with CMYK color values or PMS spot colors, if you are using them. If you are working with a printer, make sure you discuss color output before you send linked image files. Some printers will request that you convert your image files to CMYK, while others will prefer to do the conversion themselves. Some will accept and print only a PDF file and will have preferred profiles for exporting the PDFs. For those that prefer to work with the source file, make sure that all linked images and text are included, and that images all have an effective PPI above 266 pixels per inch, which is the point at which a human eye can't easily make out individual pixels.

With few exceptions, graphics that are not continuous-tone photographs should be saved as vector files. While a raster file describes an image as a group of contiguous boxes, a vector file describes a form as a collection of points with specific types of lines and fills connecting them. Since a vector file is all about the relative position of points and lines, they will appear the same at any scale. Font files, too, are bundles of vector files, and also appear the same at any scale. One thing to watch as a designer is the line weight. Depending on the process, any line weight below 0.5 point may or may not appear as you wish it to appear, especially if it's not composed of a solid color. Unfortunately, the only way to really know is to test line weights in the process you plan to use or see an example.

Web/Desktop

Using the word "production" to talk about the web is not exactly accurate. You can't produce a website any more than you can "produce" a garden. Websites are continuously renewed, adjusting to changes in content or feedback from readers or analytics. Still, there is a divide between the design of a site and the making of it, even if the making is not a one-time event. For a responsive site, where the website readjusts its layout to the screen size a reader is using, the production notes here extend to mobile as well.

This process can be organized in a variety of ways. Designing for the web offers the unique opportunity to craft what you have designed, so many designers choose to also code the website. Web design has also come a long way in the past twenty years, in that there is a much greater range of expression, more tools, libraries, and frameworks to make what's desired, and an ever-increasing array of resources for learning. This is not always possible or even desirable, so designers will also frequently work with developers, either as a two-person team or as one part of a much larger team. As with print design, the more people are involved in the production process, the clearer the design documents need to be because they cannot just be drafted in internal shorthand. Unlike print design, the design of the process itself has to think into the future to points where new designers or developers will be looking at layouts or code and will be able to access and modify them.

Implementing the design of a website used to be relatively straightforward, if inefficient. A designer would put together a full-scale pixel-perfect static raster file in Photoshop, and then a developer would slice it apart to build a website using HTML and CSS. Now the documentation is both more extensive and less precise: A designer is more likely to put together broad

style frames along with key images showing what the site will look like in different media, in different states, or with different actions applied, and will work with a developer to fill in the parts that haven't been as precisely detailed. Any content management system will also present both opportunities and constraints that affect the design and production of the site.

There are two key production considerations that are not an issue in print. First, there are two sizes to every image: its actual size, measured in pixels, and its file size. Every web page, and everything it references, costs a reader a discrete amount of time that correlates directly to file size. This is especially true of mobile devices. A reader following a link could be going to a page on a giant monitor connected to a blazing fast CPU, wireless connection, and graphics card. The same reader could come across the link on a Twitter feed on a smartphone while in transit. A page that has more than 150K of data can potentially take more than a second to load, at which point, your potential reader is gone. Delivering a quality experience at each of these points requires expertise in delivering the smallest possible file for the highest quality of content. Even if you are not coding the site, you will likely be responsible for delivering graphic content, and training editors and writers to prepare images and videos.

One of the surest ways to keep file sizes down at varying scales is to use SVG (Scalable Vector Graphics) files for logos and other graphics. SVG files are XML-based vector files that can even display some limited animation. The one downside is that they are not supported in every browser: Users with older versions of Internet Explorer will likely need an alternative or plug-in, and a particularly complex graphic with many points may be larger in some instances than a raster file, if the image has a small footprint.

Where an SVG file is not appropriate, an image that has just a few colors will be smallest (and highest-quality) as a GIF file. A GIF file is made smaller by reducing the number of colors used, and you will see the difference in quality if you use the "save for web" function in Photoshop. For continuous-tone or photographic images, JPEG compression often produces the best results for a small file size. Depending on the image, however, an overly compressed JPEG image can be lossy, introducing artifacts into the image that are most visible in images that have large areas of continuous color.

For both graphics and continuous-tone images, especially those that have sharp transitions between color areas, PNG images can sometimes offer the highest-quality images at small file sizes and have great support for transparency as well.

Images are not the only items that bulk up the file sizes on a page. Custom fonts, long style sheets, long scripts in a header, queries to third-party servers, and even an excess of space and commentary in HTML and CSS code can slow load times. A properly produced website will look beyond images toward incremental solutions in each of these areas to lower the amount of time it takes for a website to load.

The second major consideration that is not an issue in print is that a web page that can only be read by humans will not reach many humans, and will exclude many of those that do come. The accessibility of any individual site also promotes the larger long-term health of the web. This is achieved through the use of web standards, which are commonly agreed-upon principles and practices that envision the web as an open, dynamic, and interconnected field. Designing with web standards means that what things look like in any static moment is a lower priority than how it connects and maintains its integrity independently from how it is presented. Doctypes, metadata, tagging, and linking are all invisible or nearly invisible components of a website, but determine how the website will be discovered, where it will be listed, and what it will be associated with. Designing with web standards also means that open-source technologies, where the code is not kept secret, are used whenever possible. Both the standards themselves as well as markup validators are free for public use on www.w3c.org.

Design habits that are geared toward making a site accessible to a nonsighted or low-sighted person will also make it attractive to search engine robots. If the HTML is ordered by hierarchy, and HTML tags are used to hierarchicize information instead of visual cues, the most important content will always be differentiated from less-important content. Using alt tags for images, labeling input fields properly, not hiding information or controls behind JavaScript actions, and avoiding pop-ups are also necessary.

Tablet and Mobile

A responsive site is often an ideal solution for publishing across platforms, especially when content is being added daily or even hourly. However, for publications that publish infrequently, it can be overly restrictive, and for a publication that has enough scale to build its own applications, unnecessarily efficient. Building a tablet or mobile application can also be a nice way to distinguish between related content that is not identical. For example, many blogs that publish continuously have begun to anthologize in the form of tablet and mobile apps, or even downloadable PDFs scaled for smaller screens.

Coding in Objective-C, or hiring someone to code in Objective-C, may be the best way to create an app, but it is also the most time-consuming and expensive. While large publications take this route, smaller ones will customize or use a mobile platform. For those who already have some knowledge in coding HTML and CSS, using the open-source Baker ebook framework in concert with the Laker Compendium is currently the best way to publish to iPads and iPhones. Online tools such as Mag+ online apps like Readymag promise the ability to create apps on your own without any coding involved. If a publication already exists in InDesign, Adobe's Digital Publishing Suite is also a way to create an application, though it has limits. Even more limited is Apple's iBooks software, though its ease of use can sometimes outweigh its limitations. Available platforms and software will change rapidly in the coming years, and each will have its strengths and weaknesses, but as with the web itself, apps will be easier to make, and the limitations will fall away, one by one. What will be left is the strength of the design itself, and its empathy for the reader.

Case
Studies &
Interviews

Case Study: BuzzFeed

WEBSITE: BUZZFEED.COM

FREQUENCY: CONTINUOUSLY

FORMAT: WEBSITE, IOS/ANDROID APPS

LOCATION: NEW YORK

EDITOR: BEN SMITH

VP OF PRODUCT: CHRIS JOHANESEN

FOUNDER/PUBLISHER: JONAH PERETTI

YEAR FOUNDED: 2006

Anyone publishing news or content of any kind on the web in 2013 had to look at the BuzzFeed phenomenon and ask themselves, "How do they do it?" And by "it" we mean hit six-digit site traffic numbers daily and create sponsored content that its readers unquestioningly want to engage with.

BuzzFeed's publishing model is unique in that it's a digital-first publication that was designed around the "social web" and sharing. The site's claim to fame is the pictorial "listicle" (list article) format that takes crowd-generated news from sites such as Reddit and repurposes it into scannable and sharable stories. On the flipside, BuzzFeed has also invested in quality, long-form political journalism. What makes it possible for high- and low-brow content to coexist? In a 2012 memo that tech entrepreneur Chris Dixon shared on his blog, founder Jonah Peretti explains the secret to his success:

> Most publishers build their site by stapling together products made by other companies. They get their CMS from one company, their analytics package from another, their ad tech from another, their related content widgets are powered by another, sometimes even their writers are contractors who don't work for the company. This is why so many publishers' sites look the same and also why they can be so amazingly complex and hard to navigate. They are Frankenstein products bolted together by a tech team that integrates other people's products instead of building their own.
>
> At BuzzFeed, we take the exact opposite approach. We manage our own servers, we built our CMS from scratch, we created our own real-time stats system, we have our own data science team, we invented our own ad products and our own post formats, and all these products are brought to life by our own editorial team and our own creative services team. We are

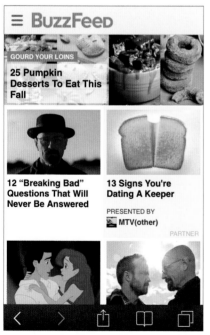

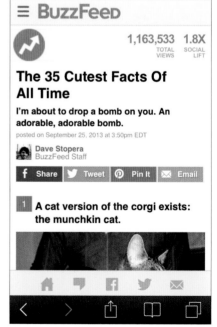

BuzzFeed's home page on a smartphone offers an infinite scroll of content upon request. Sponsored content is highlighted with "Presented By" and "Partner" labels, while others wear reader-reaction badges such as "LOL" and "WTF?" Story pages lead with buzz statistics, and tools for sharing the whole page or a specific image are featured prominently.

what you call a "vertically integrated product," which is rare in web publishing. We take responsibility for the technology, the advertising, and the content, and that allows us to make a much better product where everything works together.

BuzzFeed is one of the very few publishers with the resources, talent, and focus to build the whole enchilada. And nothing is tastier than a homemade enchilada.*

* http://cdixon.org/2012/07/24/buzzfeeds-strategy/

This desktop screenshot of the BuzzFeed.com home page captures the top 1.5 percent of what's available. There are links to hundreds of stories as the user scrolls down the page.

Chris Johanesen
VP of Product, BuzzFeed

Tell us what you do at BuzzFeed.
I am VP of Product, so I manage the product team but I also do a lot of my own product design and management because we're a small team. I was BuzzFeed's second employee and first designer, so I've been designing and building our products from day one. As we grew, I took on more of the product management duties from Jonah and eventually started hiring other designers and project/product managers.

What was your background prior to BuzzFeed?
Short story: I'm a generalist and have done everything from coding, to print design, to web design.

Long story: I grew up in the New Jersey suburbs, spent my teenage years teaching myself how to program on my family's early PC. I went to college for computer science, but I also discovered the internet in 1994, and started making websites and playing with Photoshop. After a few years at school, I realized that what I really wanted to do was design websites, and my interest in programming was really just a way to implement my designs. So I switched [my major] to visual arts and got a degree from Rutgers. All this took a very long time because I worked full-

time for a computer company while going through school and amassed way too many credits due to switching majors. By the time I graduated, the first dot-com boom had already bust. After a little while designing and building websites as a freelancer, I saw a posting on Kottke.org of a new start-up that wanted a designer who could code. That turned out to be BuzzFeed.

There seem to be some clear editorial "buckets" at BuzzFeed, ranging from very viral (LOL/Cute/OMG) to the more serious and long-form (BuzzFeed Politics, BuzzFeed Reads). Could you identify the main types of reading experiences that BuzzFeed offers?

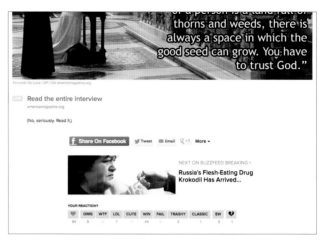

A BuzzFeed listicle page—that is, a list-formatted article—is designed so that individual list items can be shared. In the hover state, pictured at left, social-media tools appear, as if to say, "You know you want to share this." At the end of a story, pictured above, readers are offered share tools yet again, as well as a prompt to select a reaction. These reactions then influence the story's ranking on the site and whether or not it earns a badge.

There are some clear buckets but also a lot of gray areas. Our editorial team is constantly experimenting with this and pushing the boundaries. We have a distinction in our CMS between "lists" and "articles," but there are a lot of articles that use a listlike format but have a more narrative feel to them.

The thing about lists is they are super digestible. You know what you are getting up front and can decide at what point you want to start reading. Some posts have the trappings of the list format (images, big headlines) but are really more narrative articles and need to be consumed linearly.

The big thing about lists is each item can be somewhat independent. We have sharing buttons on each list item, and a lot of readers share or comment on their favorite items.

How does the design communicate both the seriousness of the subject matter and the time involved (i.e., how long it will take to read, how new the content is, how ephemeral its subject)?

To a large extent, we let the content tell that story, and we don't do much from a product/design perspective to communicate those things. We tend to take the simplest tack with things like this: present the content simply, all on one page, and let the reader decide how to consume it. One big exception is with our numbered lists. You can tell a lot about the post if it's "10 Things …" vs. "143 Things …"

What's the staffing structure, and how many people work on design at BuzzFeed? What are the skills they need?

Different departments work differently, but overall, we still have a fairly thin hierarchy and work collaboratively. The product team is currently made up of nine people. Besides myself, there are five designers, three product leads, and one project manager. Skills for designers can vary somewhat. Web design really requires a very specific mix of visual design acuity, a strong sense of interaction and user experience, and a solid understanding of technical constraints. Our designers do a mix of front-end coding and Photoshop. We have a fairly fluid and flexible process. Sometimes,

The BuzzFeed iPad app, with its visual pinboard-like appearance, offers a less chaotic browsing experience as compared to BuzzFeed.com. Only one story gets the hero-image treatment, while an infinite list of thumbnails and headlines populate the screen as the user swipes upward. The drop-down menu takes readers to their custom feed, what's hot, and all the usual sections.

On any given article page, a scrolling list of what to read next appears along the left side of the screen. The active story is highlighted in blue, to orient the reader. Sharing and liking buttons are easy to find.

We tend to take the simplest tack with things like this: present the content simply, all on one page, and let the reader decide how to consume it.

projects are taken 90 percent by a product manager. Sometimes, a designer is really responsible for the interaction.

Do you like to read?
I'd say I have an interest in reading, but I don't end up reading that many books, unfortunately; iBooks on my iPhone has made reading books somewhat feasible again, but it still seems to take me forever to get through books. The last book I read was Nate Silver's *The Signal and the Noise*, which I enjoyed a lot. But I mostly read articles that get passed around on Twitter or that I find on Kottke.org. And like everyone, I spend a lot of time researching random things that come up. And lots of BuzzFeed, of course. •

Case Study:

Huffington Post

WEBSITE: HUFFINGTONPOST.COM

FREQUENCY: CONTINUOUSLY (WEB),
WEEKLY (TABLET)

FORMAT: WEBSITE, IOS/ANDROID APPS

LOCATION: NEW YORK

PRESIDENT/EDITOR IN CHIEF:
ARIANNA HUFFINGTON

VP, DESIGN & UX: JOSH KLENERT

HUFFINGTON MAGAZINE DESIGNERS:
ANDREA NASCA, PETER NICEBERG,
MARTIN GEE

OWNER: AOL (ACQUIRED IN 2011)

YEAR FOUNDED: 2005 (WEBSITE); 2013
(TABLET APP)

A social news platform unburdened by a print legacy is an exciting and daunting prospect. When the *Huffington Post* was first launched in 2005, it needed to convince readers that it could be a trusted source for information. Establishing credibility is essential to any type of journalistic endeavor, so *HuffPost* needed to establish trust with its audience. With an editorial selection ranging from serious world news to celebrity gossip, and through a mixture of reposting and aggregating, Arianna Huffington's namesake website proved itself to be a combination of the liberal response to Drudge Report and the future of news. Jonah Peretti, who later went on to create the social news site BuzzFeed, was part of the founding team and was influential in highlighting the importance of search rather than modeling the site after the front page of a newspaper. In a *Fast Company* interview, Peretti explained the site's high-ranking search results:

"Partly it was the right keywords, partly it was being fast when the story would break, partly it was knowing which sort of nouns were important and how to write headlines and make an authoritative page, and the thing that was unfortunate about all of it was that the person who decided whether you were successful or not was a robot."

Those words might not be reassuring to a traditional news journalist or news designer, but it's a reality of the web, which *HuffPost* has mastered. As the site has grown into a multi-armed media network, publishing hundreds of stories and producing live video from its newsroom at AOL each day, design has played a greater role in communicating the brand across platforms and in creating more opportunities for instantaneous news on the desktop and phones, while the free weekly *Huffington* magazine offers slower reading experiences on the tablet.

The landing page for *Huffington* Business, a vertical within HuffingtonPost.com. The *Huffington Post* focuses on the personalities of its contributors to generate interest. **Opposite page:** A typical front page of the *Huffington Post*, dominated by a massive headline and hero image, with comment/share stats underneath, instead of an image caption.

Josh Klenert

VP, Design & UX, Huffington Post

Josh Klenert has worked in magazines and editorial design for much of his career. He studied graphic design at RIT, where he also designed his school paper. An internship with the Hearst publication *SmartMoney* led to his first job, working for Don Morris Design, where he worked on numerous magazine redesigns, and later the full brand experience for the Sundance Film Festival. At *Billboard*, he set the creative direction for everything from the website to the music trade publication's awards events. By 2008, he was a creative director for Clear Channel's iheartradio, and in 2011, he joined AOL Mobile, parent company to the *Huffington Post*. A former president of the Society of Publication Designers who still serves on its board, Klenert shares insights on the inner workings of *HuffPost* and the state of digital publishing in general.

Huffington *magazine, the weekly iPad app, was the first project you undertook with* **HuffPost.** *Tell us about it.*
Yes, Arianna and [then-executive editor] Tim O'Brien were investing in original, long-form journalism—3,000 to 5,000-word stories—what you call your traditional magazine feature. They had done an amazing job, assigning and creating these pieces—the first for-profit, digital-only website to win a Pulitzer for original reporting. But the web on a desktop computer is not the best environment to read a 5,000–word story. It's not a good user experience. They had been toying with the concept of a magazine-like product. As a website, we have over fifty verticals and publish hundreds of stories every day. It's a lot to take in. My first week at AOL was in Palo Alto, whiteboarding and designing with the *HuffPost* design and editorial team along with the AOL Mobile team—a flashback to my old magazine design days. So we did a rapid prototype for a weekend magazine where the best stuff could rise, and you could read it in a more lean-back experience. We prototyped it in January 2013, released it in the

The *Huffington Post* native app for the tablet takes some cues from the web page (such as the giant headline for the lead story), but is more refined. For article pages, swiping brings the article layer over the main image, creating a sense of depth.

spring, and it debuted at number one in the iOS App Store.

What's the structure of your design department? How do designers at Huffington Post collaborate with developers and editors?
Physically, it's a very open environment. We're in a newsroom-type setting. Design works closely with editorial, technology, and sales, so everyone sits close by. In the instance of doing native applications, our designers are literally sitting right next to the developers. And we found that to be incredibly productive.

Are the designers you hire identify more as product designers or editorial designers?

When you say "editorial designer," I think about designers who can tell a story and create a package. Whether it's redesigning a blog entry for desktop or a photo gallery for mobile, I'm looking for people who can tell a story through type, image, and layout—the traditional storytelling elements. Sure, it needs to be applied to a digital screen and, yes, there are challenges that come up through user experience, but there's a certain core essence of editorial design that is storytelling, and that's something that I look for when I hire.

I came up in a design studio background, and we were designing magazines, but we were really designing the underlying architecture that could then be handed off to the

magazine's staff to do on a regular basis. That's really what digital design is about: You're creating the underlying architecture, and then the picture is being painted by the news and content that comes flowing in on a regular basis. You can teach the digital side; you can learn the flow and the specs of an iOS app versus an Android app. But these guys have, through years of experience through magazine design, learned to package. And because they're great with building templates and packages, they have applied that mindset to digital design.

Even as it has grown, the overall look and feel of HuffingtonPost.com seems like it's always been. It still looks and feels like a blog.

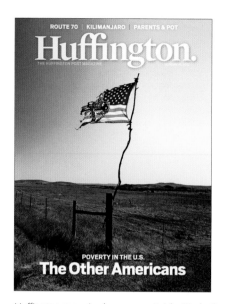

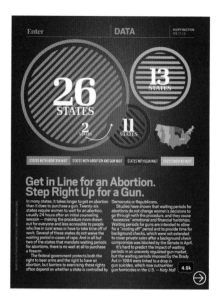

Huffington magazine has a separate identity, both on the cover and within, that brings it closer to the world of printed news magazines.

I think if you had asked Arianna, she's very proud of the fact that in the eight years that it's been in existence, they've never done a full redesign. But if you look at it today, it is vastly different than it was at the outset. We employ a very iterative process. We rapidly work on different modules of the website. So rather than doing just a massive redesign from top to bottom, we'll focus on modules of the site. How do we improve commenting? How do we improve recirculation? How do we improve the sign-in process? How do we improve the sharing process? We'll take those discrete areas, and because we have a general style guide and a general look and feel, we can apply those principles to those areas. We'll iterate and increase and evolve the design over time, but we always take a very modular approach.

Do you launch new features and see how users respond, or are you testing with users ahead of time?
We're definitely inspired by data, but it's not data driven. I think data driven means that if a predominant amount of people say, "blue, blinking, upper right," whatever, then you do that. We like to balance the data with the editorial mission and design best-practices technology to come up with the best product.

If you look at even some of the larger companies that have, over the years, done purely data-driven design—the Googles, the Amazons of the world—they're reining that in a little bit. You can't just go by the numbers. You need to have a broader strategy to your design. That's ultimately going to lead to a better place. But we'll A/B test. We'll get in front of people. We've got a very vocal community. If you compare us to most traditional publications and websites, our commenting community is significantly more engaged. Sometimes, you'll look on the top article, and it'll have thousands of comments within an hour. It's pretty intense.

Some sites are deemphasizing their home pages as the first place readers go, but the home page is still hugely important for HuffingtonPost.com.
Well, in the desktop environment, definitely the front page is our place

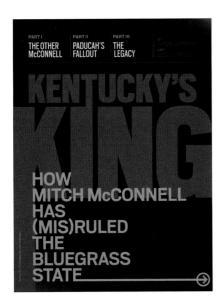

to say what's the most important thing right now. That large splash image and story at the top is editorially curated. Our editors are constantly picking and choosing what are the most important stories at any given second. So that's a very important curated editorial product. But that said, we're highly engaged in social media. So we're getting a lot of traffic from social sites such as Facebook and Twitter. And those users are coming in the side door to the article, and they may not go to the front page, but we want to keep them engaged and going from story to story to story, and that's definitely the case as we start to update our mobile products. Starting on mobile, we've begun employing an "article as home page" strategy.

What do you see happening now?
It's been amazing to see the rise of iPad design over the past few years. I still say we're in its infancy. We've been doing web for 15+ years. We're at year three for the iPad. I think we have a ways to go. A lot of traditional print publications are still just replicating their print product and not designing for this new platform, they're not rethinking it or reformatting it; they're just replicating it and adding a layer of multimedia, which reminds me of 1994 *Blender*. "Oh, we can add a video onto a CD-ROM. Great." But at the end of the day, people want to read this content.

That really influenced the design of our *Huffington* magazine. It's really stripped down. We carefully consider adding anything to this because we

want it fast and fluid and simple. We've got an easy-to-navigate, no-instructions-required approach. I really think the future is in something that is a combination of great, bespoke, traditional magazine design but that's also being updated frequently. And we're not making magazine designers design in multiple orientations for a variety of platforms. It needs to be more fluid and more responsive, and work on anything from an iPhone to an iPad to an Android to a Kindle. We're only going to get more fragmented in the coming years as far as designing for devices. So we need to be smarter about the systems that we create that allow us to be everywhere people expect us to be. •

Paul Ford
Content Strategist, Writer, Programmer

Time is an essential element in all editorial experiences, but particularly online. How long will it take a reader to digest a story or a slideshow or a video? How quickly will it load? How long is that piece of content's shelf life? How long will it take the author to create that post in the first place? And for how long will its container be relevant or will it need to be rebuilt?

Issues of time can be maddening, but they don't seem to faze Paul Ford. He's an author and developer who is currently writing a book on the web page and has spent a lot of time thinking about time. In 2007, while working for *Harper's* magazine, he single-handedly archived every one of its back issues, page by page, going back 157 years, so that they could be searchable and downloadable for subscribers, well before the *New Yorker* and other magazines followed suit.

His commencement address to the 2012 School of Visual Arts' MFA Interaction Design graduating class, titled "10 Timeframes," is required reading. In it, he implored students:

> We're constantly switching accelerations; we're jumping between time frames. That's what we're asking people to do every time we make something new, some new tool or product. We're asking them to reset their understanding of time. To accept that the sequence we're asking them to follow is the right way to do a thing.... And I want you to ask yourself when you make things, when you prototype interactions, am I thinking about my own clock or the user's?

What you said to the School of Visual Arts (SVA) MFA Interaction Design class seems so essential and not stated often enough: that we should be creating things and experiences that are worthy of people's time. Time is such a valuable commodity.

If people were more sensitive to time and not to the project—not to the design, not to the layout, not to the editorial strategy, but just to where the minutes are going to go and who's going to spend them—they could think a little bit differently about all of this stuff. By "they" I mean the people who are making the systems or making the decisions as to what gets built. We keep presenting designs, and no one ever says how long this particular CMS approach will take, or no one optimizes for ease. They optimize for certain kinds of elegance. It's very rare for someone to say, "This will only take an editor a minute." Right? They work backward from the design they want. They work backward from the look and feel. So that really drives everything, but it doesn't make for flexible systems.

When I archived *Harper's* magazine, I learned to start thinking in terms of enormous multiples. So it was a quarter million pages, and you say, "Well, that's kind of manageable." But I started to multiply it out by a minute. It took a minute per page. That turns into years very quickly. So I think that all comes out of that experience for me, which is that anything you do that has sufficiently enough human or historical data, doing one thing to all of it quickly begins to take years.

The systems that we're building, people don't think about them in terms of years, but they represent that. Every content management system that everyone hates was designed to solve a problem at hand, and there was never any budget to fix it four months out from the initial launch. I was talking with someone this morning about how they're trying to collect civic data, and what they really need to do is add a few fields to their content management systems. If they could just plug in a couple of boxes, they could get everything they needed. But it's brutal to change the system; it's exhausting. Strangely, there's always a lot of corporate politics around that stuff.

At Harper's, *you were involved in the site's design, but did you have a design background at all?*
No, I was always really sensitive to design, but that's because I was interested in the web. So early on, the web shows up—I'm thirty-eight now, so the web shows up when I'm like nineteen or twenty when I'm in college. I was a lit nerd, an English major. I picked up some HTML skills, which was enough back then. I'm very guilt motivated, so I'm like, "Well, I need to learn about design because people are asking me to build these pages, and I don't know what they're really supposed to look like. I should go figure that out."

The assumption that I'm doing it wrong has been really valuable throughout my life, and it is continually valuable. I showed up in New York City in the late 1990s, the dot-com boom. I went from company to company for a bit and worked for a branding firm. Then I went freelance as a copywriter on things like, "We have a line of synthesizers, and there are 200 of them, and they each share 1,000 qualities." Every single one of the qualities would need a bit of copy so that it could all be assembled in an online catalog, and it would all need to be written in a very bare-bones way so it could be translated into fourteen languages. So I was the copywriter to whom you could give that problem, and I would go, "Can I just do it straight in the database?" And they'd be like, "Yes, great!" It was ugly work.

Then I started to write more and more. I always had little personal web pages, and I built my own blogging system. The word "blog" wasn't there yet. I started a site called Ftrain.com, and that became my calling card. I was a pretty good writer, and I knew technology, and so I started to get a lot of calls. I got a call from NPR for "All Things Considered," so I started being on the radio to talk about mostly tech in general, but also personal essay kind of stuff. They just got a kick out of me.

So then that got you the gig with Harper's. How did the archiving project come about?
I adapted my blogging software and that ran *Harper's* website for a couple years. I wrote archive posts and thought technology thoughts for them. There really actually wasn't a lot for me to do at first. The publisher is kind of anti-web in a very open, public way. He just doesn't like or believe in the internet as a force. It's a nonprofit organization with unusual revenue needs, so it's not a priority in the same way that it is elsewhere. I was a web guy at an organization that didn't really care that much about the web. There wasn't much original content for the web. So I started to spin my wheels. Then, I figured out that they had actually done a giant bibliography of every article back to 1850, and that all we would need to do is scan and do

about a year of work, and then we could have the archive online.

So that became a huge, all-consuming project for a while because there were no resources. I bought a scanner, got a high school kid to help me, ended up hiring my fiancée at the time, now my wife, to help me. Wrote a back-end system. Figured out the database and so on. There was no one to tell me no, because it was so cheap to do. Then we built it and launched it, and it got lots of subscribers, and it was neat for people to have an archive that went back to 1850 that came for free with their subscription. That was exciting. I know for a fact that it created anxiety with other large magazines, and that was very satisfying.

Did you study library science at all? How did you know what to do?
No, and again I always felt really terrible and guilty. *Harper's* was so cheap, I couldn't get a designer, so it had to be me. I couldn't get a professional archivist, so it had to be me. I got the scanner, and I did research on what the best quality would be. At that point, I knew a lot about XML and structured data, so the gap between library archival work and structured data nerds is not that great. I really just needed to know a few specs.

The only thing I really hedged on and couldn't pull off was the goal—the metadata standards called for uncompressed TIFF images of each page, and that meant 100 MB per file. I just couldn't afford the storage. So instead I got nice high-quality JPEGs at 600 dpi. I figured if you could see the grain of the paper, there weren't any artifacts, and you had a pretty good color range, you'd be fine.

I always sensed that someone was going to descend and yell at me,

but it was more interesting to move forward and wait for that to happen. And the truth is, no, it's all fine with libraries. They were happy with the quality. I freaked out over the fact that the pages would sometimes be a tenth of a degree off because that was just the way they would scan. Or that people would be upset over the fact that you had to look at the pages to get the text or download PDFs rather than having the articles, but of course that would have been hundreds of thousands of dollars to get everything retyped. People didn't care!

> *The assumption that I'm doing it wrong has been really valuable throughout my life.*

A friend of mine who is a programmer has a great line. He said to me, "You really only want to get it to the point where it seems like magic and then stop. Anything after that point, and you are wasting your time."

And it worked.
It had tons of flaws but it worked. It was real. *Harper's* actually has a proper content management system now instead of the one that was cobbled together by me, but they kept that; the archive is kept intact, the URL structure, all the core architecture has remained there.

One of the big lessons is the design is very fungible; that's always going to change, the CMS itself is going to go away. But if you can create a really good structured set of data that is adaptable—and even if it takes a week or two to write the adapters because it's going to go in WordPress or whatever—that's the job. So the entire archive as it was has been imported over to the new system as a big blob of data. At some level, I've come to realize that my job as a web-edit whatever—I don't even know what I am right now—is to help create and then serve as the caretaker for the data structures. Everything else can be taken care of elsewhere. But it's a sort of archivist–librarian style impulse. My job at *Harper's* turned out to be getting the huge bibliography lined up with

sulted?" Do you still think that's what differentiates the web from other media?
I still stand by that piece. The gist of that piece is that the web allows this kind of two-way communication: People want to be consulted, and when given an opportunity, they will exercise that, and that will be continual. It's ridiculous, because they don't get paid, it takes their time, it generates traffic and money for someone else. That sense of power and authority and connection that they get from commenting is really important. That's one of the reasons people use the web. There's a Twitter account called Don't Read Comments [@avoidcomments]. Once a day it will put up a little

around them and having a tribal moment, except it's the thing that makes that moment possible. That to me is one of the big places that we're all negotiating. We just assumed that if you give people a voice, that people are great and they'll do right by each other and try to move towards a common goal, but that takes an enormous amount of coaching and help. They don't do it on their own.

What do you think about comments as part of the editorial experience?
Honestly, I would love to see students become committed commenters on a couple different sites, to embed and see what those communities are like and compare the experiences. People spend more time using commenting

People don't think of the systems we're building in terms of years, but they represent that.

the pages and then getting that on a hard drive in such a way that other people could do interesting things with it. Flaws and all. And just accepting the flaws and not freaking out over them, and letting that 5, 10 percent and the ripped pages in the 70s, that still bug me, and so forth, just letting it happen and moving it as far forward as I can.

When I think about this stuff, it's not the front end, and it's not the design necessarily—it's "what gets created as a big blob of data and how you hand that off" that is the job.

You wrote a piece about the web ("The Web Is a Customer Service Medium," ftrain.com/wwic.html), which so perfectly reduced the feelings of every person on the internet to "Why wasn't I con-

tweet like, "One of the things you might want to do instead of read-ing the comments is: Visit with your grandmother!" It's sort of like this slow-motion life coaching.

I know as a writer, I avoided writing for a while because I got so burned out. The audience is pain-ful—the inability to see the author as a human being who is actually one of you, to me started to feel like an actual moral failing.

It used to be that we could all quietly hate the media amongst our-selves, or bitch and moan amongst ourselves. But now that you can talk back, it really changes that dynamic because [the media are] still actually in a superior position, they're still tell-ing you what to think, they're telling you how to do things. It's almost like readers are rejecting the hierarchy

systems probably than editors do the CMS's. The editor wrote the piece in Word and pasted it into the CMS and probably spent about five minutes total in that environment to get that piece published onto the web, and then 300 to 400 people have then posted comments on top of that. You're talking about probably a dozen or more hours per piece being dumped in those boxes. They're seen as secondary experiences, but if the system works, the volume is intense.

You're writing a book about the web page, which is a fascinating topic. And currently we're seeing tools such as Readability—where you're an adviser—and Instapaper that are stripping down what's on the page for readers. What's your take on this trend?

It's funny, the aesthetic is supposed to be this collage; we're supposed to take text and image and video and put them all together into a stewpot and that's the web, right? Content management systems need to do that. That experience is supposed to define what we do. But there's a real reaction to that. It's almost like people have said, "Nah, it's too much. Just simplify this for me."

We're in a weird transitional zone. What is an article? Why are all these media types on one page? Is that actually good or not? Maybe embedded YouTube videos aren't the answer. It looked like that was the way tech should go. I mean, dress it up, sound and video. But then you look at something like Readability, and it has a lot of users, and people don't want that. Or they want to read it on a dedicated device or a dedicated app on their phone, such as in the Kindle. We're having these almost tribal moments where we're saying, "These guys don't get along. Let's separate them back."

People keep trying to give you the entire context at once, like here's the video, here's the audio. I don't know if people want to watch the video in the middle of the piece or listen to the sounds as they're reading. I'm trying to figure it out. Those are the puzzles.

What does this mean for the design of good web pages?
We've started to define "a good page" in a really specific way: The type is a little bit larger; if there's more line spacing, it's fairly wide; it uses a Typekit font instead of a default font; white background; may have a header, may have a footer,

We've started to define "a good page" in a really specific way . . . if you do a redesign, new text is 99 percent of the time going to look that way.

but it's a central column; multimedia; the pictures are wide. As I'm saying it out loud, it's funny how much of it I've internalized. That's becoming the default for smart text online. If you do a redesign, new text is 99 percent of the time going to look that way.

As sites redesign, there's now total comfort in scrolling. The early consensus that people didn't like to scroll is completely gone. We just assume now that people will scroll or swipe like crazy.

I was having a conversation the other day about how the web used to be so much sillier. You would have animated horizontal bars with little rainbows on them, and it was black backgrounds and blue text, and the rules weren't there yet. I remember the tremendous debates in the 1990s like, "Can you ethically edit your own piece after you've published it?"

The norms and the tribal standards start to emerge, and then there's a very clear line and aesthetic understanding between what the good text looks like and what the bad text looks like. Of course that's great because God knows there's more readable text on the internet than there used to be. People would do insane, terrible things. On the other hand, I always feel a little sad when the norms emerge because that period of ridiculous shenanigans is over. It's like *The New York Times* puts animated GIFs on their

home page or on some page, but they're not animating kittens running around. They're subtle, elegant, beautifully done. They have figured out a way to line up the aesthetics, and everybody's happy. And it's progress, and it's great, and it's modern, but I just love when somebody just throws a lot of glitter in the air and runs around crazy. That was really the web to me. ●

Case Study:
The New York Times

WEBSITE: NYTIMES.COM

FREQUENCY: CONTINUOUSLY (WEB), DAILY (PRINT)

FORMATS: PRINT, ONLINE, MOBILE

LOCATION: NEW YORK

EXECUTIVE EDITOR: JILL ABRAMSON

CHIEF CREATIVE OFFICER: TOM BODKIN

DIRECTOR OF DIGITAL DESIGN: IAN ADELMAN

OWNER: THE NEW YORK TIMES COMPANY

FOUNDED: 1851 (PRINT), 1996 (WEB); 2008 (MOBILE APP)

The New York Times may be the most closely scrutinized newspaper in the business, not only for the quality of its journalism but also for its innovations in everything from monetizing content to inventing new forms for storytelling. All newspapers have been struggling to remain relevant as technology changes reader expectations, and paid subscriptions become harder to retain. And yet in so many ways, *The New York Times* has been doing the right thing, taking on each challenge in a highly considered and on-brand way. Over time, the media company seems to be shedding some of its "Gray Lady" austerity and even its "New York–ness" in order to compete with the *Huffington Post*s and BuzzFeeds of the world. As our interview with Paul Ford points out, who would have thought *The New York Times* would ever use GIFs on its home page? Or build elaborate storytelling experiences such as 2013's "Snow Fall" avalanche report that exploited the web's capacities to its fullest? The investment in design and technology is noticeable and keeps things in a continuous state of evolution.

During this writing, the feature pages of the print edition underwent a subtle redesign. And a new article page design for NYTimes.com was unveiled, reflecting a similar content-forward sensibility—again with an increase in white space and improved typography. Supervised by Ian Adelman, director of digital design, the site is undergoing its most significant design changes since 2006, including a redesign of the home page. The

Tom Bodkin
Chief Creative Officer, The New York Times

Tom Bodkin has been in publishing since his high school days in Great Neck, New York. For most of his career he worked for *The New York Times*, where he began as a designer for the Home section in 1980 and has risen steadily from there. In 2013, his title changed from design director to chief creative officer for the New York Times Company, a top-level title that's a first for the media company or any newspaper, reflecting the growing recognition of design and user experience as essential to its entire mission.

How did you get started as an editorial designer?
I was the editor of my high school paper. There was no art director or formal role for a designer, so the editor did the design. Like any editor, I wrote editorials, edited copy, and assigned stories, but I also laid out the paper every month. That's really the first time I started thinking about design, although I'm not even sure I called it that. But I liked laying out the paper! And I didn't like writing. Writing's hard. Laying out the paper was more fun. It was hot type in those days, so an outside printer did the work, and I would go to the printer with my layouts, and they would set it up, and I'd see how that happened, and I really liked the production aspect of it, too.

I was a good student. I was on a trajectory to go to an Ivy League school, which I ended up doing for a short period. I went to Brown for only three semesters—I'm a dropout. I got frustrated because I wasn't sure what I was doing there. I took a few classes at the Rhode Island School of Design because I was interested in art, but I wasn't prepared to go to art school. I was studying English and history and a little economics, and I never got to the point where I had to declare a major. I worked on the daily paper at Brown, and that was partly why I dropped out. I was the production manager, which meant long hours, and a lot of sleeping through classes. They wanted to set up a cold type shop, and I was just inher-

design specifics are less significant than the thinking behind them, so we spoke to chief creative officer Tom Bodkin about his macro vision for design at *The New York Times*, as well as content strategist and blog specialist Jeremy Zilar, whose more granular focus leads to creating better tools for authors and better experiences for readers.

Front page of *The New York Times* print edition, October 21, 2013.

ently good at that. With typesetting capability, we began to take on other projects, which gave me experience designing other material. After I left Brown, I came back to New York City. I needed a job, and I had this skill, so I answered an ad in the *Village Voice* and started working at a little trashy magazine. I was hired because I knew something about production. Again, they didn't have an art director, and so I did the design.

After a while, I applied to transfer to Columbia University and was accepted. But just before I was to start, I got a job offer from Ralph Ginzburg, publisher of *Eros*, *Avant Garde* and *Moneysworth* magazines. I couldn't turn it down. There, I worked very closely with Herb Lubalin, who designed all of Ginzburg's

publications. It was an incredible experience, and that's where I started to learn about real design.

From there, I went to CBS and worked for Lou Dorfsman in the in-house design group, which mostly dealt with advertising, collateral, and corporate. That was another incredible training ground, but I felt like I really wanted to be in publications at that point. So I applied for a job at *The New York Times*. It was 1978, and I didn't get hired. But Lou Silverstein, who was the design director at *The New York Times* at the time, sent me over to *Us* magazine, which *The New York Times* was just in the process of starting, and I was hired as the founding art director. I was 25, and this was a national consumer

publication. I was in way over my head, but I did it.

For how long did you do that?
Two years. I left when *The New York Times* sold it. They started with the idea that it would be a more sophisticated version of *People* magazine, but after a while, *The New York Times* was embarrassed by it, and it was very frustrating for everybody who worked there. They went through six editors in two years. But I did a lot of design work, and I oversaw other designers, so I got some management experience. When *Us* was sold, Lou Silverstein brought me into the newspaper, and I began as the art director of the Home section.

Iterations for the cover of the Book Review section of *The New York Times.* The features sections underwent a print redesign in Spring 2013, led by Kelly Doe, Design Director for Special Projects and Brand Identity.

ScienceTimes
The New York Times

THE NEW YORK TIMES **SCIENCE TIMES** MONDAY, MONTH 00, 2012

Well

Arena
HIGHLIGHTS FROM TMAGAZINE.COM

36 Hours
MIDCOAST, MAINE

Passport
TOPIC SENTENCE TO GO HERE

On The Street
Bill Cunningham

The Hunt
Headline or Topic Here

Residential Sales
AROUND THE REGION

N.F.L. Sports Headers
SUPPORTING MATERIAL

ON LOCATION
Merida, Mexico

THE MIRROR
Tweeting 101

CHECK IN
THE RADISSON BLU AQUA, CHICAGO

COLUMN NAME | BYLINE NAMEHERE

COLUMNIST NAME

COMMENTYS   CORRECTIONS

---

2 THE WEEK
Chimps, Mars and a look ahead. JENNIFER A. KINGSON

3 ENDANGERED SPECIES
Saving the Tasmanian devil by moving it. CARL ZIMMER

4 WELL
Are we doing too many mastectomies? TARA PARKER-POPE

5 PERSONAL HEALTH
Is the annual physical overrated? JANE E. BRODY

ONLINE
In a time-lapse video, sculpturing a fractal from cards.
nytimes.com/science

AskWell, a forum for readers.
nytimes.com/well

SCIENCE | MEDICINE | TECHNOLOGY | HEALTH

ScienceTimes
The New York Times

TUESDAY, JANUARY 22, 2013   D1

How High Could the Tide Go?

Fossil beaches miles inland offer critical clues on sea level rise in a warming world.

By JUSTIN GILLIS

BREDASDORP, South Africa — A scruffy crew of scientists barreled down a dirt road, their two-car caravan kicking up dust. After searching all day for ancient beaches miles inland from the modern shoreline, they were about to give up.

Suddenly, the lead car screeched to a halt. Paul J. Hearty, a geologist from North Carolina, leapt out and seized a white object on the side of the road: a fossilized seashell. He beamed. In minutes, the team had collected dozens more.

Using satellite gear, they determined they were seven miles inland and 64 feet above South Africa's modern coastline.

For the leader of the team, Maureen E. Raymo of Columbia University, the find was an important clue as she tries to determine just how high the oceans might rise in a warming world.

The question has taken on new urgency in the aftermath of Hurricane Sandy, which caused coastal flooding that scientists say was almost certainly worsened by the modest rise of sea level over the past century. That kind of storm tide, experts say, could become routine along American coastlines by late in this century if the ocean rises as fast as they expect.

Researchers exploring ancient rock formations on South Africa's coast.

TEMPERATURE RISING
Sea Level and Science

In previous research, scientists have determined that when the earth warms by only a couple of degrees Fahrenheit, enough polar ice melts, over time, to raise the global sea level by about 25 to 30 feet. But in the coming century, the earth is expected to warm more than that, perhaps four or five degrees, because of human emissions of greenhouse gases.

Experts say the emissions that may make a huge increase of sea level inevitable are expected to occur in just the next few decades. They fear that because the world's coasts are so densely settled, the
CONTINUED ON PAGE 6

MIND | BENEDICT CAREY

Avoiding Cold Feet Down the Aisle

Women who suppress lingering doubts are more likely to seek a divorce later.

HIS CHARISMA WAS BIG ENOUGH to make his bad habits seem small, more like quirks than flaws. The cigarettes on his breath; the extra weight around the middle; the indifference to clothing and appearances — surely these were minor things, correctable in time.

In the months leading up to the wedding, in 1988, even the fact that he'd been living with his mother at age 38 seemed somehow explainable, if not ideal.

"How about that for a red flag?" said Jincey Huck, a state court employee in St. Louis, of her first husband, who has since died. "Deep down I knew it was a mistake, but I wanted to be married, I wanted kids, all that. I had cold feet the entire time," said Ms. Huck, now 51.

Psychologists have studied decision-making for more than a century, trying to tease apart how biases, emotion and personality affect big choices and small ones. They have studied people playing invest-

ment games. They have taken brain images during hypothetical moral decisions. They have compared the accuracy of snap judgments to long deliberation, trying to gauge the value of subconscious instincts.

But it's a lot harder to simulate in a laboratory the sort of big life decisions that are risky and hard to reverse: Whether to move across the country. Whether to take a new job, or buy a new house, even switch from PC to Mac. And, perhaps biggest of all: whether to walk down the aisle or split up.

"Virtually every big, real-life decision requires the decision-maker to resolve 10 fundamental questions, or what I call cardinal issues," said J. Frank Yates, a professor of marketing and psychology at the University of Michigan's business school. People only feel real confidence, he said, when they begin to address them all, including trade-offs and timing.

Most people, of course, aren't experts in decision science. They decide based on their own beliefs, whims and their gut.

So how instructive are gut feelings — particularly cold feet — when there are so many moving parts and the stakes are so
CONTINUED ON PAGE 7

Outside the Box
The beauty of math emerges from fractals made of business cards. On View, Page 3.

TO OUR READERS

Science Times has a new design and an array of features to reflect the growing role of science, medicine and health in the news and society. Among them are The Week, a review of science news and a look ahead; and AskWell, in which journalists and experts answer readers' health questions. We welcome comments on the changes, which can be e-mailed to scitimes@nytimes.com.

Dozens of iterations of various page types brought about new rules for differentiating headlines, kickers, subsections, and bylines. The new rules, paired with a more flexible grid structure, allow the photography and illustrations to take center stage.

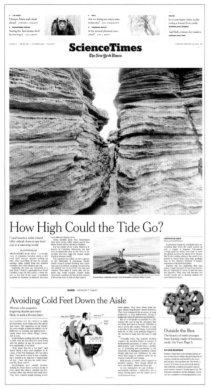

Feature section first pages of *The New York Times* after the 2013 redesign. Putting them side by side illustrates how much flexibility and variety the system allows without diluting the newspaper's identity.

I try to figure out what it is that an editor and designer are trying to do and try to help them to do it better.

You've held so many roles in thirty-plus years.
The role hasn't really changed drastically. The place has changed a lot, though, digital being the biggest change. It's just grown tremendously; even without digital, it's grown. But at its core, my job has remained the same.

How would you define it?
The job is setting and maintaining design standards and managing a large creative group. It's interesting because, again, I don't have a formal education in management. I learned on the job from great designers, particularly Lou Dorfsman, Herb Lubalin, Lou Silverstein, and Roger Black. They weren't all great managers, though. I learned how to design from their example, but much of my management training came from avoiding their mistakes.

I try to do a lot of listening and teaching. I try to figure out what it is that an editor and designer are trying to do and try to help them

to do it better. I think of myself to some degree as an editor, and I think a good publication designer needs to be as much an editor as a designer. The two things are inseparable. I think you need to speak the language of an editor, and they need to see you as central to the process of telling a story, not just somebody who makes things look pretty. I've always felt that that's what's interesting about publication design—the content and the substance of it and how design is so integral to that act of communication, not at all superficial. There's an aspect of it that can be superficial, but that's not successful design.

So how has that approach to nonsuperficial design played out on the interactive side?

This is where the history of digital design against the history of print design becomes really fascinating. At the beginning, digital design was "skinning," because that's all you could do, at best. The challenge has been to bring sophisticated design to the digital world because it wasn't there from the beginning. I've always been focused on integrating the principles of good graphic design with the interactive capabilities of digital. In a lot of places, they're still very separate. There was digital design and there was print design, and there was no overlap; and the print designers and digital designers really didn't trust each other. There was a big divide.

At one time, The New York Times *and NYTimes.com actually were two separate companies. How did they eventually combine?*

Digital was not only a separate company, it was in a separate building. When we first started the website in the 1990s, I found a designer to work with them, and later I found the first NYTimes.com art director. I would meet with that person every couple of weeks and talk to them, but they didn't report to me. I was not overseeing digital design; I was more like a consultant. And that went on until Khoi Vinh [former NYTimes.com design director, 2006–2010].

Through the Khoi Vinh period, we started merging the newsrooms, and then Khoi eventually reported to me.

I think a good publication designer needs to be as much an editor as a designer.

And that's when I got more actively involved in digital design. I learned a tremendous amount from Khoi. At that point, my focus was to integrate the art departments. I felt strongly that the greatest advantage we had was that we had both a strong foundation in classic graphic design

A story page on NYTimes.com before (left) and after (right) the new design, introduced to beta users in March 2013. The new layout features a tray of articles along the top, a larger headline and hero image, wider paragraphs, bigger type, more white space, and less noise.

> *If you were a designer graduating from school in the early 1990s, and you immediately went into Web design, you never really got a chance to learn or use many basic design tools.*

and a digital design group that was well versed in interaction and already producing a very successful website.

We have to remember that engineers created the internet in the 1980s to talk to other engineers. It wasn't created as a design platform or as a wide-ranging publication platform. And so it didn't have the tools that graphic designers are normally used to using.

If you were a designer graduating from school in the early 1990s, and you immediately went into web design, you never really got a chance to learn or use many basic design tools. You didn't deal with type in any sophisticated way because you only had the four typefaces that were resident on everybody's machine. You never assigned an illustration, because there was no appetite for

illustration online at that time. You didn't deal with concepts, because it wasn't about concepts, it was about templates. The beginnings of the internet involved designing forms into which content was flowed, but I knew then that this medium, kind of like television in the 1940s, was going to change tremendously. The tools were going to get a whole lot better, and there would be an appetite

Top left: Another story page, oriented horizontally. Notice the similarities with the redesigned web page on the facing page. Many of the decisions made here influenced the new web page design, in part to recognize and aid readers who access *The New York Times* on both platforms. ***Below left:*** Tapping on the top left corner summons a view of the contents list in the iPad app, which lets readers customize their home pages by "starring" the sections they want to read first. ***Above:*** A redesigned article page in the iPad app, oriented vertically.

for high-end design where there wasn't at the time. So you had digital designers learning to make the best of the limited tools available, becoming very adept at creating templates and starting to understand interactive behavior, but not learning anything about type or concept or story—they weren't doing storytelling. None of the people in our digital design group had ever assigned an illustration when they came to this building. The magic was in combining classic print design skills with the new digital interface skills. I thought the best way to do it is to get these people to work together.

How hard has it been to bridge these skills, to make print designers more aware of interaction and interactive designers more aware of graphic design principles?

There are basic principles that apply to publication design no matter what the medium is. It's always about communication. That's what you're trying to do. You're trying to either communicate information or tell a story. Sure, it's nice to surprise people and give them pretty stuff to look at, but that's secondary to telling a story. And that's critical. In many ways, it's the same challenge in print and digital; you're telling a story, but using different tools.

I remember when we started printing in color—everybody thought it was going to be terrible. I kept saying to people here, that our underlying principles are the same, and color's just another design tool, and we'll use it for the same purpose we use other design tools. People thought they would never get used to it, and two weeks later, they were used to it. Adherence to fundamentals makes the adoption of new tools and forms of media relatively easy.

In 2003, the newspaper redesigned in a big way. The recent changes have been much quieter.

We narrowed the width of the paper and went all Cheltenham type. But we never actually just ripped up everything and started all over again, the way many papers do redesigns. I've always looked at it more as an evolution, adapting to new technology,

The New York Times iPhone app in iOS7. From the "top news" landing page, outlined here in blue, tapping the top left corner brings up a list of sections (outlined in green). Tapping a section brings up a section front, here the national section (pink). Tapping "Photos" brings up a wider selection of images in reverse chronological order (purple), designed to be browsed in slide shows (orange), and with captions upon request (green). Photos and video are set against a black, lightboxed background, in contrast with the article pages that are always on white. Photos are zoomable and browsable in vertical and horizontal orientations.

Tapping on any part of an article slug brings up an article page (orange), and swiping left at any point during a scroll will bring up the next article (red) in that section.

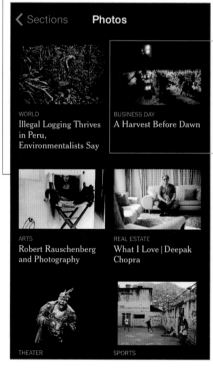

China's Arms Industry Makes Global Inroads

By EDWARD WONG and NICOLA CLARK

Last Updated: October 20, 2013

Members of Aviation Industry Corporation of China displayed a model of the JF-17 jet at an exposition in Beijing last month. SIM CHI YIN FOR THE NEW YORK TIMES

BEIJING — From the moment Turkey announced plans two years

develop more

d from Beijing
Clark from
tributed
Kong. Patrick
tributed

hine

CITY ROOM

New York Tod: Marriage Cros

By ANDY NEWMAN and SAM F

Last Updated: 10:42 AM ET

Rich Kiamco, left, and Davi gay couple married in Jerse REENA ROSE SIBAYAN/THE JER ASSOCIATED PRESS

Updated 10:32 a.m. |

CITY ROOM

New York Today: Gay Marriage Crosses the River

By ANDY NEWMAN and SAM ROBERTS

Last Updated: 10:42 AM ET

Rich Kiamco, left, and David Gibson were the first gay couple married in Jersey City this morning. REENA ROSE SIBAYAN/THE JERSEY JOURNAL, VIA ASSOCIATED PRESS

Updated 10:32 a.m. | On the day that

A Harvest Before Dawn

In the predawn chill of a September morning, Mario Bazán, his wife, Gloria, and their crew of about 10 workers arrive to harvest sauvignon blanc grapes grown on a plot near their Napa Valley home. Here, Mr. Bazán maneuvers a tractor, positioning the lights for the workers.

JIM WILSON/THE NEW YORK TIMES

The New York Times

Snow Fall
The Avalanche at Tunnel Creek

By JOHN BRANCH

T he snow burst through the trees with no warning but a last-second whoosh of sound, a two-story wall of white and Chris Rudolph's piercing cry: "Avalanche! Elyse!"

The Pulitzer-winning article "Snow Fall: Avalanche at Tunnel Creek" has become synonymous with immersive interactive storytelling online. The parallax-scrolling, six-chapter story—built with HTML5, CSS3, and JavaScript—uses full-width high-res images, animations, data visualizations, and video that unfurls with each narrative twist. Above, the opening image and title frame at **nytimes.com/projects/2012/snow-fall**.

I remember when we started printing in color—everybody thought it was going to be terrible.... People thought they would never get used to it, and two weeks later, they were used to it.

adapting to new forms of communication. It's always a very practical approach. If you go back and look at the paper fifty years ago, it does look very different. But it's an evolutionary change, where we make adjustments as we come up with new ideas.

It's important when the Sunday paper lands on your doorstep that it all feels as one piece. You want to evoke a certain feeling and emotion, a familiarity—that's what builds habit. You want people to see a section of *The New York Times* separated from every other section and still know it's *The New York Times*. That's all about design continuity and consistency, and finding that right balance between consistency and variety. Digital is another piece of that. Those are the challenges of designing a large product with a whole lot of sub-products within it.

What do you see happening next?
I don't see another revolution in media like digital has brought for a long time. Obviously, we're not quite television in 1940s, but we're television in the 1950s, and it's still got a long way to go. I think there will be a continual move toward people consuming more and more of their information digitally. I think it's inevitable because of its convenience.

That's where I see the basic principles of good design as critical, whatever the platform. The stuff you design needs to make sense, be well organized, be accessible, and be visually exciting. It has to do with basic principles and smart concepts. Good video isn't the same as good written narrative. But there are certain qualities that make both successful—qualities of excellence—that can be applied across all media. •

From top, left to right: As the reader scrolls down, the already-seen images and content are covered over as a video element fades into view. At the bottom of the first section, a view of the area rotates and stops. To keep the reader from feeling lost, persistent navigation hovers in a horizontal bar along the top of the browser window.

Jeremy Zilar

Content Strategist/ Blog Specialist, The New York Times

It's easy to forget that it was once a radical concept for newspapers to have blogs. For editors to relinquish some measure of control, for reporters to take on "more work," and for readers to understand the connection of this more-opinionated content with the main publication has not been instantaneous or easy. The blogs at *The New York Times* are no longer controversial—they're an essential means for providing additional commentary in an immediate and engaging way.

One of the nimble minds behind that balancing act is Jeremy Zilar, who joined the NYTimes.com design team in 2006 and has shepherded more than 200 blogs into existence. More recently, his work has expanded beyond blogs toward content strategy across the *Times*'s websites. Zilar studied painting, drawing, and digital media at the Rocky Mountain College of Art and Design and also briefly taught preschool, which he says is helpful in his current occupation. "You need a good amount of patience and a good amount of handholding and understanding because people get very scared of technology," he says. "And if they're scared, they can't actually make good use of it. So you need to find the level at which they're comfortable and see if you can raise

them up one level from there." We asked Zilar about creating and growing this critical element of *The New York Times* online experience.

How did blogs at The New York Times *come about?*
I was hired in 2006 to figure out blogs—everything from building them to how they're going to be integrated with the site to designing them. There were only about three or four blogs at the time, and they had been publishing on WordPress, which I was very happy about..

It was a very big, open landscape. A lot of newspapers were just starting to launch blogs. Here, we had a lot of entrepreneurial editors or writers pushing editors, saying, "We've got to make this happen."

(From top, left to right): "Snow Fall," continued. A diagram animates over an aerial view of the mountain valley; archival photographs are tiled alongside text; an icon indicates a pop-up slideshow of images; an animated data visualization tracks the storm that triggered the avalanche.

There was a team of 30 people or so working on the other content management system that runs the rest of NYTimes.com, and then there was just another designer and me working on the blog templates. I was designing and building out all of them.

Within a year, there were 100 blogs. One of the wonderful things about WordPress (and also about the internet) is if you structure things right, you can create a system in which you can do a lot of work across an array of things while allowing each thing to feel unique and distinct. So for example, all the blogs shared the same skeleton template, but I created ways in which each one could be customized, so now if I need to update something across all of them, it's as easy as updating something on one of them.

What was the mission for blogs at the Times?

The goal from the start was not to make it feel like a separate identity but actually fold it into *The New York Times* reading experience online. First, it was figuring out how these things fit into the larger organization visually and from the readers' experience. What you had in the paper was a very news-driven, very orchestrated, very tightly edited set of articles that contained very little of the writer's voice. And when the voice of the writer shone through, it was labeled as such, like "News Analysis"

or "Column" or "Opinion." These are distinctions that matter a whole lot here. Then all of a sudden you have this blog, and one of the key things from the beginning was finding a way to let it be more voice-y. Letting the writer say "I." Or telling a story and letting the writer's voice be part of that reading experience, which is very much a part of the web.

There are fewer than twenty sections of the printed newspaper but more than 100 blogs.

Actually, we've launched more than 200. We've performed a lot of different experiments along the way. I mean, once I built things into a stable place, someone would say, "The pope's coming in for two weeks, and

Animations throughout the article engage and explain. "Snow Fall" was assembled by a stellar team of writers, editors, photojournalists, documentary filmmakers, developers, and designers. For more about how they built it, we recommend reading this account: **source.opennews.org/en-US/articles/how-we-made-snow-fall**.

he's going to tour, and we want to blog about it." Little experiments like that allowed us to see what topics and time scales would work for blogs.

So a blog could last for only a two-week period?

We didn't always intend to make something into a brand or make it really big. Sometimes a blog was a venue in which to try something, to experiment with publishing on the web. That's been the biggest gift that the blogs offered to *The New York Times*, to figure out how to do online publishing, which is very different than print publishing. In addition to that voice that needs to be rolled in, you need to start thinking about links, embedded media, and building

a different type of narrative than the pyramid structure that a lot of journalists learn in journalism school. In a blog or on the web, people expect the story to be a lot more woven and interconnected. The context matters as much as the links within it.

How much of the time are you working on the design of each of the blogs?

The majority of my job has actually been in training and coaching in a lot of ways, and observing and watching people work and making changes based off of that. You can only do so much design work before you need to do the training work to get people to use the design that you built. It takes time to get people up to speed to use

the tools to their full capabilities, to start to be so familiar that you start thinking about new ways to craft what it is you're doing.

Do the blogs serve as a design incubator for other parts of the website, a way to try out technology?

I would say not a design incubator but more so a writing and editing incubator, and a tools incubator. Publishing's at this weird state, and if you look around at other publications, you can see that they have the same problems. They have a content management system that is largely built for print articles. How do they deal with web-only articles, and how do they integrate them? Do they

From the *Times* blogs: (above) The Well blog, which covers health matters at **well.blogs.nytimes.com**; (opposite page) the Sinosphere blog, about the future of China, at **sinosphere.blogs.nytimes.com**; and Deal Book, a blog for the financial markets, at **dealbook.blogs.nytimes.com**.

separate them out as blogs, or does it all feel like one natural report?

Back in the day, and actually still today to some degree, blogs were started at publications because they were easier to use, easier to build. Most newspapers had some sort of legacy content management system that was just unchangeable, so if you wanted to put a blog in there, it was impossible. So that's why blog platforms such as WordPress or Movable Type caught on.

Was there also a benefit to giving blogs their own look and feel as opposed to the paper?
Yes, because you had articles that were written for the paper, but then how do you identify the articles that are only online? This is the thinking:

"Well, the online articles will go in the blog, and that way each will have its own home." Yet that always undermines the experience of the reader who only reads online and doesn't read the paper. They may not get all the politics coverage, because some of it exists on the blogs, some of it exists over in the Politics section, and they're not mixed together at any point. And that's kind of problematic.

What are other ways content online can have a different kind of exchange with readers?
Comments need a big step in evolution as well. As opposed to comments being this totally open-ended space where anybody can say anything, you could start to create something a little bit more interesting if you find

ways to control that or guide that conversation better. We're starting to do that now with structured Q&A's on the Well blog, so people can ask a question like, "Why does my foot hurt after I run?" And then if other people have similar questions like, "What's going on with my foot after I exercise?" the moderator can take all those questions, group them together, and try to answer them better for readers.

It's helping to define a type of content. I draw a lot of parallels to magazine editing and magazine design because as you move through the book, you want there to be big things and small things to keep you moving and keep you reading. In a lot of ways, you want that online as well. If everything just has headline

> *As opposed to comments being this totally open-ended space where anybody can say anything, you could start to create something a little bit more interesting if you find ways to control that or guide that conversation better.*

and text, headline and text, you lose that amount of texture. Because a lot of the text in articles or blog posts occurs below the fold on the screen, you're really just seeing headline and text, and then you're scrolling a bit, and how do you get to the next thing?

If you can find ways to add more texture to that reading experience, so it's not just "headline, text," it's actually an interactive question. Maybe I can vote it up or vote it down. Maybe I can actually participate in a different way. This thing that I landed on is not a traditional article, but it's something more. That becomes interesting for the reader and also it becomes something that we can start to identify and craft and work into shape.

What do you most enjoy about creating these new editorial experiences on the web?

I like creating systems and frameworks for people to create really great work. Setting up the right conditions is one of the biggest parts of what makes something successful. When I see successful publications coming out with a new launch or a new identity, or I see a blog that's starting on a new clip, I think that's largely indicative of the environment they're working in, the ways that they're probably communicating

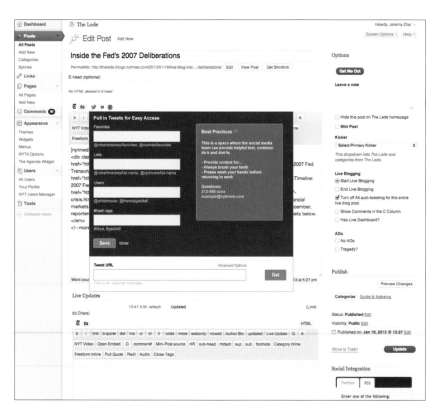

A new Twitter embed tool that is being built for **thelede.blogs.nytimes.com**, left, will help editors populate a templated live blog (opposite page, left). More complex tools come into play when pulling in live data during special events such as elections (see election night coverage on the NYTimes.com home page, far right). But the principle is still the same: sound tools for reporting the news in real time.

about the thing that they're making and the ways they are sharing their ideas. That's largely what I try to craft and create here: the right environment for creating great work.

A lot of that is the tools—you need to love editing in the thing that you're editing in. You need to feel in control. I think most people, especially on the web, want to feel like they can touch the internet. I think when that quality comes through in the writing, it produces really great content. It doesn't feel extremely distant, like it's been through the hands of six or seven editors. There needs to be something there—maybe it's a turn of phrase that ends in a link. Maybe it's just the right headline or a photo that takes it beyond or ties it in with

I think most people, especially on the web, want to feel like they can touch the internet.

another story. You want to feel like somebody actually touched this and pushed it on to you and that they're waiting for you to read it because they're excited for you to read it. I get excited about that. •

Case Study:
The Guardian

WEBSITE: GUARDIAN.CO.UK

FREQUENCY: CONTINUOUSLY (WEB), DAILY (PRINT)

FORMATS: PRINT, ONLINE, MOBILE

LOCATION: LONDON

EDITOR: ALAN RUSBRIDGER

EDITOR, GUARDIAN.CO.UK: JANINE GIBSON

CREATIVE DIRECTOR: ALEX BREUER (2013), PREVIOUSLY MARK PORTER (1996–2012)

CHIEF DIGITAL OFFICER: TANYA CORDERY

OWNER: GUARDIAN MEDIA GROUP

FOUNDED: 1821 (PRINT), 1995 (WEB), 2009 (IPHONE APP), 2011 (IPAD APP)

The history of the *Guardian* goes back almost two centuries—it was first founded as the *Manchester Guardian*, in 1821, before becoming simply the *Guardian* in 1959, and centralizing its editorial operations in London in 1964. But its design history only got interesting in 1988 when David Hillman, tasked with giving the broadsheet a "modern, newsy, busy" look (as per the brief by then assistant editor Michael McNay), introduced the paper's first grid system and a contemporary masthead that combined Garamond italic ("The") with Helvetica bold ("Guardian").

Eleven years later, then design director Simon Esterson and associate art director Mark Porter made a number of improvements, which they explained in an article titled "Design to create pages people want to read" (*Guardian*, April 18, 1999). "Newspapers have to try to keep up with the standards set by magazines," Esterson commented. They modified the grid, made the overall hierarchy of information clearer, and replaced the use of the typeface Garamond with Miller by Matthew Carter.

In 2005, Esterson and Porter radically redesigned their own work and Hillman's, changing the masthead and reducing the broadsheet size to the Berliner format, unique for a British paper, and began printing color throughout. They commissioned custom typefaces such as Guardian Egyptian, a suite of fonts used for the new logo, set inside a blue banner, and its companion Publico, both by Commercial Type designers Christian Schwartz and Paul Barnes. The *Guardian* website has evolved alongside the paper and surpassed it, unsurprisingly, in worldwide readership. Neville Brody, one of its original designers, explained to the British Design Council about his 1998 version of what was then called the *Guardian Unlimited* (Guardianunlimited.co.uk): "We weren't going to be conventional for a start . . . It was going to be centre of the page—or screen—and that was quite unusual at the time. The top of the page was going to be full of blocks that could be combined in any way to form any kind of meaning without the use of heavy images . . . We wanted the simplest navigation possible, and the simplest way to understand the site was to have less on the page. I pointed out that digital white space was infinite. White space is a lack of information, and it doesn't cost anything," to which a commenter wrote "What a relief to not be all crammed and cubey."

When Mark Porter explained his redesign of that site in 2007, he focused on the home page experience, while noting that over the next eighteen months, improvements would take place sitewide, affecting half a million pages. By 2008, the site was rebranded as Guardian.co.uk. In late 2012, a responsive mobile site was launched at m.guardian.co.uk and at m.guardiannews.com for U.S. visitors, making it more usable. In 2013, the *Guardian* began experimenting with more cinematic storytelling under creative director Alex Breuer. And in May 2013, it launched its own media-rich feature, "Firestorm," and made global headlines with its groundbreaking coverage of the United States National Security Agency's surveillance programs.

While the print edition has a circulation of 213,000, the website draws close to 4 million unique, global daily browsers. The *Guardian*, like *The New York Times*, has broken new ground with blogging and more cinematic storytelling.

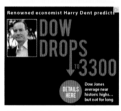

Sections of the *Guardian*, such as "Environment" and "Comment is Free" (opinion) are color-coded to accustom readers to the type of content within.

The "Firestorm" article in the *Guardian* is often compared to "Snow Fall" in *The New York Times*, as they are both emotional stories presented in an interactive way. The *Guardian*, however, uses the medium more as an interactive video, where scrolling brings up either images or videos overlaid by text, audio, or both. The story was selected to compete in the prestigious Sheffield documentary festival, and was produced to coincide with the launch of *Guardian Australia*.

Alex Breuer

Creative Director, Guardian News and Media

Alex Breuer is creative director at the *Guardian*, overseeing its print and digital products as well as contributing to branding work for Guardian News and Media. Prior to joining the *Guardian* in January 2013, he was the digital design director at the *Times* (of London), overseeing the design of its web and native products. Before crossing into the world of news media design, Breuer was an art and creative director for consumer magazines including *Esquire* and *Men's Health*.

You've been at the Guardian *for less than a year. What are some of the initial challenges you've faced?*
I joined at a time when there was a great appetite for change, in terms of workflow, improving the digital products, and establishing The *Guardian* as a global brand. At the heart of this is that task to develop a consistent design and interaction language across all digital platforms. Currently, our web apps all have a very different look and feel. This is a huge undertaking, as you can imagine. But basically, I am developing an underlying grid and design system that serve both a fully responsive web presence and a universal app. Also, very much part of this process is looking at all editorial workflows and patterns. The content as well as the design needs

to be responsive for this to work. How people consume our content across different platforms is not just driven by the size of viewport, but also by time of day, week, etc. So it has been really important to understand in great depth not just the behaviors of current users but also those new users who we wish to bring to brand.

The brand work is also an interesting challenge. Much of the development of our current digital products has leant on recognition of the print brand. The lack of a print legacy in the U.S. and Australia (our main target markets) means we have to rethink our message and visual identity. So getting the balance right between establishing our identity in new markets whilst still bringing loyal

readers in the UK with us is a very delicate process.

You must have played a large part in the "Firestorm" project, launched in May 2013. Could you share what was involved in that massive, multimedia undertaking?

This involved a hugely talented multi-disciplinary team: literary journalists, video journalists, audio journalists, designers, and developers. Our goal was always to develop a new form of narrative, one that was a real meld of literary journalist skills, broadcast journalist skills, and eyewitness/user content. My role in this was to gently shape the storyboard or narrative of the project, balancing the flow and duration of content types so the users got the clearest journey through the content, and that we used the right form of storytelling (visual, audio, literary) for the right narrative strand. Getting this right was only half the challenge. Bringing together complete narratives from different content types and splicing them also required a very sensitive approach in dealing with the creators of that content, who were more used to seeing their work shown in its entirety and placed alongside other forms rather than having them combined.

How is the Guardian unique compared to other places you've worked for?

The organization structure is much less hierarchical. People are empowered to take risks and initi-ate their own projects. A focus on well thought-through and expertly executed design as part of the story-telling experience is rated as highly as the literary, making this probably one of the best editorial design jobs in the world.

We noticed that on your LinkedIn page you haven't listed any post-secondary school education. Are you self-taught?

Yes, I have not been formally trained as a designer/art director. I had always been interested in design and art from a very young age, devour-ing books and exhibitions. My first encounter with editorial design was working with my father on a univer-sity magazine he edited. After school, I decided to take a break from formal

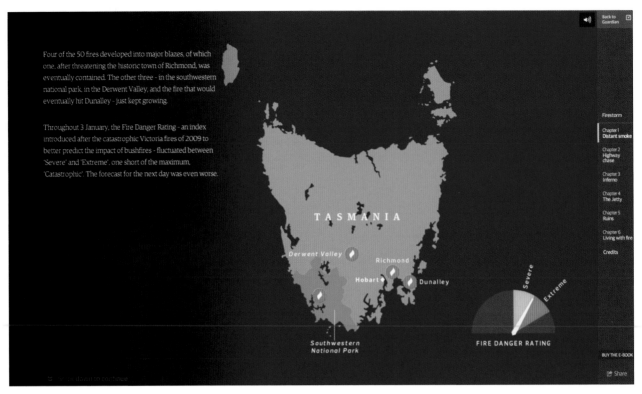

Four of the 50 fires developed into major blazes, of which one, after threatening the historic town of Richmond, was eventually contained. The other three - in the southwestern national park, in the Derwent Valley, and the fire that would eventually hit Dunalley - just kept growing.

Throughout 3 January, the Fire Danger Rating - an index introduced after the catastrophic Victoria fires of 2009 to better predict the impact of bushfires - fluctuated between 'Severe' and 'Extreme', one short of the maximum, 'Catastrophic'. The forecast for the next day was even worse.

TASMANIA

Derwent Valley

Richmond

Hobart

Dunalley

Southwestern National Park

Severe

Extreme

FIRE DANGER RATING

Back to Guardian

Firestorm

Chapter 1
Distant smoke

Chapter 2
Highway chase

Chapter 3
Inferno

Chapter 4
The Jetty

Chapter 5
Ruins

Chapter 6
Living with fire

Credits

BUY THE E-BOOK

Share

A dynamic map in the first chapter of the Firestorm story allows the reader to see the context of the story over time.

... the key attribute across all teams is the ability to communicate simply and clearly the value and reasons for their work to nondesigners.

education to pursue music with the intention of going to art college in due course. However, my musical abilities didn't match my aspirations and so I sought to explore a career in editorial design. I was fortunate enough to get a very junior job working at Haymarket Publishing.

Two things really helped me learn and develop my skills. First, the advent of Apple computers and sophisticated, but easy to use, design software. But mostly I was fortunate enough to be mentored by some of the best editorial designers in the business—initially by Roland Schenk and then Mark Porter, who was a creative director at Haymarket at the time. Effectively, I was probably getting the best possible apprenticeship I could hope for. Subsequently, I also worked for another great editorial designer, Simon Esterson, at his consultancy. Interestingly, none of my mentors had formally studied design either so I gained a huge amount of confidence from this.

One of the key things that struck home to me through this early period

is that at the heart of the editorial design process was the need to have an understanding of storytelling and journalistic narratives as keen and clear as that of a journalist. This reinforced the difference between great editorial design and decoration.

How is the design department structured at the Guardian?
Currently, the department is split across disciplines and products. I have a department of "digital designers" who focus on UX/UI across web and native products; a news design team dedicated to producing the daily sections of the paper; and a features design team who work across magazines and weekly newsprint sections. The print graphics and interactive teams are integrated together

Firestorm

Chapter 1
Distant smoke

Chapter 2
Highway
chase

Chapter 3
Inferno

Chapter 4
The Jetty

Chapter 5
Ruins

Chapter 6
Living with fire

Credits

BUY THE E-BOOK

Share

Chapter Two
Highway chase

Scroll down to continue

The story is broken down into six chapters, each of which opens with a full-screen video.

as native, as their work is complementary. Going forward, I plan to begin to use print art direction talent to feed good editorial design thinking into digital iterations of stories. I see this as distinct from the core digital design for platform and product development.

What skills are required for designers on your team?
A keen editorial design eye, attention to detail on typography, ability to interpret and understand a story to enable simple and clear art direction. Recently it is even more important that digital designers have some understanding and hopefully practical knowledge of front-end development. But the key attribute across all teams is the ability to communicate simply and clearly the value and reasons for their work to nondesigners. Editorial environments can be combative and contrary, so you need the ability to stand on your own feet and stand up for your ideas. •

David Sleight

Creative Director, UX and Product Designer, Developer

David Sleight is a web designer who cares about readers. He's a former creative director for Businessweek .com (prior to its acquisition by Bloomberg) and has consulted on user experience and product design for Readability, a web application that, among other things, lets users control the visual noise of webpages. As a philosophy and history major, he developed an interest in design as a student working on an early version of his college website. Sleight spoke to us about the first wave of iPad magazines and how the print-artifact mindset can stand in the way of reader-friendly interactive editorial design.

As someone who's been designing reading experiences for digital platforms since the early 2000s, what are the most significant changes you've noticed in how people read online?
As a web guy, I tend to get hyper-sensitive when people say you can't do long-form content online. I've always felt intuitively that that's not the case. With the most-read articles on a service such as Readability, people spend more than four minutes on those pieces—that's the average. The high end of the scale is way more than that. That's about as much time as people spend on print articles for monthly or weekly periodicals. We need to do more experimenting to find out for sure, but one conclusion is that we're see-ing design influencing the amount of time people spend with content and the way they interact with it. And that activity is in the apps, but it's also on the web. People actually are spending time reading stuff on desktop and laptop screens. What we're doing with design is having an impact.

In what ways have you noticed editorial experience design evolving?
It's weird to me that editorial web design ossified so quickly onto the inverted L: header at the top, navigation on the side, this column over here. Then in the past two years or so, we've started to see experiments with a more graceful editorial layout. My hope is that it trickles down and infects everybody. Even ESPN.com, where you wouldn't expect it, has stories that are beautifully clutter free, with involved layouts. I actually found myself reading this very long-form journalism and long-form designed article, and it had everything to do with the design of the article. All the things we were doing before were hurting our content. We can take a piece that somebody wasn't spending any time on, refactor the design so it's humane, and suddenly someone will spend double-digit minutes on it.

What do you mean by a more humane design?
A table of contents on a single page is an act of humane design. I can look at this, and I can comprehend, with one sweep of the eye, where everything is. The idea that wayfind-ing can be spread out over several pages in a print magazine always drives me batty. The most important rule of thumb is empathy—putting yourself in the reader's place. If I am reading the site, does the design let my eye travel? Do I see what the most important parts of it are? Do I have space to read? And if it is long-form content, am I giving the article comfortable amounts of white space, comfortable typog-raphy, images that actually add to the editorial rather than take away from it? Is the advertising hostile, is it jumping out and getting in your face? Is the designer being humane to the reader? Are they present-ing something that they would feel comfortable with reading?

Readability and similar tools such as Instapaper, Pocket, whatever else is coming—don't they undo all of the work of the editorial experience designer?
Reformatting does not represent infidelity on the part of the user to your design—it only represents infidelity when they do it out of spite. We get a lot of users who are like, "Thank God I ran Readability, so I could read this page," because a page has a really hostile design or it has a nondesign. A big user community for Readability is people who need it as an assistive tool, and that has benefits for all of us. For the sites that are well designed, we actually see a little bit of competi-tion there, upping the bar on the humaneness of the editorial design online as a result.

What's another misconception you've noticed about reading experiences either online or on tablets?
Online, or interactive, is an inher-ently flexible medium. I've read a lot of critiques of iPad magazines, and I agree that the walled garden

approach is bad, and design moves such as page flips don't mesh. But it's not as if those are indelible, inherent properties of a magazine on an iPad. It's a bitmap screen, and you can do anything you want with it, within some broad limitations, and the same thing goes for the web.

These experiences are inherently informed by a print legacy where literally you did at one point hit print, and it became an artifact. Once you do it, it's done. Then on the computer science side, people approached it as if they were creating one deliverable to be fixed, because they were used to a QA [Quality Assurance]-driven process adopted from building software. However, any QA system is going to be broken because it's not adapted

A website's home page seems to be tied to an old medium—the front page of a newspaper—and there are people who say you don't need one anymore because people are reading content through Twitter, Facebook, even Readability. What do you think? Does the home page matter?

In terms of news, I'd say an emphatic yes. For an editorial home page, particularly for news, you don't know what you don't know. You're coming to a home page to be informed. You need the editor to come through and tell you, "This is what's important," or at the very least "This is what's going on." Hence, it's the designer's job to assist the editor to tell the user that this is what's important. It gets dangerous because you don't want to get too preachy. That tends

mind. But when you're news driven, that doesn't actually work. The main navigation has cues to say things like, "We have a large style section. You might not have known that, but it's here, and it's discoverable."

How do you determine if something is more "readable"? Do you test that?

Until this point, it's been quite intuitive. A lot of the rules are the ones that Robert Bringhurst, author of *The Elements of Typographic Style*, would teach us. We have a general notion of what a decent line length is and leading proportions. Those are still true online; they're just modified. How do we test new stuff to figure it out? We're still kind of grasping our way through that. And really that is straight-up user testing online. User experience testing is mainly about, "were you able to achieve a goal?" We don't often define a goal as, "did you find it comfortable to read?"

What interests you about this area of design?

I want to push the cause forward. I want to further content. I want to give people more tools. I also want to nudge a designer and see how they respond back. Any friction that creates movement is important. •

The new medium is still being understood in terms of the old one.

to something that's going to change over time.

The new medium is still being understood in terms of the old one. I think we're just getting out of that wave now. It's been a two-year tablet mania of shops making very fixed editorial layouts. We web designers predicted that they were not going to be successful because the audience has been educated to have more liberty with the content. The grand scheme of progress doesn't go in reverse. Once you've been given these tools, you can't take them away. So we're still in the early phase. And in this case, we skipped everything we learned with the web and interactive design and went back to print and started over again.

to put the editor and the designer in a position of authority, and we need to do that diplomatically, as if to say "We're here to teach and assist." Sometimes it's "This is absolutely what's important, and I'm not going to show you anything else, you must look at this thing." And then editors will say, "How come they didn't click on that story that they were really supposed to?" It's a little like parenting: You can't actually tell your kid everything to do, but you can put up some guidelines.

Someone at Businessweek.com once advocated that the home page be turned into a search field. The argument was, "It works really well for Amazon." Well, in retail situations, you usually arrive with an idea in

Case Study:
USA TODAY

WEBSITE: USATODAY.COM

FREQUENCY: CONTINUOUSLY (WEB), DAILY (PRINT)

FORMATS: PRINT, WEB, MOBILE

LOCATION: MCLEAN, VIRGINIA

PUBLISHER: LARRY KRAMER

EDITOR: DAVID CALLAWAY

SENIOR VP, DIGITAL PRODUCTION AND DEVELOPMENT: MARK KORTEKAAS

BRANDING AGENCY: WOLFF OLINS

DESIGN DIRECTOR: LISA SMITH

INTERACTIVE AGENCY: FANTASY INTERACTIVE

OWNER: GANNETT CO.

FOUNDED: 1982 (PRINT), 1995 (WEB)

USA TODAY is the third largest newspaper in the United States (after *The Wall Street Journal* and *The New York Times*, according to a March 2013 audit, reaching nearly 2 million readers daily). James McCartney wrote about it in 1997, fifteen years after it debuted, for the *American Journalism Review*: "It was brash, multicolored, gimmicky, a paper created—its founders said—for the TV generation . . . It was to be a quick read for a world in which nobody has much time."

Today, the world still hasn't got much time, and instead of TV being the catalyst, it's the web that's most drastically changed reading habits. And all those "gimmicks" that made it frowned upon in the beginning have become standard fare: full color, information graphics, scannable, bulleted stories. Having not only embraced visual storytelling early on, the paper has also invested in quality journalism, earning it some measure of respectability. The news organization continually strives to deliver the types of news that the most readers will want and in all the formats that they might want it, investing widely in video and mobile platforms.

In 2012, with the help of branding firm Wolff Olins, *USA TODAY* unveiled a new identity and redesigned newspaper, website, and new apps. The typeface of the logo was changed to Futura Today, a customized update of Futura by Dutch designers Bold Monday, and the former globe icon flattened into a solid dot. Blue remained the primary color for the brand, but the dots change color depending on the newspaper section (including green for Money, red for Sports, teal for Travel, purple for Lifestyle) and can contain useful, news-related (not promotional) information.

Wolff Olins design director Lisa Smith explained the reasoning behind the mutable logo: "To have something static doesn't seem appropriate for a news organization that changes every single second, so its brand needs to be adaptive in the same way."

The new website, designed by Fantasy Interactive, takes cues from tablet-style navigation, with arrows on either side of the screen to go "ahead" or go "back" from one section to the next. And in the style of Boston.com, the "Big Page" features a single full-screen image that takes over the page as a means of using photography to communicate and spotlight the biggest story of the moment.

USA TODAY sections are color coded and accompanied by dots that can either be left alone or illustrated for a specific purpose.

The full-screen website, designed by Fantasy Interactive, takes cues from tablet gestures to make navigating on a desktop screen more intuitive. **Above:** the home page; **Below:** the Opinion section.

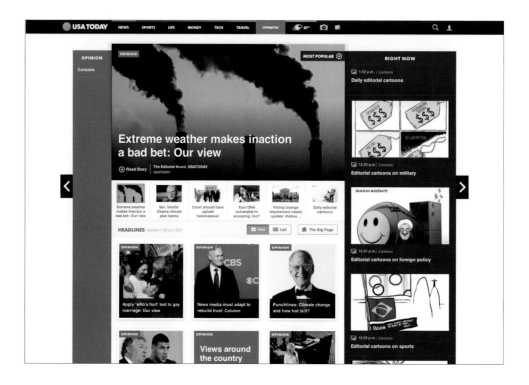

Above: An information graphic illustrates a story on extreme weather conditions in the western United States.
Below: Users tap the speech bubble to open a drawer with comments.

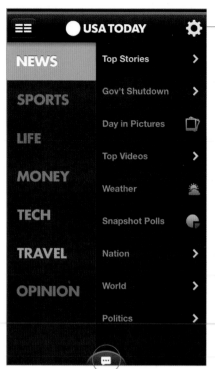

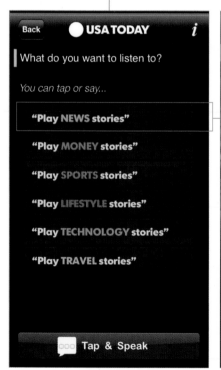

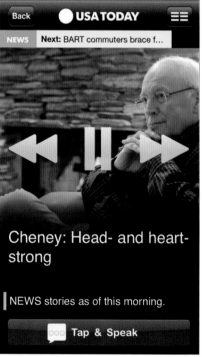

The mobile iPhone app includes a speaking feature that is useful for those who would like to hear the news while walking or driving. When commanded to play stories from a particular section, the screen shifts and plays the stories in order of publication.

Jeanette Abbink

Founder and Creative Director, Rational Beauty

Jeanette Abbink has an impressive portfolio of editorial design—she was the founding creative director of *Dwell* and has been an art director for *The New York Times* sports magazine *Play*, *Martha Stewart Living*, and *American Craft*—but she considers herself more simply as a designer, with as much experience in packaging and branding as editorial design. Growing up in rural North Carolina, she worked on her high school yearbook. "I remembered laying it out and doing photography and thinking, this is kind of cool," she says. While earning her bachelor's degree in visual design at North Carolina State University, she explored textile design, in part inspired by her mother, who was a seamstress and military wife. Through Abbink's curiosity about textiles, she discovered an interest in designing patterns and "fiber storytelling" that complemented her graphic design focus.

Her first job was doing desktop publishing at *PC Computing*, a Ziff-Davis magazine, "when it was more about the culture and less about electronics," she says. She was living in San Francisco, picking up various freelance design work, when an identity she designed for the restaurant Slow Club got her noticed by clothing brand Esprit's creative team, who would meet at the restaurant for drinks and dinner after work. For Esprit, she designed catalogs, a magazine called *Esprit de Corp*, and a newsletter called *Perspective*. Later, she worked with David Turner at Turner Duckworth, where she got into packaging design for clients including Nike and Levi's.

In 2000, Abbink was doing branding work for BP with Landor when the opportunity to work for a new magazine called *Dwell* came up. That she's been able to switch gears between branding and editorial so seamlessly results from her core conviction: "As graphic designers, we tell visual stories, whether it's announcing or selling something or defining how a complicated system works: from an organic cotton fashion line for Esprit to prefab architecture for *Dwell*. Boiling down to the essential communication with visual flair is what is important to me." Abbink reunited with *Dwell* in 2013 to redesign the magazine and help create a cohesive identity across its platforms, which now include a conference and e-commerce site.

Tell us what it was like starting Dwell *from the ground level.*

I was pretty happy doing brand work for BP. But then I met Lara Hedberg Deam, the founder of *Dwell*, and Karrie Jacobs, the founding editor, and I was inspired. I had an enormous interest in the subject, and to start a magazine from the ground up was an opportunity too good to be true. I had always admired Karrie's work as a design critic, especially for *Colors* magazine, and had all of the issues that she had edited. Both Karrie and Lara were visionary. *Dwell* was going to stage a minor revolution. That it was possible to live in a house or apartment by a bold, modern architect, to own furniture and products that are exceptionally well designed,

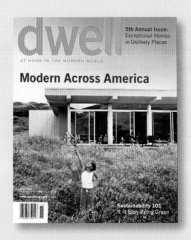

Dwell's 5th Annual Issue showcasing exceptional homes in unlikely places, November 2009

and still be a regular human being. That good design is an integral part of real life, and that real life has been conspicuously absent in most design and architecture magazines until then. That was the *Dwell* ethos. After understanding the editorial direction, I was able to craft a team together and create the identity. Karrie did the content part, and we did the visualization of that. She really trusted us to do what we were hired to do.

To capture real-life design and the mindset that modernism could be down to earth, we worked with portrait photographers instead of architecture or interiors photographers. We relied on fine art photographers such as Todd Hido and Jim Goldberg to show portraits of houses and help us communicate what a space feels like. *Dwell* thought that modernism should be friendly, and that you didn't need to be an architect to appreciate it. *Dwell* was interested in how people were using and creating their domestic space and how they interacted with architects, and hoping that architects would in turn also become more approachable.

Dwell *invented a whole new language for speaking about the domestic space. The term "shelter magazine" came out of this whole idea of not being an interiors magazine or an architecture magazine, but something else.*
That was the vibe. The first year, we were really struggling because a lot of people didn't get that we didn't want to use architectural photography. When we'd call a portrait photographer, we'd have to do all this convincing, like, "No, you're our eyes. We want you to go in and capture the space, just like you would do a person."

We wanted the layouts and typography to feel designed and systematic, like architecture is, so there was a big rationale behind the design of *Dwell*. Production-wise, we played a lot with CMYK colors of web printing. There was a lot of magenta, a lot of cyan, just because it's easy to

We wanted the layouts and typography to feel designed and systematic, like architecture.

reproduce. So we were playing with modernist design tenets, like reduction with impactful photography. We wanted the photography to show people in their spaces along with all of the quirks, and for the layout to play more of a supportive role. But then the design started having a big identity, too, even though it was trying to pull back and let the photography pop. And the language—the writers were really great.

Later, in 2007, you moved to New York and worked on a redesign of **American Craft** *magazine. Could you tell us about that?*
American Craft had a lot of history, more than fifty years of publishing, that I was able to go through and look at with editor Andrew Wagner, and then map out what the new look should be based on its history and to try to make it relevant for today. It was a lot of fun. Back in the 1950s, Robert Brownjohn designed several issues while he was at Chermayeff & Geismar, so I got all his issues and looked at them. It had a real heritage of graphic design. It was only since 1990 to 2000 that the design unraveled. Whereas in the 1950s and '60s, there would be amazing stories, like about a new illustrator, Andy Warhol! I would be reading stories about some shoe design, and be like, wow, that's what craft is. It meets all aspects of our lives. Andrew was really interested in that—craft as a verb, as a culture. The logo originally designed by Kiyoshi Kanai in 1979 was redrawn by my husband and type designer, Mike Abbink, who redrew it to work with DTL Fleischmann—which I was super in love with. I saw it and said, "That's the one! It will solve all our problems." DTL Fleichmann, designed by Erhard Kaiser, is a modern interpretation of a 1700s typeface. The font is beautifully crafted and considered, making it ideal for use in both text and display. We used the unique ligatures

in the headlines and decks, and that became a strong visual element in our identity.

You took a similar approach at **Dwell**, *too, right? Why did you want to use only one typeface?*
Well, we actually used a few fonts: Proforma, Trade Gothic, and Franklin Gothic. We knew that we didn't want to use typefaces like Helvetica or Univers. A few of the new humanistic sans serifs like Meta and Scala didn't feel right either. We wanted the type to feel truly American, so we turned to Trade Gothic and Franklin Gothic. Because Trade Gothic and Franklin Gothic did not have all of the weights needed to detail the content, we hired Mike to create an extra bold version and old style numbers for all of the weights. So I feel like people in the '80s and '90s were using all kinds of fonts just to try to help communicate because the fonts weren't really built out—not for humanistic sans serifs. Today, I feel like there are really beautiful, well-crafted fonts available that can work across all these mediums that will help reduce the noise and keep everything really sharp. You have to have your palette, and you've got to make sure that the photography, the typography, they're all working together to help communicate that story and not have to rely on fifteen fonts. Also who wants to deal with it from a technological standpoint, too? That's a pain.

Let's talk about **USA TODAY**. *You worked as a designer on the team at Wolff Olins that designed the new brand identity and guidelines in 2012. What are some things you can tell us about that experience?*
That was an awesome project because Wolff Olins was hired to

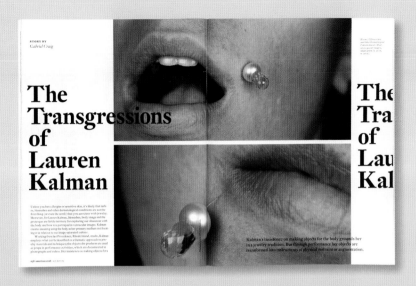

American Craft feature opener on artist Lauren Kalman's jewelry in performance pieces documented in videos and photographs by the artist herself., November 2009.

reinvent their brand. *USA TODAY* was going to celebrate their thirty-year anniversary and unveil their new identity. They wanted to go back to their roots in storytelling, with really bold graphics, very impactful, very simple. They started working with a web team [Fantasy Interactive], and Wolff Olins worked with them to make sure that it was implemented. They decided that Wolff Olins should do the newspaper because it was the flagship product. And then Wolff Olins put a team together and hired me to help work on the newspaper. A lot of the framework had already been decided, like using the dot as an infographic. So primarily what I did was basic graphic design and layout, figure out how many stories should be on a page and come up with lots of templates for how these stories could look.

They have a very interesting workflow, a proprietary program called NewsGate that all of the Gannett publications use. So if a story happens in Chicago or a small-town newspaper, *USA TODAY* could

grab it. It was very cool from an information flow and design perspective, but it looked like something from the 1990s. It was really clunky, and a lot of my time was spent bridging the design over to their system, helping get NewsGate's templates usable so their people didn't have to build pages, because they weren't always designers but rather editors, copy editors, and technicians.

How would you describe the results of this project?
I think it's getting rid of unnecessary noise. You want to create a palette that makes music and gets rid of the static—unless you're going after punk rock and want to make everyone really unsettled. But all the products that I've worked on, it was more about, we want to talk to more people, let's get our hands around the masses.

Could you tell us about the typography?
We worked with Dutch type designers Bold Monday on a beautiful cut of Futura. It is legible, and it looks great small, which the old Futura didn't. Futura Today distinguishes itself by featuring shorter ascenders and descenders, a number of redesigned shapes—lowercase *j, t,* and *u* are the most obvious changes—and a dramatic improvement in quality of contours. All glyphs have been completely redrawn. The spacing and kerning have been built up from scratch, too, to ensure the highest quality and consistency. In the newspaper, Futura Today is used in conjunction with Chronicle from Hoefler & Frere-Jones.

If you could do anything next, what would you do?
I would love to do a project where I could incorporate technology and work with type designers and photographers, and really kind of create a new way to communicate to the masses. While I love the print piece—I have an emotional connection because it speaks to my era—as a creative person, I feel like it's limiting to say, "Oh, I just want to do print." It's not exciting to me. I respect it, if that's what one's choice is, but I feel like it's going to be very limited. •

Case Study:
Bloomberg Businessweek

WEBSITE: BUSINESSWEEK.COM
FREQUENCY: WEEKLY (51 ISSUES)
FORMAT: PRINT
LOCATION: NEW YORK
CREATIVE DIRECTOR: RICHARD TURLEY
EDITOR: JOSH TYRANGIEL
OWNER: BLOOMBERG L.P.
FOUNDED: 1929 (PRINT)

Businessweek's history goes back as far as 1929, beginning at first as *The Business Week* and launching just before the stock market crash that put the U.S. economy in the Great Depression. "*The Business Week* always has a point of view, and usually a strong opinion, both of which it does not hesitate to express. And all the way through, we hope you will discover it is possible to write sanely and intelligently of business with-

out being pompous or ponderous," Malcolm Muir, president of McGraw-Hill, the former parent company, once said. As it tried to compete against *Forbes* and *Fortune*, the magazine struggled to stand out. In 2009, financial data company Bloomberg acquired the ailing title from McGraw-Hill and forever changed its course.

Although giving it a very long title—*Bloomberg Businessweek*—seemed ridiculous at the time, the new publishers wisely brought in editor Josh Tyrangiel, whose journalistic background includes *Time* and Time.com, as well as *Vibe*, *Rolling Stone*, and MTV. Since his arrival, the magazine has taken on a more attention-grabbing approach—one still steeped in solid business news reporting, but for an era in which CEOs such as Facebook's Mark Zuckerberg and Apple's Steve Jobs are more like rock stars (albeit nerdy ones) than stuffy suits. Creative director Richard Turley, who previously had been based in London and working as an art director for

the *Guardian*'s daily arts supplement *G2*, was recruited to give form to Tyrangiel's editorial vision.

Ever since the reinvention of *Bloomberg Businessweek*, which officially relaunched in 2010, it has earned recognition for its smart journalism and unpredictable art direction. A solid grid and handful of typefaces—including a revival of Neue Haas Grotesk, essentially the original Helvetica—provide just enough structure for the organized chaos Turley and his team unleash in each issue through risqué illustrations, surprising photography, and instructive, yet often humorous, infographics.

Bloomberg Businessweek's bold use of images and typography on the interior and on the covers set it apart from other business magazines. Clever, edgy art direction of photography and bright, complex, and engaging graphics make the magazine instantly identifiable.

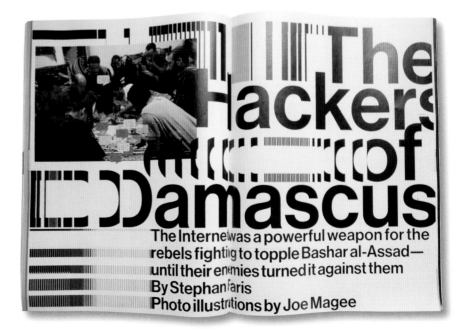

Bloomberg
Businessweek

November 19 — November 25, 2012 | businessweek.com

Syria's Virtual War

Facebook and Twitter were once
instruments of change in the Middle East.
Now they're lethal weapons

$4.99

Richard Turley

Creative Director, Bloomberg BusinessWeek

Richard Turley, who previously art directed the *Guardian*'s *G2* daily arts supplement and worked with Mark Porter on the sweeping redesign of the *Guardian* newspaper in 2005, spoke to us about leading a creative team of people who "shouldn't really be designing a business magazine."

How did you become interested in editorial design?
The graphic design that I was interested in always tended to be in magazines, like David Carson; he's quite important to me. And then the English magazines such as *The Face*, *Dazed & Confused*, *Sleazenation*—those were the magazines I read. They were all design heavy and design led, and I suppose that's the stuff I was most interested in at the time.

While in school in Liverpool, I kind of engineered an opportunity to do a university magazine, which was really bad at the time. My friend and I just sort of told the university that we were redesigning it and we did. I really enjoyed doing it, and then we won a design competition, and I got an internship at *The Guardian*

newspaper and stayed on for almost ten years.

I started off in the marketing department and did a lot of advertorials, ads, invitations, any sort of marketing. I then got another job at a magazine, which closed. When I came back to the *Guardian*, I ended up assisting Mark Porter, who was then the creative director. It was never really formally announced that I was his assistant, but I helped him on a lot of projects, and he taught me just about everything I know. When the main *Guardian* newspaper got entirely reconfigured in the early 2000s, I learned just about everything about design and typography.

Were you always artistically inclined? What made you choose to be a designer?

I was always good at art. I wasn't terrible at other subjects. I liked English, I liked history. But I did a lot of art. I could draw. I found myself in a graphic arts course and that's what I fell into. I like music, so record covers were very important. At one point, I think I would have hoped to design record covers, but then this magazine thing took off.

"This magazine thing" is pretty impressive. Bloomberg Business- week is quite well regarded, earning awards from the Society of Publication Designers (2012 Magazine of the Year) and the American Society of Magazine Editors (2012 award for General Excellence).

I think we're quite surprised by the way it's been picked up on. It's not that we weren't ambitious for that, but I don't think we ever really thought that that was possible.

Were you looking at other business magazines when you approached the initial redesign?

The only magazine I really looked at was *New York*. There's a way that Adam Moss, the editor, has made that magazine where you can graze it, and you can take out little bits and bobs, but then you can also really read the magazine…that was very influential to me. I didn't look at any business publications. One of the reasons I think we were quite successful is that we're a lot of people who shouldn't really be designing a business maga- zine. We're not people who thought in a million years that we'd be designing the magazine that we design. So I think our expectations and our inter- ests are a lot different from the usual business publications.

How does the fact that everyone sits together—design and editorial— help the design process? For instance, you sit across from editor Josh Tyrangiel.

We have about fifteen design people, including photo editors. We have probably ten on staff and five freelancers on contract. There's a lot more communication here, and decisions get made quicker because of that. People aren't hiding away in offices. For people who are used to offices, it's a bit freakish, but I've always been used to working in a newsroom.

Create a Workplace People Never Want To Leave

I feel productive

I am listening closely

I really need you

90 91

PHOTOGRAPHS BY ELIZABETH RENSTROM FOR BLOOMBERG BUSINESSWEEK

Christopher Coleman

The No. 1 thing is to listen to what employees need. We found that they need a lot of diversity. There are so many ways to work—as a team, solo—and so many kinds of workers, from introverts to extroverts and so on. We create many different places so people can be as productive as possible—from formal and informal conference rooms to open spaces to stretching and yoga areas and gyms. One trick is to design spaces with a diversity of scale, light, and mood. It's really hard to do, and it looks like we're just making up these crazy spaces, but it's very scientific. We have information from Googlers on what works and what doesn't, we do post-occupancy surveys, we ask questions, and we listen very closely. When we design a space, we usually offer a few solutions people can react to. We go back to the drawing board, go down to two or three options, and pick one. Next we define aspects like mood, lighting, and furniture. Then we build it, and people are happy–hopefully. ¶ With all this input, they're basically designing their own space. One of the earlier amenities we provided were micro-kitchens. It was an amazing, vibrant place where people connected before they started their workday. Now we have micro-kitchens that are libraries, micro-kitchens that are game rooms. Also, health is very important. A few years ago we introduced sit-stand desks, and they're used extensively now. It changes the worker's environment all through the day and gives them flexibility to work how they want to work. ¶ We look at every single detail through the Living Lab, which is a space where the Real Estate and Workplace Services team can experiment with innovative ideas for the office. We're trying out three ventilation systems, six lighting systems, and furniture from 10 manufacturers. In the end, though, we're actually very frugal in our approach to design. It's more about creating character than money spent. ● *Coleman is global design director at Google. As told to Venessa Wong*

From the look of the design, it would seem like you have a lot of creative freedom and few constrictions. Is that true?

No, because I've got to make the editor happy. That's my big constriction—and it's not as if that feels particularly constrictive. That's my client, if you like, and he's got to be happy with what we do. If it's a cover, it's not as if I sit there and propose stuff and get angry when he says no. We go back and forth all the time. There's an exchange of views and ideas.

And you are working on the print magazine only. Are you interested in having more of a hand in the digital products: the website, the tablet apps?

No, not really. Design for apps and design for websites is architecture, it's about building structures and cylinders to hold information, and that's just not something I've ever been particularly good at or interested in. I like ideas. It's the content that interests me. I'm not really interested in typography; I just want to communicate. I understand how an underlying type structure helps you tell stories, but once you've done that, then I lose interest, and I just want to tell stories, and I want to find the best way of articulating ideas. So digital design has never really interested me because it's very rarely about that design perspective, and it tends to be about back-end stuff and making stuff look smooth rather than the things you can do with a magazine, which is about selling an idea and articulating an editorial vision, and just communicating.

You do very interesting things with typography, though.

I have a very good relationship with Christian Schwartz at Commercial Type, and we work very quickly with each other. And I think he quite likes that relationship as well, because typographers tend to move kind of like an ocean liner, turning enormous circles, and everything takes ages. We probably buy about three or four fonts from him a year, which is a lot for bespoke type.

What do you think makes someone a good editorial designer and a good fit for this magazine, in particular?

You can't lose your temper too much. Pick your battles. My design style is very loose, and I like when it's rough, and that's beneficial to me because it means you don't obsess about things.

*Bodhi, a 3-year-old Shiba Inu, likes bacon, peanut butter, and half-windsors. See more looks at mensweardog.tumblr.com.

**BAND OF OUTSIDERS
WIDE DIAGONAL
STRIPED TIE**
$455
barneys.com
Steven Alan single
needle shirt, $109;
Levi's denim
jacket, dog's own

**BARNEYS NEW YORK
CO-OP TEXTURED TIE**
$70
barneys.com
Charvet poplin dress
shirt, $445; J.Crew
blazer, dog's own

J.CREW SILK TIE
$64.50
jcrew.com
Alton Lane
Egyptian cotton
shirt, $165;
A.P.C. blazer

**BANANA REPUBLIC
STRIPED SILK TIE**
$59.50
bananarepublic.com
John Varvatos
point collar dress
shirt, $225;
Bonobos' The
Fleetwell
blazer, $458

**THOM BROWNE
NEW YORK SILK TIE**
$185
thombrowne.com
Turnbull & Asser
solid poplin
dress shirt, $315;
A.P.C. dark navy
double-breasted
blazer, $556

**ETRO STRIPED
LINEN TIE**
$156
etro.com
Steven Alan single
needle shirt,
$198; Steven Alan
Caleb blazer, $395

**ALTON LANE
COTTON STRIPE TIE**
$75
altonlane.com
Jean Machine
Bonk shirt, $176;
A.P.C. blazer

**JACK SPADE
WASHED SILK-COTTON
STRIPE TIE**
$98
jackspade.com
Façonnable
classique fit solid
cotton Dobby shirt,
$185; Seize sur
Vingt khaki cotton
jacket, $720

THE TIE MAKES THE MAN
Bold stripes are every where—Bodhi the Menswear Dog models summer's coolest neckwear options

80   81

EDITED BY AJA MANGUM. PHOTOGRAPHS BY JAMIE CHUNG FOR BLOOMBERG BUSINESSWEEK

Just the amount of work we produce each week, it's impossible to obsess over everything. There are designers out there who would obsess over every detail, so I think being nonobsessive is quite useful. Really, you've just got to like communicating with people. Just enjoy the fact that you're putting out this product, that you're talking to people in quite a direct way.

I hire on instinct, if I just feel that I want to be around them and they could teach me some stuff. Very rarely have we hired someone because we needed something specific. It's just that we saw someone, and a role came up, and we had an opening, so we hired that person whose work I liked.

And has that worked out well?

It's the content that interests me. I'm not really interested in typography; I just want to communicate.

It has, actually. It's worked out for me because I like working with them, and it's fun to come to work. We have a close relationship, and we trust each other and understand each other and push each other as well.

What do you look for in a magazine?
I just want to see something a bit different. With magazines, increasingly it's about an object. And as we become more digital, I think magazines and printed products need to be more aware of their status as an

object. It's in the paper choice, the shape of it, the size of it, the density of it, that's becoming increasingly important. And I think magazines that play around with that and understand the fact that it's an object are more successful.

What do you most enjoy about what you do, and how do you keep things fresh from week to week?
It's a repetitive act, a magazine, but it is a dialogue. I just enjoy it. As long as we keep doing slightly new things,

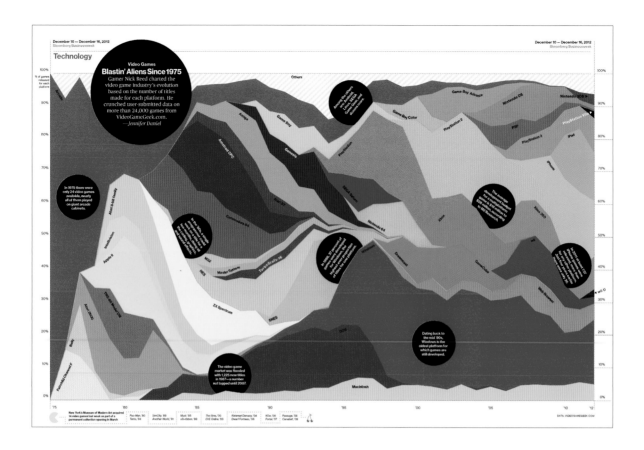

It's a repetitive act, a magazine, but it is a dialogue.

whether it be a slight redesign or special issues—as long as there's something just ahead of me that I don't really know what it's about. As long as it feels like an opportunity for change in the way that we do things, or an opportunity to think about the magazine in a different way. A lot of these special issues we do, they're just blank pieces of paper, really; there's no template, there's no format at all. And those are definitely the most rewarding.

People have asked me, who are you making the magazine for, or who are you trying to impress? I just try to impress the people I work with. If they're happy, then I tend to be happy. It's that internal drive. It's the people in this building or this little area of it that push me more than anyone else. We're all very ambitious, and I mean, ambitious to do some-thing different and not repeat ourselves, and to keep pushing and pushing and pushing. ●

What's the best online service for sharing holiday photos? p82

Photo FAQ & Liberal Moppets & Gobblers

Etc.

The little orphan gets all hopey-changey. Forward! Tomorrow! p90

Business by the Bard

The son of a famous Hamlet has created a management seminar that actually seems to work. A story told in five acts. *By Claire Suddath*

Illustration by Wesley Merritt

Etc. Rant

It's the 2% vs. the 1%: Associates are getting squeezed while partners make millions

WILL DEFEND 4 $$$

Poor Young Lawyers

No, seriously. *By Elie Mystal*

It's bonus season in America, and at the nation's biggest and most prestigious law firms, associates—attorneys who do not hold equity in the firms they work for—will be receiving yearend checks greater than the full salaries of many of their contemporaries. Cravath, Swaine & Moore, which sets the market for many top New York firms, announced in late November that its bonuses will range from $10,000 for the most junior associates to $60,000 for those closest to the partner level.

That's still a far cry from the levels before the financial meltdown: In 2007, senior associates got $110,000 on top of their annual salaries. But no one's making as much as they used to, and the bonuses are way up from 2011, when the top payout was $37,000. So this lucky group should be out celebrating at some stodgy lawyer bar. Right?

Not quite. In a twist that will probably delight the 99 percent, these associates, who are in the top 2 percent of wage earners in the country, are getting economically squeezed by other, more important lawyers who are in the top 1 percent. That's because the partners who own these law firms—most of whom have seen their profits rebound to pre-recession heights—are hoarding a bigger share of the pie than ever before. Yep, the older lawyers who helped structure the instruments that wrecked the economy in the first place and who constantly give sound bites about how worried they are about business prospects are sitting like dragons atop piles of cash. *American Lawyer* reported that the average profit for a Cravath partner in 2007 was $3.3 million. In 2011 it was back up to $3.1 million.

I know, I know, #TwoPercentProblems. Crocodile tears flow for a fifth-year associate making $230,000 in base salary and a $34,000 Christmas bonus. But it's worth keeping in mind that in 2007 the bonus to the same fifth-year associate—for the same work—was $95,000. In New York City, the difference between a $95,000 bonus and a $34,000 bonus is the difference between saying "rent is high in this city, but I can afford it" and "I'm living paycheck to paycheck in my crappy one bedroom." After Simpson Thacher & Bartlett, another top New York firm, announced they'd be matching Cravath's bonuses, one associate complained that his measly $10,000 check was an insult, given his $220,000 law school debt.

And let's not forget that these partners are paying out these reduced bonuses to a much smaller group of people than in the boom times. In the summer of 2008, right before Lehman Brothers collapsed, Cravath brought in 161 summer associates. "Summers," as they're referred to, are the main way top firms hire fresh talent; most summer jobs translate into entry-level attorney positions. In 2011 the firm brought in only 53 summers according to the Association for Legal Career Professionals. In 2010 the firm had a mere 22. That represents far fewer mouths to feed—there would be less profit-sharing even if firms were paying out the same generous 2007 bonuses.

In fairness, Cravath's partner pool has also shrunk. In 2007, 90 equity partners raked in that $3.3 million-per-partner haul. In 2011 the firm split the profits among 80. Essentially, that just means lawyers, both partners and associates, are doing more with less. Cravath's gross revenue in 2011 was $568 million. Even in 2009, in the teeth of the recession, its gross revenue was $569 million. While 2012 numbers aren't available yet, the firm figures to again post over half a billion dollars in gross revenue. The pie is still being made—it's just that associates are getting a smaller slice. Sounds like a good lawyer joke if I've ever heard one. ◑

Etc. Gift Guide ● Get Up and Go

7:00am

"A woman may race to get a man a gift, but it always ends in a tie."
—Earl Wilson

The all-purpose blue work tie, good for fathers, brothers, everyone. $465; angelogalasso.com

A Tory Burch tote for schlepping in style. $650; toryburch.com

A Fox umbrella, because he's going to the office—not the golf course. $295; bloomingdales.com

Stocking stuffers: Carolina Herrera for Target • Neiman Marcus stationery and pencils. $15.99; neimanmarcus.com

Brown and brogue and great for stylish office dudes. $1,450; angelogalasso.com

Ditch the canvas bag! Mark Cross's attaché case is all grown up. $1,795; markcross1845.com

Luxe leather gloves for the sophisticated lady. Hermès gloves. $630; hermes.com

Coach men's Bleecker pebbled leather notebooks. $168; coach.com

Bold-pattern shirts by Angelo Galasso, terrific for hard-to-impress hedge funders. $940; angelogalasso.com

Keep your little guy warm with this animal hat (and mitten set). $49.95; redenvelope.com

Remember: Just one spritz for the office. Pomegranate Noir cologne, $200; Cologne Intense, $250; jomalone.com

"It's after six. What am I, a farmer?" —Jack Donaghy, Bottega Veneta silk bow tie. $190; bottegaveneta.com

Winter fun for little ones: Mini Boden hat and mitten set. $38; bodenusa.com

Snapchat And the Right To Be Forgotten

The world's hottest photo-sharing app, which features self-destructing pictures, isn't just a better way to flirt. It's about taking control of your digital self. By Felix Gillette

Etc. How To

Navigating Love At the Office

New data reveal that 39 percent* of workers have dated a colleague. If Cupid strikes, how should you proceed? *By Claire Suddath*

SCENARIO 1	SCENARIO 2	SCENARIO 3	SCENARIO 4	SCENARIO 5
Dating The Boss	**The Fling**	**Forbidden Romance**	**In Bed With the Competition**	**Going Into Business Together**

Dating The Boss

"Proceed very, very carefully," says dating coach Tracey Steinberg. "If you get together with your boss, you'll get a reputation for sleeping your way to the top," Steinberg explains. "If you're the boss, you could be accused of abuse of power. If things go wrong, the person could say they felt pressured into the relationship." No amount of success will make you immune to accusations. According to a 2010 Center for Work-Life Policy survey, more than 60 percent of working professionals said they suspected that an underling sleeping with the boss would get preferential treatment.

WHAT TO DO:
Consider a mate more lateral to you. Otherwise, see Scenario 2.

The Fling

If it's still in an early stage, "your co-workers don't need to know about anything that might not work out," says Chiara Atik, a dating expert at HowAboutWe. Once you've established a relationship, your colleagues will inevitably start gossiping. Megan Hopkins knows what that's like; she met her husband when they worked at a marketing company in Plano, Tex. For months they were the subjects of speculation. "We showed up to a co-worker's going-away party holding hands, and people were like, 'I knew it!' " she says. After that, the talk died down and the couple relaxed. But they still only made out in private.

WHAT TO DO:
Until it's serious, "Hide it at all costs!" Atik says.

Forbidden Romance

In some offices, dating a colleague is a fireable offense. But "our ability to suppress strong emotions is not very good," says Eli Finkel, a professor of social psychology at Northwestern University. He warns that attempts to quell desire might result in sleepless nights and depression. The upside is that secret relationships are much more passionate. In a 1994 behavioral study, Harvard psychologists asked strangers to surreptitiously play footsie underneath a table and found that they rated each other more attractive than those who didn't play footsie.

WHAT TO DO:
Our official opinion is that you should abide by official company policy.

In Bed With the Competition

Getting romantic with someone at a rival company is fine, Steinberg says, as long as you agree to never trade company secrets. You may even have stumbled into a promising situation: You're both passionate about the same topic or industry, but you don't have to see each other at the office every day. "As long as you guys have ground rules for what you talk about, I almost think you're better off dating your rival than dating a co-worker," she says. She should know–before becoming a dating coach, Steinberg worked as a lawyer. "I dated a lot of my adversaries," she says. "It was fun. I just made sure never to share case notes before we argued in court."

WHAT TO DO:
Never go to bed angry, and always say you're sorry (even if you don't mean it).

Going Into Business Together

Brian Strom was married to his wife, Andrea, for five years before they opened Crapola, a granola company in Ely, Minn. The Stroms spend at least six hours of their workdays together, and they don't have any rules about what they can and can't talk about at home. "Sometimes when you're in the thick of a stressful situation, you can't process it right then," Brian says. "If your business partner is also your life partner, whatever you don't get done at work you can talk about over dinner." Of course, this isn't always a good thing. "Work time isn't romantic time–and vice versa," Atik says. "You have to make sure you make room in your life for both."

WHAT TO DO:
Unless you want to spend 24/7 together, don't do it.

According to a CareerBuilder survey

A fling or the real thing? According to CareerBuilder, a third of secret office romances end in marriage.

Contents ▶ Mobile apps for bigger screens 31 ▶ For Web browsers, it's evolve or die 32 ▶ Innovator: What if your smartphone had X-ray vision? 33 ▶ Charlie Rose talks to Sequoia's Mike Moritz 34 ▶ Edited by Doug Cantor

February 11 – February 17, 2013
Bloomberg Businessweek

Technology

Hacked? Who Ya Gonna Call?

▶ Mandiant is the go-to responder for cyber-espionage attacks

▶ "It's a reputational thing. They play well with law enforcement"

The brand-new operations center of cybersecurity firm **Mandiant** is deceptively tranquil. Rooms in the third-floor office, overlooking a lagoon in Redwood City, Calif., are playfully named after locations on the Starship Enterprise from *Star Trek*, including a kitchen called 10-Forward.

In one large central room, dubbed the Bridge, a dozen security analysts peer quietly at their computer monitors, looking for anomalous activity on the computer networks of Mandiant's hundreds of corporate clients around the world. A large computer display on the wall shows an image of the earth, seen from space, that highlights inbound and outbound network activity in each country. Mandiant monitors the entire planet, yet a printout taped to the desk of one analyst suggests that these days, the company has a more specific focus. "To accuse the Chinese military of launching cyberattacks without solid proof is unprofessional and baseless," reads an excerpt from a recent Chinese government statement. Jennifer Ayers, who manages the Redwood City facility, removes the printout and folds it in half. "We're not supposed to editorialize," she says.

Last week, a succession of news stories divulged that the computer systems of major news organizations including the *New York Times*, *Wall Street Journal*, and *Washington Post* had been breached by hackers with connections to the Chinese government. Unsuccessful attempts were made to infiltrate the computers of Bloomberg LP, which owns *Bloomberg Businessweek*, as well, says Ty Trippet, a company spokesman. China's censors are apparently trying to stifle dissent by reaching across the ocean to expose the anonymous sources of Western journalists who have written negative stories about the country or its government. After detecting the breaches, papers including the *Times* and *Post* contacted Mandiant, a 9-year-old Alexandria (Va.)-based company with a reputation among industry insiders for technical proficiency and large egos. It also has a budding business on the front lines of U.S. national cyberspies.

In a wave of cyberattacks beginning in 2009, dubbed Operation Aurora by security firm **McAfee**, sophisticated hackers based in China breached the corporate networks of **Google**, **Yahoo!**, **Juniper Networks**, **Adobe Systems**, and dozens of other prominent technology companies and tried to access their source code. China's hackers seemed narrowly focused on military technology and telecommunications companies as early as 2000. They were seen as a way to purloin intellectual property and narrow the marketplace advantages enjoyed by U.S. rivals over Chinese companies like **Huawei Technology** and **ZTE**, neither of which has been implicated in cyberattacks.

Now China's targets appear to be much broader. Wiley Rein, a prominent Washington law firm working on a trade case against China, was hit in 2011; the White House was targeted last year. Last month, hackers breached the website of the Council on Foreign Relations and rigged it to deliver malware to anyone who visited it.

Hacking groups with ties to the Chinese government have also aggressively targeted Western oil and gas companies (and often their law firms and investment banks) as a way to get proprietary financial information, sometimes in advance of an acquisition by a Chinese company. In 2011, when debt-plagued **Chesapeake Energy** put billions worth of its natural gas holdings on the market, its investment bank, **Jefferies**, was targeted around the time a Chinese government official visited Chesapeake's Oklahoma headquarters. "You can almost think of it as part of their due diligence," says Richard Bejtlich, Mandiant's chief security officer, who says the data are often stolen by military-sponsored hacking groups and then given to Chinese companies. "It's almost like they're thinking, 'When we report our financ-es, they're all garbage, so yours are probably garbage, too. I'm just going to steal it straight from you and get the real story.'"

To stop such hacks, Mandiant uses unconventional methods. Teams of three to five specialists are assigned to track each victim company's computer system, a painstaking process that can last for months. After they have identified every security hole and piece of malware in the customer's network, Mandiant gives the bad guys the boot, in some cases by replacing every infected machine within 48 hours. For companies that fear their secrets might be lost before the hackers are cut off, it can be a white-knuckle wait.

Mandiant says it booked more than $100 million in revenue in 2012, up 76 percent from the year before, and counts 30 percent of the Fortune 100 as clients. Its business is booming because of hackers' ability to steal data on a far greater scale than with traditional methods of espionage. "The fact that you can do this from a safe harbor thousands of miles away with no risk or repercussions has changed the game," says Kevin Mandia, the company's 42-year-old founder and chief executive officer.

Mandia has been training to take on hackers his whole career. A square-jawed former football player at Lafayette College in Pennsylvania, he joined the Air

---

What   Crash?

In bellwether Phoenix, real estate is back. Will the turnaround spread?

By Susan Berfield
Photographs by Michael Friberg

Case Study: Rookie

WEBSITE: ROOKIEMAG.COM

FREQUENCY: THREE TIMES DAILY, TWICE ON WEEKENDS

FORMATS: WEBSITE, BOOK (ANNUAL)

EDITOR: TAVI GEVINSON

DESIGN: RUMORS

FOUNDED: 2011

Tavi Gevinson wasn't even yet a teenager when she started writing about fashion on her blog, The Style Rookie. By the time she was thirteen, she had attracted 4 million followers, becoming a news sensation in her own right. Then in September 2011, she launched Rookiemag.com, an online magazine that speaks to the interests and concerns of the audience she knows best: teen girls. Like her primary readership, Gevinson goes to school (she's still in high school as of this writing), so the publishing schedule of *Rookie* is designed to reflect that. Unlike other editorial sites and blogs that flood readers with dozens of posts a day, *Rookie* will only publish three times per weekday—once after school, once at dinnertime, and once more at bedtime—and once a day on weekends, a defining statement that's communicated clearly in the website's design.

As the rare teen publication created by and for teens, *Rookie* is almost by default authentic. It isn't as though Gevinson isn't being helped by smart grownups: Anaheed Alani is the editorial director, and Renda Morton designed the site through her studio Rumors, currently being led by Andy Pressman. The site is polished but just rough enough around the edges to feel like Gevinson's personal touch is there. The hand-lettered logo and section headings are reminiscent of a private journal, only it's one that welcomes readers and makes them immediately feel part of its inner circle. The content is aspirational and smart, so much so that regular video features such as "Ask a Grown Man," in which nice-guy celebrities like Jon Hamm and Paul Rudd answer readers' questions in a frank, not-condescending way, are equally popular with the postadolescent set. *Rookie* also doesn't hold back when it comes to sensitive subjects, such as what it's really like to get your period, and a well-moderated and active comments section ensures that the site feels trustworthy.

In 2012, after completing her freshman year as editor in chief, Gevinson compiled the first annual *Rookie Yearbook One* (Drawn & Quarterly), a beautifully designed hardcover edition reproducing some of the site's most popular features and placing them into context in high-school yearbook fashion. In October 2013, it was followed by a softcover *Rookie Yearbook Two*.

Opposite page (from top): The *Rookie* home page presents the day's content under a handwritten header announcing the month's theme. Three placeholders represent the day's three posts, published after school, at dinnertime, and before bedtime. Visit at 4:00 p.m., say, and you'll see the one live post and grayed images hinting at what readers can look forward to in a few hours. The background image reflects the theme: in this case, Victory. Below, a month at a glance.

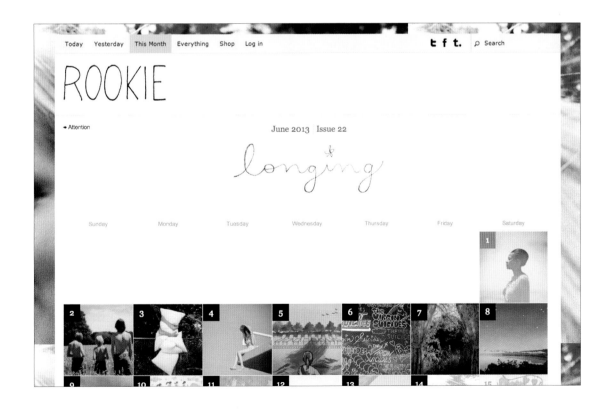

An article page for recurring features Ask a Grown Man (above), and Secret Style Icon (opposite page). On both pages, you'll see a Post-It–like note that calls out to readers for submissions and clues them in to the next month's theme.

Renda Morton
Designer

Although Renda Morton is no longer part of the design studio Rumors that she founded with partners Andy Pressman and Holly Gressley, she was pivotal in giving form to Tavi Gevinson's initial concept for *Rookie*. The reason the site is so well-suited to a 16-year-old editor in chief is because of Morton's spot-on interpretation of the brief. Having studied print and sound design as part of her web and multimedia environments major at Minnesota College of Art and Design, Morton defines herself as simply a designer—albeit one who is skilled at designing editorial experiences. Morton

left Rumors in 2012 to join the staff of NYTimes.com as a lead designer. Prior to that, she had consulted on an early app prototype for *The New York Times Magazine*, designed *American Craft* magazine's website with Jeanette Abbink, and freelanced for studios including Local Projects and Flat. Although she no longer has time to work with Rumors or *Rookie* now that designing for NYTimes.com is her full-time occupation, we asked her about getting *Rookie* off the ground.

Do you remember how you started the design process with Tavi?
First, I had to talk to her dad, which is really smart because no one should let their child start talking to adults without talking to them first. Tavi

wanted to do an internet magazine, but it had to be done in a month before she went back to school. I asked them what other websites are good for teen girls, and they didn't know. What I found was really tacky and not very well done. The content wasn't very good. *Rookie* is not like other sites that are always trying to trick you into constantly coming back by constantly putting out low-quality stuff. There's always new stuff on *Rookie*, too, but from the beginning they said, "We're going to post three times a day: after school, at dinnertime, and right before bed." And when they started, it was just weekdays, though now there are also Saturday links and a Sunday comic.

ROOKIE ROOKIE YEARBOOK ONE EDITED BY TAVI GEVINSON

style

Secret Style Icon: Shirley Kurata

Talking tacos and the benefits of being a nerd with the smartest stylist around.

04/24/2012   **Leeann**   autumn de wilde, fashion, fashion styling, horror movies, interview, mod, rodarte, secret style icon, shirley kurata

Hey guys. Next month's theme will be PASSION. We're looking for work (visual/written/filmed/whatever) about the very strongest kinds of love: friendship, romance, unrequited love, and the kind of intense connection you can have with a song or a book or a movie or whatever. Also, anything about FEEEEEELINGZ, chasing your dreamz, lust, anger/fury, hunger, pain & suffering, and all kinds of angst. Send your stuff here, and thanks!

More to See

How to Find the Vintage Eyeglasses of Your Dreams
It's basically exactly like online dating.

Other than the publishing schedule, how else does the site communicate that it isn't like other teen magazines?
Tavi was really into these sites that were very clean and black and white and fashion-y, and that's how she talked about what it should be like. But I wasn't quite sure that that was really the best idea for *Rookie*. We wanted it to seem really accessible to all different types of teenagers, for boys and girls. So we came up with this idea to have a changing background image because it's something that's such a social media thing. Like if you're a teenager, you always have this background, and you can always change it. So we came up with a scheme where they could change the background every day, but then the content layer on top of it would be

very clean. And every month has a theme, so we came up with this idea that there could be a custom type thing to announce the theme in the style of what it is.

They weren't quite sure how to execute the timed publishing idea or how the interface should be, what should happen on the home page. I helped them figure out how to do this so that it made sense to readers. Everyone is used to blogs being in reverse order, so we had to communicate what was happening.

What was the process like?
We showed them wireframes, but it was kind of confusing because they had never really worked with a designer before. So we just started to design it in WordPress. Also, we

We wanted it to seem really accessible to all different types of teenagers, for boys and girls.

didn't have a lot of time, so I made three different directions for the home page and for the story page, and we talked a lot about it. I don't remember what the other two were, but the one we went with, with the image background, was the best one, and they saw that. •

Mandy Brown

Cofounder, Editorially

Designing the Editorial Experience interview

 # ABOUT YOU

Where did you grow up? What and where did you study?

I was born in Okinawa and grew up in Northern Virginia, not far from Quantico. Mine was a military family. I attended the College of William & Mary, where I double-majored in English and Physics. (I have something of a Renaissance approach to education.)

What and how do you like to read? Have your reading habits changed over the last few years?

I have pretty catholic tastes in reading, both as far as topics go and in media. I read lots of nonfiction, novels, and criticism. I read essays on every subject imaginable. I read news from many sources. About the only things routinely absent from my reading are graphic novels (which I was

In February 2013, Mandy Brown and Jason Santa Maria, the former editor in chief and creative director, respectively, for A Book Apart, and Ethan Marcotte, the designer/developer who "started that whole responsive web design thing," stopped what they were doing to create a new form of web-based application "designed to help writers and editors work more effectively together." What does content creation software have to do with editorial design, you might wonder. Well, there's merit to the theory that the better the experience of getting ideas onto the page, the better the experience of reading them will be, too. And by creating content in an interactive environment *for* an interactive environment, the writer and editor are going to naturally consider how the reader will engage with it as part of the writing process. We asked Brown to tell us about the path that led to her spearheading this collaborative tool.

Could you tell us about your editorial design background prior to Editorially?
I came up through traditional publishing, at the venerable W. W. Norton & Company, home to the Norton Anthologies and Norton Critical Editions. I worked first as a layout artist, then as a print designer working primarily on catalogs and advertisements, before graduating to web design. Later, I worked at

Typekit, a service that allows people who make websites to use real fonts on the web, and helped build a small press, A Book Apart, with Jeffrey Zeldman and Jason Santa Maria. Editorially emerged out of wanting to take what I'd learned about product design at Typekit and apply it to some of the problems we were facing at A Book Apart.

What motivated you to go from being an editor to addressing the writing experience itself?
I've always been someone who wore many hats. In just the past five years, I've worked as a designer, editor, product lead, communications director, and founder, with all its attendant business- and company-building components. I was working actively as a designer before I was working as an editor.

Is there a correlation between better writing experiences and better reading experiences?
Probably. Part of writing is sitting back and reading, and many of the

same principles—of good typography and white space—are universal across many experiences. But designing for reading and designing applications are each disciplines in their own right.

Have your reading habits changed over the past few years?
Some of my habits have stayed the same, and some have changed. I continue to acquire paper books at a moderately obscene rate. I also buy e-books and send many articles found on the web to Pocket; both are often consumed on my iPhone. I read more than I ever did, across mediums, and on more diverse topics than in the past (owing primarily to the web's facility for discovery).

What should be the priorities of a designer today who gives form to editorial content?
A pleasing reading experience that will translate across every kind of device and screen size. Content today is read on phones and televisions and cars and tablets and just

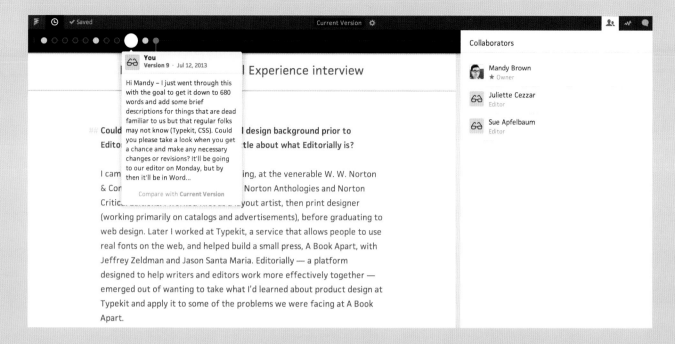

Above and left: Screenshots of a beta version of Editorially, which, fittingly, was the tool we used to conduct our interview with Brown. The interface features a linear versioning timeline, a list of all collaborators, and a place for conversation.

about everything else flat enough to put a screen on it. The design needs to work everywhere. And the content needs to be able to survive without that design. Good markup is a prerequisite for good design.

What kinds of tools do you imagine editors, writers, designers, and developers will use in the future?
I can tell you what kinds of tools I want now. There's a big gap between Photoshop—a photo manipulation tool that we've hacked for the purposes of design—and the browser, a tool designed for consuming, not building. Most of the current discussions about whether designers should code are really about finding something that's more appropriate to the medium than Photoshop, but easier and faster than writing style sheets in Cascading Style Sheets (CSS), which is in principle easy, but with the increasing complexity of browsers and the diversification of screens and devices, ultimately more difficult in practice.

I also think there's a great deal of overlap between the work of the editor and the designer, but as yet no space for the two to engage. Part of Editorially's ethos is that writing and editing should be native to the medium in which we publish. That's among the reasons we chose to support Markdown.* I also think writers and editors will need to become more engaged in HTML and CSS, and tools will emerge to enable that.

And what about the reader? Is reading going to fundamentally remain the same? Are there things that the reader will need or want that we aren't even considering yet due to our limitations?
I think most readers want good stories, and that's not changing. Good design enables those stories, as does good editing. But at the end of day, both are in service to the words. •

* http://stet.editorially.com/articles/why-markup-and-markdown-matter

Case Study: Pitchfork

WEBSITE: PITCHFORK.COM
FREQUENCY: CONTINUOUSLY
FORMAT: WEB
LOCATION: CHICAGO
FOUNDER: RYAN SCHREIBER
CREATIVE DIRECTOR: MICHAEL RENAUD
TECHNICAL DIRECTOR: MATT DENNEWITZ
EDITOR IN CHIEF: MARK RICHARDSON
FOUNDED: 1996

Physical, packaged music and magazines have quite a bit in common. Both industries have been radically transformed by the web, for better and for worse. Music journalism exists predominantly online now, and with good reason. Who really wants to return to a time before you could instantly listen to the music you were reading about? Founded in 1996, Chicago-based *Pitchfork* is something of a pioneer in its field and is one of the most widely read music journals regardless of medium. Started simply as a blog to discuss new music, *Pitchfork* had by the early 2000s become the ultimate authority on what was worth hearing, and its ratings could make or break an album. Although less likely to cause controversy today, *Pitchfork* has remained an influential resource, with content ranging from the quick-hit 24-hour newswire to deep, long-form immersions with its full-screen, magazine-style "Cover Story" format for desktop readers.

Along with in-depth writing and skimmable news briefs, music discovery is key to the *Pitchfork* experience, and one of the ways it accomplishes that is by making it easy to enjoy music continuously—start playing a song on one page, and it'll keep playing as you click to the next. Then mark it as a favorite if you want to save it to a playlist, and that playlist is stored in the user's cache; it'll be saved for the next time you return (no logging in is required). The result is an experience that leaves music fans unrestricted and able to explore to their hearts' content.

Michael Renaud
Creative Director, Pitchfork

Michael Renaud started at *Pitchfork* as a freelancer in 2008 and is now the brand's creative director. Self-taught as a designer, he majored in advertising at the University of Illinois and earned the distinction of being "the only salesman who designed his own ads," for student newspaper the *Daily Illini*. Following that, he was the marketing and art director for the Sun-Times News Group and its ninety-six newspapers and websites. In 2007, he started his design consultancy, Renaud Co., in a storefront in Chicago's Humboldt Park neighborhood. A self-proclaimed magazine junkie, Renaud tells us about how *Pitchfork* creates experiences for reading and music discovery, and what he considers the "good problem" of keeping up with technology.

What do you do in your current role at Pitchfork***?***
My job is to find solutions and produce experiences, and that can require any number of disciplines, given the challenge. I oversee the day-to-day visual aspects of the company. I established *Pitchfork*'s most recent brand identity and worked with the in-house team to develop the current website design, which we continue to improve and revise every day. We also work with national advertisers to build unique connections with their audiences, generate imagery for editorial pieces, and give graphic assistance to our TV department. And I've directed the design of *Pitchfork*'s music festivals in Chicago and Paris since 2008. Also, with Chris Kaskie, *Pitchfork*'s president, I started our visual culture and retail brand Nothing Major.

The web is ideal for music coverage because readers can hear what they read about. When you started, there weren't as many ways to hear music for free online as there are now. How is Pitchfork ***keeping up?***
Our development team, led by technical director Matt Dennewitz, has created a music player that I haven't seen matched by any other site.

Pitchfork.com's home page indexes its five daily album reviews from the previous four days as well as annual staff lists. A built-in player is accessed at top right, and festivals are linked at top left.

When tracks are posted to our CMS by editorial in the form of MP3s, or streaming from sites such as Soundcloud and Bandcamp, it pulls them all into one player, seamlessly making a site-wide playlist that keeps playing as you navigate the site. You can mark songs as your favorites, which are stored in your cache, so when you return to the site, you have the option of listening to a playlist of your favorite songs that have appeared on *Pitchfork*. Everything we do, we do with our readers in mind, and one of our primary goals is to help them discover new music to fall in love with. This player gives them a running document of their discoveries and is an interactive trove of new music waiting to be found.

Pitchfork *is perhaps best known for its music reviews, but you've also experimented with new editorial approaches, such as the cover stories. Could you describe what you did with this content format?*
The "cover story" format is an ongoing experiment. It was originally devised as a way to call more attention to some of the great features that were being generated by our editorial staff. *Pitchfork* is most known for its daily reviews, but there was so much great long-form writing being done that we felt it deserved as much attention as we could get for it. But it also gives the design and development teams an excuse to break the format of our site's day-to-day environment and investigate

new techniques in presenting our content, which can eventually inform site-wide changes.

There are no real rules in terms of consistency each time we do one, and the only tenet that we vehemently stick with is that it needs to be an engaging, highly legible, and enjoyable experience (and environment). There will never be a replacement for print, but we're trying to challenge the statement that "reading on the web will never be better than print."

The Bat for Lashes piece was very well received. The most common piece of congratulatory feedback was that it could be the future of reading on the web, which although flattering, I don't think is true for a few reasons. One is, we can't possibly predict what

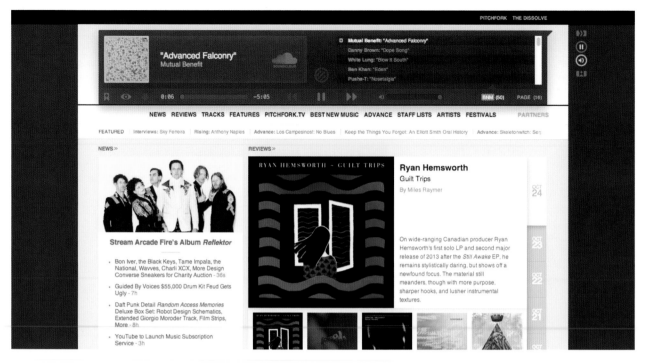

Pitchfork.com features a music player that can be summoned and then hidden, playing relevant tracks and following readers as they navigate around the site.

that will be, and at the rate things are being innovated, the future is destined to hold many more iterations of possibilities. But also, these stories so far are not mobile focused. They're meant to respond to a print environment, incorporating big visual elements and plenty of negative space. Because of the smaller size, legibility dictates a simple interface and elements for the mobile experience, and we need to subtract a few of the techniques we use for the desktop version for an adequate solution.

There isn't a Pitchfork app (yet). What are your thoughts on app development?
Right now, we're just concentrating on a well-done mobile version of the site. Streamlining our content through a responsive system is a priority for us before developing an app. I think when we do an app, we'll do it because there's a specific and alternate way we think our readers would like our content presented to them that we can't accomplish with a mobile version of the site.

What does "editorial design" mean to you?
Editorial design is a responsibility to communicate and present content in the most efficient, legible, and engaging way possible. It's giving your readers every opportunity to immerse themselves in the words and imagery you've created without distraction. Today, the saturation level of information is difficult to comprehend, and as a result, it's difficult to wrangle a focused voice. I believe it's the editorial designer's responsibility to act as a producer and the final filter that can key in on what's important and execute and protect the overall mission effectively.

Are there any editorial design principles that are universal, regardless of the platform?
Having a content strategy all parties agree on and understand is essential for the foundation of a great publication. From there, listening to your audience and knowing when to make concessions to your primary goals for the sake of the editorial subject matter and your readers is very important. Attention to detail is fundamental, as is a strong sense of hierarchy and organization. I also

Published in October 2012, *Pitchfork*'s cover story on musician Bats for Lashes (Natasha Khan) was among the first to forge the parallax-scrolling rich-media storytelling trend, in which it created a flipbook effect of gorgeous black-and-white photography by Shawn Brackbill, elegant typography, and, of course, music. **pitchfork.com/features/cover-story/reader/bat-for-lashes**

Great communication transcends visual design capabilities, and editorial design is more about communicating than it is decorating.

think the best designers are great writers, too. Great communication transcends visual design capabilities, and editorial design is more about communicating than it is decorating.

What do you like most about designing an editorial website?
There is a soul here. Years and years of pushing and pulling through changes in the music and publishing industry have yielded a very passionate and complex foundation. In many ways, it was built from the heart and ideals of many people who put everything they are into it, and designing around that and within that soul is more meaningful to me than, say, finding a solution for a brand's new identity or working on one singular idea via an advertising campaign.

What is the hardest thing about designing an editorial website?
The biggest challenge has been the compartmentalization of web design and not being able to utilize many principles of traditional layout design, typography, grids, and hierarchy due to technical limitations. But all of that is changing and loosening up, which is great—but it poses a new problem of needing to adjust more often as the possibilities expand. Which is a good problem to have, most of the time! •

Another *Pitchfork* cover story, this time about Janelle Monae. With photography by Glenford Nunez and video by Winston Case, this feature, from September 2013, bumps up the typography, adds graphic elements for pull quotes, and plays with color saturation. Each of these features can be read in dynamic (pictured) or standard mode. **pitchfork.com/features/cover-story/reader/janelle-monae**

At the Atlanta headquarters of Janelle Monáe's Wondaland Arts Society, a giant turkey has been roasting slowly for hours, and cups of something called Wondapunch are being passed around. From the front, the place looks like any other home in the surrounding suburban McMansion development, which is otherwise populated by middle-aged and elderly professional types. But inside, Monáe and her team of collaborators have worked to cultivate a hidden artistic oasis.

The living room is carpeted with grass and adorned with a long bench swinging on ropes from the ceiling. In one bathroom is an issue of *Vogue* with Michelle Obama on the cover—Monáe

Later on, Chuck and Nate lead me into a small guest room to screen a rough cut of the video for the slyly doomsaying single "Dance Apocalyptic", which finds Monáe shedding her standard tuxedo getup for an all-white ensemble and loose hair. There are a couple of stray wine glasses in the room, and the bed is unmade. Monáe, they confess, might be upset if she knew I was in here—she wouldn't have wanted anyone to see the mess.

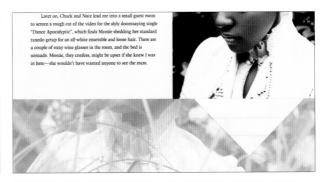

> "
> Diddy is very
> ... mess it up,
> ... of her artistic
>
> ... he should be.

relationship with Chuck and Nate, who helped her ramp up her sound while sticking to her creative scruples.

In turn, the producing pair were entranced by Monáe's sphinxlike on-campus reputation and her laser-sharp focus on her art. "She did one show where she told everyone to drop out of school," remembers Nate, shaking his head and grinning. "She was like, 'Y'all might not even need to be in school! You're wasting your parents' money. You need to go out and find what makes you passionate!'" Though she wasn't even technically a student, she "ran the school," according to Chuck. Walking alongside the petite Monáe—not more than 5'2" and wearing a black-and-white checkered blazer, fitted black slacks, suspenders, patent-leather flats, and Prada sunglasses—it's not hard to imagine her days as an elusive and eccentric character on campus.

At the time, she was working a job at Office Depot, where she'd routinely use the store's computers to update her Myspace page and correspond with fans—a move that would eventually lead to her firing. But the song she wrote in the wake of her exit from the store, "Letting Go", would make its way to the ears of

"Last time [with *The ArchAndroid*], I was really focused on the performance, and I didn't want to do radio," she says. "This time, I said, 'Let's try it and see what happens. I believe in these songs even if they don't make it on the radio, but why not try?'" When we meet at Atlantic, she's mapping out a month-long promotional radio tour that'll have her paying visits to local stations in the hopes that "Q.U.E.E.N." will land on the airwaves. (As of press time, none of the three tracks released from *The Electric Lady* have cracked Billboard's Hot 100.)

So while her ambitions are intact, Monáe is loathe to admit that she'll do anything to sacrifice an ounce of her vision to attain them. "We're focused on getting great music on the radio," she explains, and again I can almost sense her referring back to her inner script. But she also knows, subconsciously, that good things happen when she's forced to put the script away. She recalls her tumultuous recent performance at Essence Festival in New Orleans, where she had a minor sinus infection and lost her voice two hours before going on stage. "I was so proud of myself, because the old me would have been over it," she says. "The audience got the most raw Janelle Monáe ever, because they saw

me adapting."

Case Study:
New York

WEBSITE: NYMAG.COM

FREQUENCY: WEEKLY (PRINT),
CONTINUOUSLY (WEB)

FORMATS: PRINT, WEB, MOBILE

LOCATION: NEW YORK

EDITOR: ADAM MOSS

CREATIVE DIRECTOR: THOMAS ALBERTY

DIRECTOR OF DESIGN AND USER
EXPERIENCE: STEVE MOTZENBECKER

OWNER: NEW YORK MAGAZINE
HOLDINGS, LLC

FOUNDED: 1968

New York magazine began as a Sunday supplement to the *New York Herald Tribune*. When that newspaper went under, editor Clay Felker and art director Milton Glaser bought it and launched it as a stand-alone glossy magazine in 1968. Through their legacy, *New York* has had a long history of excellence in journalism and design. The magazine has gone through many transitions over the years, including a time when it was owned by Primedia and was, according to a 2003 business article in *The New York Times*, "barely profitable." Under its current editor, Adam Moss, who left the same post at *The New York Times Magazine* in 2004 to help bring the publication back from near death, *New York* is now hailed as an industry and reader favorite, in part due to Moss's keen design sensibility. Another key to its success has been its ability to understand the strengths and purposes that each medium presents.

A general-interest national magazine with a city-centric bent, *New York* has been shrewd about balancing what works best in print with what web audiences demand. While the weekly is fairly slim (around 120 pages in a typical issue), it feels worthy of the paper on which it's printed and offers a complete, substantial, beautifully presented meal, with in-depth features sandwiched in between easy-to-scan, bite-size content, such as its popular Approval Matrix infographic. At the same time, NYmag.com and its Daily Intelligencer, Vulture, The Cut, and Grub Street offshoots provide a near-constant stream of news on politics, celebrities, fashion, and food, respectively. "It's a speed business," Moss acknowledged in a 2011 talk at Harvard. "[On] our collective websites, we're putting material up about every six minutes, and we're writing overnight, and we're writing on the weekends, and we're functioning much more like a newspaper in that sense. And 90 percent of our readership online is for original web content." In 2014, the magazine will come out on a biweekly basis as the web continues to take off.

Opposite page: Cover of the annual "Sex" double issue of August 6, 2012, and the post–Hurricane Sandy cover, shot by Iwan Baan from a helicopter, published November 12, 2012.

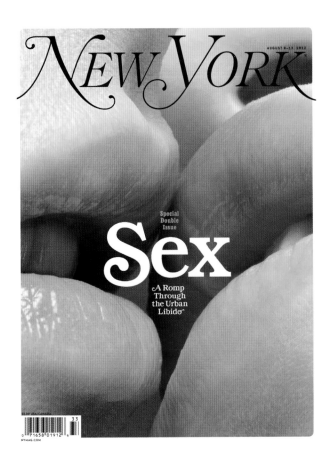

Thomas Alberty

Design Director,
New York Magazine

On the shoulders of giants such as founder Milton Glaser and successors Robert Newman, Luke Hayman, and Chris Dixon, Thomas Alberty stands confidently, yet humbly in his role as *New York*'s design director, the position he's held since January 2012. The self-proclaimed type nerd, who majored in history before switching to design at Rutgers University, started his editorial design career at *Men's Journal*, followed by *Travel + Leisure*, where he worked with Luke Hayman, before Hayman joined editor Adam Moss in reviving *New York* in 2004.

For nearly eight years, Alberty honed his art direction skills at *GQ*, under the design leadership of Fred Woodward, the former *Rolling Stone* art director and one of the best in the business. While his time at *New York* has been relatively brief, Alberty has made his mark subtly, through typographic precision and wit, in particular finding inventive ways to reintroduce typefaces from the magazine's beginnings.

How did you first become interested in editorial design?
I've always loved magazines. I loved *Rolling Stone* in the '90s—the photography, the different fonts on the cover every issue. It was just so amazing and I didn't really understand the process behind it. But I had a really great art teacher in high school

who would show the class design magazines such as *Communication Arts* and *Print*, and it exposed us to the idea that there's this thing called "graphic design," and it's a job that people actually get to be creative, and make cool work, and get paid for it, too. I had done yearbook in high school, and later in college I worked at the *Daily Targum*, the newspaper at Rutgers, doing graphics and layout. We redesigned it over a summer, and that was fun. After that, I designed the covers and center spreads for the weekly entertainment supplement. We had a lot of hand-out promo art, so I learned a lot about how to make something look fun using not-so-great raw material.

Above: The "Childhood" issue ran four different covers, using archival photos (and personal ones from director Spike Lee and actor Matthew Broderick) to bridge the experience of growing up in New York. *Opposite page:* More attention-grabbing covers

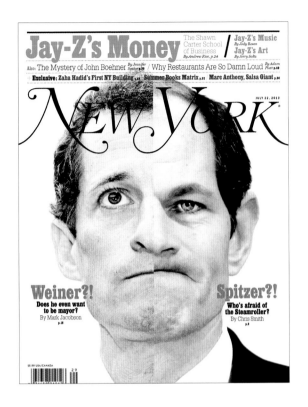

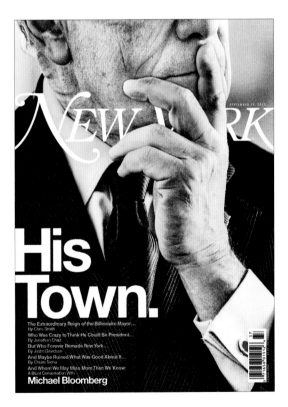

2.

… that is one New York; in another, the poor have made little progress, and homelessness has crept back to the streets.

▸ Joblessness

8.4%
New York City's unemployment rate

7.3%
National unemployment rate

▸ Poverty

The South Bronx is still the poorest district in the country.

38% of its residents live below the poverty line.

37% of its residents lacked money to buy food at some time in the past month, double the national average.

85% higher risk of obesity for a South Bronx resident than a Manhattan resident.

▸ Homeless population

50,926
June 2013

31,063
January 2001

▸ Inequality

+55%
Increase in incomes in the wealthiest neighborhoods between 2000 and 2010

-0.2%
Decline in incomes in the poorest neighborhoods

NEW YORK | SEPTEMBER 16, 2013

3.

Under Ray Kelly, the NYPD had remarkable success, bringing down crime across the board.

▸ Percentage decrease in crime rate

	MURDER	RAPE	ROBBERY	FELONY ASSAULT	BURGLARY	GRAND LARCENY	GRAND LARCENY OF AN AUTOMOBILE
2001	649	1,991	28,202	23,483	32,765	46,329	29,931
2012	419	1,445	20,144	19,381	19,168	42,497	8,093

-35% -27% -29% -17% -41% -8% -73%

4.

But its tactics became flash points of racial tension and conflict, and the NYPD's success against terrorism also came at the expense of civil liberties.

▸ Stopped and frisked

Total stops

532,911

The top precincts for stops in 2012: East New York, Brooklyn Brownsville, Brooklyn Mott Haven, the Bronx

The least-stopped precincts: The 22nd, Central Park The 17th, Kip's Bay The 50th, Riverdale, the Bronx

Frisk profile

10% White
6% Other
53% African-American
31% Latino

"Everyone's a criminal, because we live here and we're minorities. It makes you hate the presence of police. And the kids see them harass us and other people so much that they start to hate the police, too."
— Bryan Bender

"They'll escalate it, they'll conjure up a lie or whatever they can. You have to be very passive or very submissive to them. You have to be like, all right, like they ass. You can be sitting on a bench, playing dominoes. They'll come, they'll kick over the stuff, cause dust in the air. They'll do little spiteful shit. But, you know, that's just another day here."
— Tiger Wood

"They're friendly. My son hasn't been stopped. But if they do stop him, I just tell him they're just doing their job. Because this is a dangerous area. Let them do what they gotta do. And they'll send you on your merry way."
— Tony Lopez

5.

And yet New York appears palpably more coherent: The city's racial politics are more muted, and the notion of the city as an archipelago of ethnic neighborhoods has come to seem quaint.

6.

Gentrification accelerated; in many precincts the boundaries between neighborhoods became increasingly porous.

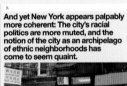

Bed-Stuy
White population
50%
1.8% 1.4% 10.9%
1950 1960 2000 2010
Average house prices
+53% 2003...$331,551 2013...$507,346

Crooklyn house
The Bed-Stuy brownstone that was the setting for Crooklyn, Spike Lee's iconic film about black working-class family life, sold in June for $1.7 million.

Central Harlem
White population
404.8% change
2% 9.5%
2000 2010
Average house prices
+85.9% 2003...$361,681 2013...$672,472

Bushwick
White population
216.1% change
3% 9.5%
2000 2010
Average house prices
+31.3% 2003...$303,111 2013...$398,017

7.

Developers pushed into hitherto untouched corners of the city.

37%
of the city was rezoned

8/20
of the tallest buildings in New York were built in the last twelve years

One World Trade Center 2013
Bank of America Tower 2009
New York Times Building 2007
One 57 2013
Four World Trade Center 2013
8 Spruce Street 2011
Trump World Tower 2001
Bloomberg Tower 2005

214,000
New housing units

▸ South Williamsburg, a partially industrial, largely working-class backwater, grew a sheaf of glittering towers and became a destination.

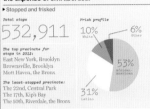

Domino Sugar Factory
Wythe Hotel
Edge
Milk Bar
Nitehawk Cinemas
Output

▸ And universities like NYU became some of the city's most rapacious developers.

"We don't want to see the Village go from an incredibly vibrant cross section of people and culture to essentially a company town with more of the same. They've continued on in an imperious fashion that's been opposed by neighbors and faculty and students who don't believe that this Manifest Destiny is in the best interest of those who go there to learn. If you look at the skyline of Washington Square South in the Bloomberg years, the Kimmel Center—the huge, hideous yellow structure right behind the arch—is a monument to their aggressive expansion. Just next door is their new law-school building, built in 2003, for which the Edgar Allan Poe building had to be demolished. Their expansion is overkill, out of scale, and having a deadening effect because of the terrible architecture and the enormous scale and the sameness that it brings to the neighborhood."
— ANDREW BERMAN, GREENWICH VILLAGE SOCIETY FOR HISTORIC PRESERVATION

▸ The Bowery, once a symbol of down-and-out, became one of the city's chicest streets.

Then → Now
Salvation Army residence → Bowery Boutique Hotel
CBGB space → John Varvatos
280 Bowery (McGurk's Suicide Hall) → Avalon Bowery Place

8.

The city's geocultural map was scrambled. Downtown became uptown; Brooklyn became the defining borough of New York, an alternate Manhattan— and a global brand.

So good to see you.

Hannah Horvath and her publisher, David Pressler-Goings, in HBO's Girls.

What the fuck is a money man doing in Brooklyn? I don't know what's going on anymore. I mean, did the East River freeze over?

I don't even know what's happening. Who chose this restaurant? I don't think it was here last week.

▸ Brooklyn around the world.

The Brooklyn Diner opens an outpost in Dubai
Brooklyn Restaurant in Sabah, Malaysia
Brooklyn Bar in Paris
Brooklyn Bar and Restaurant in Dalian, China
Brooklyn Beef Club in Berlin

Brooklyn Restaurant in Helsingborg, Sweden
Brooklyn Parlor Bar in Tokyo
Brooklyn Pizza in Manila, Philippines
The Brooklyn Steakhouse in Sheffield, U.K.
Brooklyn Coffeeshop in Curitiba, Brazil

ILLUSTRATION BY MARK NERYS. PHOTOGRAPHS: CHRISTOPHER ANDERSON/MAGNUM PHOTOS/NEW YORK MAGAZINE

ILLUSTRATION BY MARK NERYS. PHOTOGRAPH BY JEFF CHIEN-HSING LIAO.

NEW YORK | SEPTEMBER 16, 2013

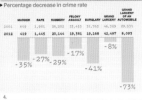

Feature article spreads from the special "Spring Fashion" double issue, February 18, 2013. Previous: Spreads from the Bloomberg issue

***Other than frequency, what was the biggest change coming to** New York **from** GQ?*
It's totally different! In terms of designing a cover, at *GQ*, a cover will always be a really great photo of an actor or athlete, with bold, clear cover lines. At *New York*, the cover can be anything. Some weeks it's a news story, other weeks it's a celebrity profile, another week is food or home design. Some weeks, a big beautiful photo, another could be bold, blocky type. Or all illustrative type, like a poster. I find the variety exciting, and a challenge.

What's the cover planning process?
Adam, photo director Jody Quon, and I meet regularly to discuss the visual strategy for future features, so we're aware of what's scheduled to run a few issues in advance. Adam will know what pieces are cover contenders, so we plan accordingly—for example, if we're shooting a subject, we'll tell the photographer to make pictures that can work on a cover. The materials are all coming together, but in the end, they'll come together very quickly.

Some weeks there might be three features competing to be on the cover, so I'll design many covers for each of those stories—different art treatments, different combinations of cover lines—and Adam will pick the cover story Thursday night. That doesn't happen too often. Most times, it's one cover subject, designed multiple ways. I'll have art usually on Monday, cover lines by Tuesday. I'll comp up anywhere from twelve to thirty versions, depending on the week. By Thursday, Adam will hold an informal focus group in his office, showing editors about six to twelve covers to gauge what photo, design, and headlines are working. What people like and don't like is always pretty interesting. After that, we'll eliminate more, refine more, and decide the cover Thursday night. It gets proofread, a little more tweaking, then it ships Friday afternoon.

How does that compare with designing the rest of the issue?
I have it the easiest! I work on the covers primarily. My crew does a huge amount of designing week in and week out. It's humbling. Throughout the week, I'm looking at layouts and approving them or asking

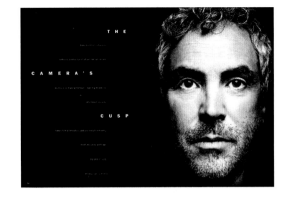

The many ways *New York* opens a feature story: with illustrations, striking black-and-white photography, and with photo illustration

for more tweaks. The magazine is like four little magazines in one: Intelligencer, the features, the Strategist, and Culture Pages. We'll know what's scheduled for the sections ahead of time, and they get worked on the first part of the week. But every week is different, in the complexity of what's going on in the magazine. One issue may have a large travel package in the Strategist section; another week may have an Emmys package in Culture Pages. It's a lot of work that comes together in a very short time.

How do you keep it from being formulaic while also needing a system to get it done each week?
Everyone always wants to do better than the last time. I feel that if we make something that's interesting to

I feel that if we make something that's interesting to us, it'll be interesting to the reader.

us, it'll be interesting to the reader. Jody is just amazing at what she does, always wanting to reinvent. And of course Adam is very visual, he pushes us to make great work, and that helps a lot.

Are infographics something you advocate for in the magazine?
Editors are interested in infographics here, so they often will suggest that we have them. Timelines, flowcharts, annotated photos, super-ranking charts, you name it. While a good

amount of planning is involved, the downside is that they are labor intensive. A designer gets the information from an editor, designs the information—then it's a collaborative conversation between the editor and the designer, a constant back and forth, adding information, changing information, trying to make the data and the language and the visuals come together beautifully and clearly. We did a story about traffic fatalities in the city, and we knew about it a month ahead, so we were able

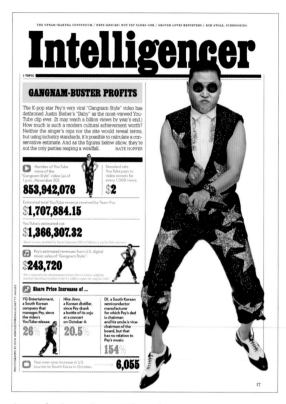

Opener for the Intelligencer (front of book) section; The Approval Matrix, on the back page of each issue, charts what is despicable and brilliant that week.

to commission a 3-D rendering of a city intersection to annotate, and that turned out great. Other times, we might only get started the week of, and it's a crunch, but it still has to turn out pretty great.

What can you tell us about desiging the iPad app?

The tablet app was in the works with the Wonderfactory before I started. Adam's vision was that he wanted to create an app that had the best of *New York*'s web content and best of the magazine built in, so you have the half-and-half presentation. Kate Elazegui was the launch design director, and I worked with her on how the magazine part would look. The architecture was straightforward to begin with, but we worked

to make things as streamlined as possible and figure out the best way to present how a feature would be structured or how a sidebar doesn't have to get scrunched in a corner, you can give it its own space to breathe. The current team has about four people who work exclusively on the tablet: the art director is Jay Guillermo, and Stevie Remsberg is the production manager and does quite a lot of designing and coordinating as well.

How would you summarize the design perspective of New York?

It's clear, it's refined, it's witty. When Luke Hayman redesigned *New York*, it had this great bookish look. Very strong bones. During Chris Dixon's tenure, it evolved more, and he

resurrected the Egyptienne typeface that was used constantly from the old days. For me, it's a balance of keeping the magazine new while maintaining a continuity with its past. •

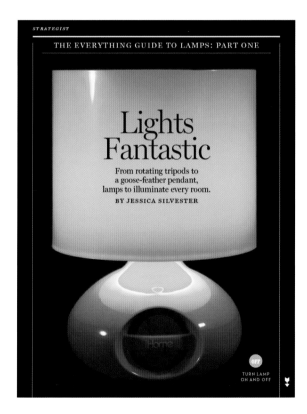

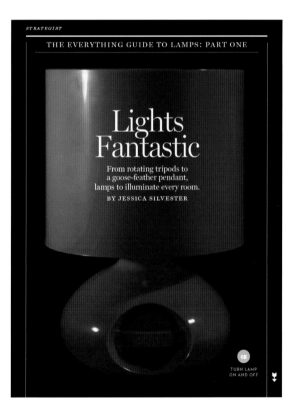

The "Best of New York" issue, March 11, 2013, marked the debut of the New York iPad magazine. Compare this story on shopping for light fixtures, shown in print (at top) and in the interactive app (above), which invites readers to tap to turn a lamp on and off.

Before: NYmag.com's home page pre-October 2013 relaunch. This version splinters off content from its Daily Intelligencer, Vulture, The Cut, and Grub Street blogs/sub-brands, using their graphic identities prominently.

Steve Motzenbecker

Director of User Experience, NYmag.com

As *New York* magazine's director of user experience and design, Steve Motzenbecker is responsible the expansive NYmag.com platform and its brand offshoots Vulture (TV and entertainment), Grub Street (food and dining), and The Cut (fashion and women's interest). All share the same high-quality genetics but have varying personalities and structures. Motzenbecker has worked for New York Media since 2004, originally as a production designer on the print magazine. He

taught himself web design on the side and transitioned to the digital team in 2007 when Ian Adelman, now digital design director at NYTimes.com, took on the role Motzenbecker now holds. The online strategy that he has helped to implement has been an iterative one, rolling out new products and features quietly, for the most part. One of *New York*'s biggest developments has been The Cut, its first responsive site. Featuring extensive slideshows of zoomable, hi-res photography, The Cut is more of a sub- or mini-magazine than simply a blog, with its own creative direction and editorial scope. Here, Motzenbecker speaks to the ways that The Cut stands apart yet within the *New York* ecosystem. We spoke in January 2013, before the *New York* iPad app existed, and before

NYMag.com's responsive redesign of its home page.

Could you explain the structure of NYmag.com and The Cut?
While in many ways we think of The Cut as a separate site, it actually still lives under the NYmag.com domain. It's likely to move to its own domain in the future but doing so would result in a significant, although temporary, depression of our search engine rankings. We chose not to complicate the launch with it.

For the most part, The Cut looks and behaves as its own website with its own branded experience. So, to most users the distinction between The Cut and the rest of NYmag.com is clear and deliberate.

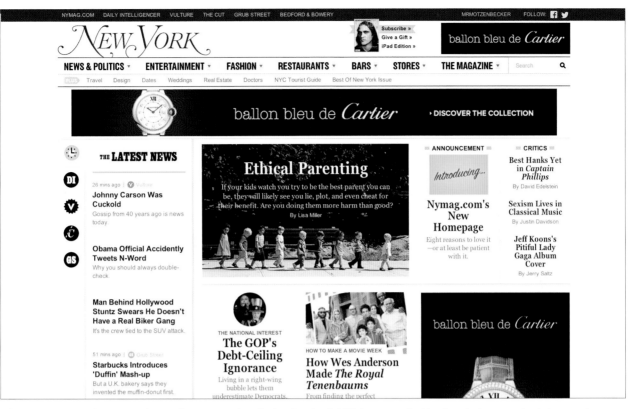

After: The responsive home page design of NYmag.com, launched on October 8, 2013, is more reader friendly, stripping away visual clutter so the content stands out, not the branding. Subtle icons along the "Latest News" rail at left help readers find their favorite verticals.

Why did you choose a responsive design for the site?

We knew that our mobile and tablet audiences were growing, and since a lot of what we were doing would be starting from scratch, it was a now-or-never kind of thing. We saw a choice between a stand-alone mobile site or building our site responsively. Both Kevin Barnett, our director of front-end technology at the time, and I felt strongly it was time to go responsive. The development and design teams were also excited for the challenge, and so we made the case to the business that it was a critical piece of The Cut's success and they were very quickly supportive.

It was a little insane, trying to do an entire site responsively without having done anything responsive yet.

Slide shows were a huge challenge. Advertising was also a huge challenge, but it's definitely been paying off. Mobile traffic is up just about 350 percent, and tablet traffic is up over 150 percent.

How do you test your designs?

We do tracking, which is literally just paying attention to what links people are clicking on and figuring out if people are using modules or not. We do A/B testing as well, which means putting up two different designs of a particular thing, for example a module that promotes more stories at the end of an article, and see which one performs better. We also do focus groups, so we bring users in and interview them about a bunch of things, like how The Cut compares

with the rest of our competitive set. We also get feedback by watching people just use the site, which usually means them pointing out things that are broken [laughs].

How often do you test?

We do A/B testing pretty frequently. And every couple months or so, we'll have a focus group come in. Focus groups are an imperfect science, but they're definitely useful. We did them throughout The Cut as we were designing, and even before we did anything visual. That helped validate some of our earlier assumptions and, just as important, not to pursue certain things.

Design and UX director Steve Motzenbecker explains that they did a lot of user testing to figure out which home page version worked best. Here are four variations that were prototyped before settling on the version pictured on the previous page.

Postlaunch we spent a lot of time bug-fixing. It's always painful to hear users' frustration when a product launches that isn't exactly up to the level you were reaching for.

different layouts, different ways the zoom experience might work, additional features, etc. We put the slide shows in front of users to get a reaction and observe how they used it.

How have the slide shows worked out with users?
It's worked out well. Users are engaging with them as expected, although when we launched they were still pretty buggy on some of the less common platforms and browsers our users were visiting from.

Although we were building a responsive site, we had to prioritize where to spend our efforts on and focus on the browsers and operating systems where the majority of our audience was. Up against a fixed

What was involved in creating the new slide show format?
In summer 2011, we started with the slide shows because a big goal of The Cut was to make it a very visual experience—all about big beautiful photography—and we wanted our slide shows to allow users to explore that. Part of the challenge was negotiating

with our photo provider to give us big photos that are upward of 3,000 pixels tall, which is a lot bigger than most sites provide. Technically, serving up these big images really quickly was a challenge for us, too. But we built an image management system to help with that. We also prototyped the slide shows several times—

launch date, some platform experiences just weren't where we'd have liked them to be. Postlaunch we spent a lot of time bug-fixing. It's always painful to hear users' frustration when a product launches that isn't exactly up to the level you were reaching for.

Tell us about the home page.
The home page is a beast. We came from a place where our home page was really just an index feed of posts. We wanted to keep the news feed on the page, but we also want to showcase all this new stuff that we're doing. It's a long page from a user experience perspective. And it's a heavy page. We actually make this page load up pretty quickly compared with a lot of others, but for the amount of stuff that we're putting on it, it's a lot. I wouldn't be surprised if in six months or a year from now, it looks and feels much different, because we'll probably remove modules that aren't performing well or redesign them. Aside from slide shows, it was also the most challenging page to do responsively because of how things are rearranged for different points. One of the ugly things about responsive design can be when you need to rely on the page being fluid, and you've got a very structured design that doesn't lend itself well to that. There are often "in-between" states where the page may look broken. The vast majority of our users come to the page and it's fine, but it's not totally bulletproof.

How often are readers coming to the home page first?
A lot of people still do come to this page, but there's no doubt it's taking up a smaller and smaller portion of incoming traffic because Twitter and Facebook are really changing how people get into a site. People are coming in the side door, landing on an article linked on Twitter or Flipboard on the iPad. They're reading the article, and then they're bouncing back into their feed.

Some people come in through the side door, end up in the article page, and then find a related article, or they might click to go back to the home page and explore that way.

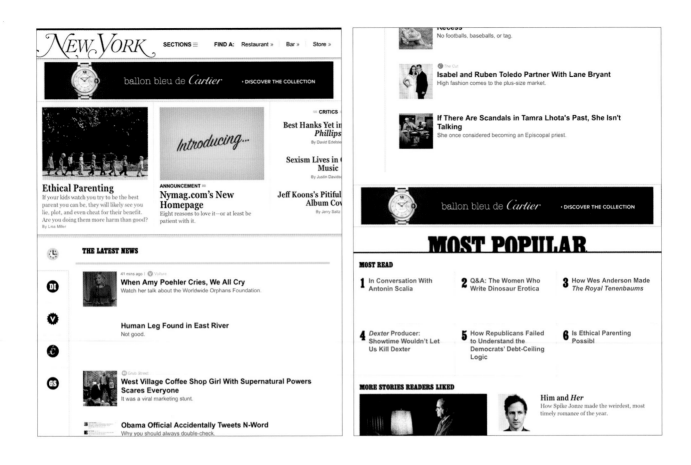

Focus groups are an imperfect science, but they're definitely useful.

That's, of course, our hope. We want visitors to find enough good content to keep them looking at more than one page if we can.

The flipside is that, for advertisers, this is an extremely important page. Even things such as section pages won't always drive the amount of traffic that you think they would, but they're very important for advertising. Advertisers want to be able to own the home page, or the Beauty section, say, and for them to see their big, beautiful takeover on there.

What is working for advertisers?
It's no surprise that banner ads don't drive a lot of engagement. Takeovers, like the big visual experiences, I think if they're done well, they can make a lasting impression that is less of an interruptive experience. If you do it well, and you do it nicely, then you're at least respecting the user in a more appropriate way than some advertisements do. That's what my job is in many ways, helping to find a balance between what is good for the user with one that gives our advertisers

the engagement and presence they're after. In the end, though, what's going to work for advertisers is engagement, and the digital advertising landscape still has a lot of work to do in that regard. •

Ethical Parenting

If your kids watch you try to be the best parent you can be, they will likely see you lie, plot, and even cheat for their benefit. Are you doing them more harm than good?

By Lisa Miller

Shutdown Because France?

Pete Sessions's head-scratcher.

Video: Insanely Brave Deli Guy Chases Away Armed Robber With Sword

This Long Island clerk is fearless.

ballon bleu de *Cartier*
▸ DISCOVER THE COLLECTION

MOST POPULAR

MOST READ

1 In Conversation With Antonin Scalia

2 Him and *Her*: How Spike Jonze Made the Weirdest, Most Timely Romance of the Year

Davidson on the Met's Opening, and City Opera's Closing

ballon bleu de *Cartier*
▸ DISCOVER THE COLLECTION

TO DO

25 Things to See, Hear, Watch and Read This Week

The responsive design of NYmag.com adjusts its layout to a smartphone (above), to a tablet (opposite page), and to a desktop screen (below). Note how elements like "Most Popular" change both in content and layout to take advantage of the format in which it's presented.

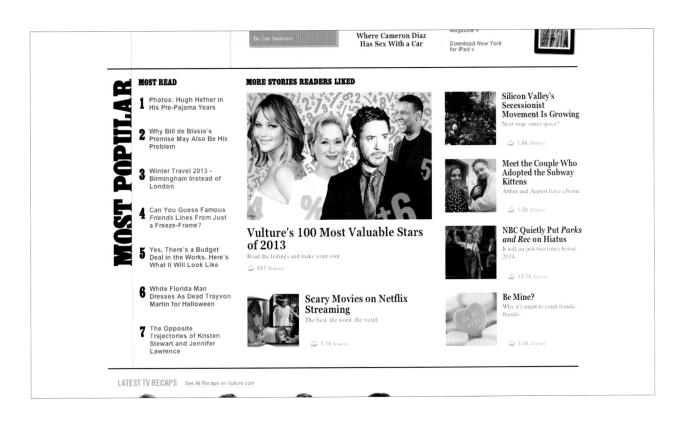

Where Cameron Diaz Has Sex With a Car

Download *New York* for iPad »

MOST READ

1 Photos: Hugh Hefner in His Pre-Pajama Years

2 Why Bill de Blasio's Promise May Also Be His Problem

3 Winter Travel 2013 - Birmingham Instead of London

4 Can You Guess Famous *Friends* Lines From Just a Freeze-Frame?

5 Yes, There's a Budget Deal in the Works. Here's What It Will Look Like

6 White Florida Man Dresses As Dead Trayvon Martin for Halloween

7 The Opposite Trajectories of Kristen Stewart and Jennifer Lawrence

MORE STORIES READERS LIKED

Vulture's 100 Most Valuable Stars of 2013

Read the listings and make your own.

857 Shares

Scary Movies on Netflix Streaming

The best, the worst, the weird.

1.1k Shares

Silicon Valley's Secessionist Movement Is Growing

Next stop: outer space?

1.8k Shares

Meet the Couple Who Adopted the Subway Kittens

Arthur and August have a home.

1.5k Shares

NBC Quietly Put *Parks and Rec* on Hiatus

It will air just two times before 2014.

33.1k Shares

Be Mine?

Why it's smart to court female friends.

3.3k Shares

LATEST TV RECAPS See All Recaps on Vulture.com

The Cut was NYmag.com's first experiment in creating a site with a responsive design that could be enjoyed on screens large and small. On a large screen, the user can zoom into unusually large photographs, making The Cut's slide shows distinctive from those of other fashion publications.

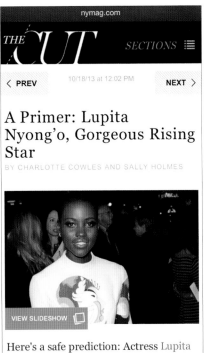

The same slide show on an iPhone. While zooming is disabled, it's easy to move from image to image with a swipe to the left.

Stella Bugbee

Editorial Director, The Cut

As editorial director for The Cut, NYmag.com's fashion vertical, Stella Bugbee defines the voice and content of the high visual impact platform that premiered in late 2012. But for four-teen years prior she worked primarily as a creative director, designing such beloved magazines as *Domino* and *Topic*, as well as issues of *The New York Times Magazine* and *New York*. Bugbee describes her current boss, Adam Moss, as a "highly visual editor," a term that could now apply just as well to her. While in school at Parsons, Bugbee studied both writing and communica-tion design but pursued graphic design as a career first. She interned with magazine design legend Roger Black, from whom she learned the commercial side of the field redesigning mass-market titles such as *Men's Health*, *Reader's Digest*, and *Rolling Stone*. After graduation, she opted to start a cross-disciplinary studio, Honest, with two of her fellow Parsons classmates and has been focused on creative edito-rial and fashion projects ever since. Her strong design background and editorial instincts are perfectly suited to the The Cut's brains-and-beauty take on style.

Your background is so varied, having worked in print and broad-cast design before becoming the editorial director for a web-based magazine. What prepared you to move from designing to editing?
Over the years, I've noticed two strains of designers: the ones that identify musically, rhythmically, and the ones that are more literary. It's just my observation.

People who read first or who identify more with a more literary side of design are perfect for the editorial experience. A really good editorial designer embodies the reader always and can project how the reader travels through a piece, devising ways of making that experi-ence meaningful and navigable. The best editorial designers that I've ever worked with can read a piece and call out what the good pull quote would be because they'll know what would make you want to jump into a piece.

At Parsons, I started an ambitious student publication called *Baseline* and also worked with some friends at Columbia on a book project. So I got the indie publishing bug, where you have control over editorial. I also worked for Roger Black my senior year of college, working on some very commercial magazine projects. I got insight into how Roger defined a decade or more of magazine design, and although no one probably credits him for it now, he is still so influential in how magazines look. The giant drop caps and rules—thick rules, thin rules—all of that stuff was super-standard Roger. He started it. At the time, when I started working with him, it blew my mind because I under-stood finally why everything looked the way it looked.

What initially drew you to making magazines?
I got David Carson's *Ray Gun* in high school, and it was just revelatory. If design isn't part of your family vocabulary, you're not likely to know about it, and then some moment happens when you're exposed to it. At Parsons, I was connecting the dots between *Ray Gun* and some of the popular-culture things I was excited by at the time, and connecting them back to graphic design.

I was really excited by language, always. Even the student publica-tion that we did, *Baseline*, was very language based. We all wrote the content for *Baseline*, and the pieces I wrote were about language, almost like linguistics. The more commercial magazines, where designers were ghettoized within the process, were the antithesis of what I liked about editorial design, that you could col-laborate with the editors. So I didn't want to do that out of college. I saw this very linear track, and where it led was not that interesting to me. You're never going to have any real impact on the publication until you're the design director, and there's still this limit.

At Honest, you tried to do your own magazine, too.
It was the second issue that broke up the company. It was clear to me that the three partners' interests were not similar. So I went to *The New York Times Magazine* in 2003 to fill in for someone on maternity leave. I also met Project Projects' Rob Giampietro while freelancing there that summer, and Rob asked me if I wanted to help his friend with a publication called *Topic*. So, I started collaborating with David Haskell—who is now deputy editor at *New York* magazine—and that was finally the experience that I was craving. Working with this very visual editor and this super strong design person in Rob, I could be this conceptual person who could think about photography and content in a different way. It was one of the best creative experiences that I've ever had. We put out several editions,

and then I didn't get to do another editorial project again until *Bene*, a custom, niche project where again, I was not just being a designer. And then *Domino* called. I knew that getting the Condé Nast experience was necessary. It was finally a design director position, so I wasn't going to be just following orders.

If something gets posted on Reddit, you're golden. And it has nothing to do with the site or the way it looks.

And how was the Condé experience after working on indie publications?
Domino was a design magazine, ultimately. It had to do with design and style, and weirdly, so many of the staff have gone into fashion-related projects since *Domino* closed, including Deborah Needleman [now the editor of *T, The New York Times'* style magazine]. But none of us had fashion backgrounds. It was fun to work on a project that felt very relevant. So I took it. And it was not easy. I realized that I really wanted to have more input into the content, and without that, I was never going to be happy. I wanted to be suggesting rubrics and formats. I wanted to bring editorial ideas to the project, not just ways of making things prettier. I think a lot of editorial designers feel that way, but there's not a path to that.

So what has your experience been at New York magazine?
It's one of the most adaptive publications. They have some type styles that are set for body copy and columns, but it's still different every single week, and it's wild. They're now doing an adaptive and amazing redesign. Adam understands that this kind of dynamic design process makes it a dynamic read. And so much of that comes from him. He meets with the design team multiple times a day. He's also insanely, deeply involved in the web, which is huge.

Let's talk about The Cut.
When I initially came to The Cut project, it was as a creative consultant. The Cut is a women's vertical for style. For a year and a half, we thought about the design and content, trying to anticipate formats that would serve us—different ways to do article layouts and different slideshow experiences—so we could spend a lot of time not thinking about the design, and instead thinking about how to publish thirty pieces a day. A third of that is original content we generate—a combination of photo stories, personal essays, and beauty posts, as well as slideshows and lists. What I like about the web is that it's so iterative. We can make observations about what's working and what's not working, and we'll get a chance to update it again. Now that I've done a web project, it's going to be very hard for me to go back to print.

You've commissioned great photographers such as Todd Cole to shoot original photo stories. How is it working with photographers for the web only?

A lot of people have been fine with it. But you know, it's funny to me that people still want to be in print mostly. Their stuff will live forever online, and way more people will see it, and it's beautiful and backlit—you can zoom in on them, and pin them and share them. Sure, I think they look better on a giant screen than on a small phone, but I don't think they look better on crappy magazine paper than they do backlit in a slideshow. Online will become the primary source of people's information and editorial experience. It's coming, even for long features and photo stories.

You're also extremely active in social media. How does that impact things such as the home page, which is less often the first impression for readers?
So we're in this middle ground of where we want to make an experience that has some cohesive tone and a top-down vision, and yet acknowledges that that model is somewhat challenged by these new ways that we get content. Half the time, you get content on your Facebook page entirely divorced from the experience where it was created. We know that it's important to have a tone and a vision and a direction, and to let some things branch out beyond that to be shared, just literally. If something gets posted on Reddit, you're golden. And it has nothing to do with the site or the way it looks. •

Case Study:
Vanity Fair Italia

WEBSITE: VANITYFAIR.IT
FREQUENCY: WEEKLY
FORMAT: PRINT
LOCATION: MILAN
CREATIVE DIRECTOR: DEVIN PEDZWATER
EDITOR: LUCA DINI
OWNER: CONDÉ NAST
FOUNDED: 2004

International editions strike a delicate balance between staying true to the flagship publications editorial mission and forging their own creative vision, with content that feels true to its readers' interests. The truth is, *Vanity Fair* has stood for many different things in the more than 100 years since the title first appeared—early incarnations dating back to the nineteenth century covered humor, society, and theater. Regardless of whether it's speaking to European or American readers, *Vanity Fair* is universally witty, cosmopolitan, and cultured.

The redesign of *Vanity Fair Italia*, launched in May 2013, came after more than a year without a creative director at the helm. When American designer Devin Pedzwater came on board in late 2012, he had a lot of cleaning up to do and worked quickly to get the publication's grid structure, typography, and color palette standardized once again. With a preference for high-quality photography ("the photography is the star," he says), Pedzwater has divined from the pages a renewed essence of glamour and sophistication.

Covers of *Vanity Fair Italia*, before (left, May 2012) and after (right, May 2013). The redesign was led by Devin Pedzwater.

Devin Pedzwater
Creative Director, Vanity Fair Italia

Devin Pedzwater is no stranger to designing magazines for a mass audience. But the size, popularity, and frequency of *Vanity Fair Italia*, which produces more than 300 pages every week, puts him in a whole new league. Originally from Pittsburgh, Pennsylvania, Pedzwater studied graphic design at Penn State University and has built a hefty editorial design portfolio that includes art direction for *Condé Nast Traveler*, *Sports Illustrated*, and *Rolling Stone*. In his eight years at *Spin*, Pedzwater was the creative director responsible for the full brand redesign in 2012, which was widely praised for playing to the strengths of each medium, but ultimately paved the way for the publisher to pull the plug on print. When we spoke just weeks after his *Vanity Fair Italia* design relaunch, he seemed remarkably calm for someone whose time is now split between two countries.

When did you start working as creative director of* Vanity Fair Italia *and how has the transition been for you?
I got the job officially over Thanksgiving 2012, and since then, I've been going back and forth between New York and Milan, doing two weeks there, two weeks here.

The work culture and also the life-in-Italy culture both came at once. Everyone involved knew that was going to be a challenge for me. I always expect the worst and hope for the best. But when I got there, the transition was very easy. The staff was very open to change; they welcomed me because they were looking for someone to help them direct the magazine into a new place.

What was the situation like when you stepped in?
The last creative director was Brian Anstey, who is now at *InStyle* magazine. He worked directly in the Milan office for about two years. In that time, he took the magazine, redesigned it, and directed the whole staff. Then, once his term was done,

he left, and they didn't have anybody there for about a year. So, as you can imagine, without having that kind of director for a time, things can start to slide. The design staff needed help, but also the magazine's goals started to shift. There's more competition on the newsstand, so they needed to recenter themselves around the *Vanity Fair* brand. So the need to address workflow and the need for rebranding came at the same time.

How did you prioritize what to do first? Did you start with rebranding or workflow?

I wanted to do everything all at once. I had to settle down, and say, okay, let's start with the fundamentals: the grid structure. The magazine had to be reset. There was a set of fonts, col-

Going through all the pages at first, it made me dizzy. There's up to 300 pages a week. I'd never seen a weekly this big before.

ors, and grids that were being used at one point, but when Brian left, they started to change and morph, and become multiple styles all at once. Each designer would pair with an editor, and there are five editors that looked after the whole magazine. And so they would operate as individual silos, not really communicating with each other. So one of the biggest problems was just communication between each of the staff members.

Once we addressed that, we could come up with a grid and fonts and styles that would work across the whole magazine.

How much did you look at the history of the magazine as a guide?

Going through all the pages at first, it made me dizzy. There are up to 300 pages a week. I'd never seen a weekly this big before. I started peeling back all the layers and studying it until I

The other, bigger underlying goal for the redesign was to get people to go home at a reasonable hour.

found where the problems were. The fonts were the real problem because there were probably fifteen or twenty in any given part. So the first thing we did was see if we could just pull it down to very small numbers. Right now, we're using Didot, which is the branded Condé Nast face and also the branded *Vanity Fair* face. And then VF Sans with VF Times, which were done originally for American *Vanity Fair*. There are a couple of other ones such as Solano, and some other detail fonts, but really it's just those two sets. That gave us a new

challenge, designing this whole massive magazine around just these two fonts, and going through the templating process, we were able to get probably to get 90 to 95 percent of it done with just those two. And that settled things down quite a bit.

The magazine had the same issue with the colors. They weren't really working from any sort of color guide. So I came up with a set of thirty-two colors that can be used in any given section. And now we're trying to challenge ourselves by only using that set, not creating new colors.

Once we had that down, the third piece was the grid. We have a twelve-column grid across the whole magazine now. The same grid for every page. So it's much easier for the staff to use. One grid, one set of colors, and just two or three fonts.

It seems like a system would be essential for putting out 300 pages per week.

Right, it has to be automated. The other, bigger underlying goal for the redesign was to get people to go home at a reasonable hour. When I was talking to staff, that seemed to be the one thing that they wanted, but didn't want say right away. But everyone wants to go home to their families and have a reasonable work life. By looking at the kind of pages that they were working on, I could

Un quartiere
residenziale che
potrebbe essere
quello (immaginario)
della serie Tv
*Desperate
Housewives*:
case basse, giardini
impeccabili e quel
gusto - molto
americano - per
l'understatement.
Soprattutto
negli abiti

WISTERIA LANE

see why they were there all the time. So I really wanted to simplify it. The system is limiting because it doesn't give you the freedom of doing whatever you want. But at the same time, it creates a much more cohesive and manageable package.

Photography is also a strong focus in your work.
For me, the photography is the star. The typography always has to fall back. *Vanity Fair Italia* has the pull to work with some of the best, if not *the* best, photographers in the world. For me, it's also important to support photographers. Because as everybody knows, the budgets are getting tight, and priority seems to be shifting away from shooting and more toward picking up and research-ing photography. So if you have the opportunity to have the photo shoots, to have original artwork, you should show it off.

Have you noticed more of a print culture in Italy when compared to the United States?
Yeah, they definitely embrace it. Just walking around the city, there are more kiosks and newsstands than there are in New York, and they're alive and part of the lifestyle and the culture still. But mobile is also huge. It seems much easier to get a mobile device and to use it. The networks are stronger in Italy, and you can use your phone underground on the subway, in the airport, everywhere.

How much does the American Vanity Fair *influence what you do?*
Vanity Fair Italia is a weekly and has its own content mix. It only repurposes about 10 percent of content from the U.S. version or from the other versions. So it really operates as its own machine. I introduced myself to U.S. creative director Chris Dixon and his team to let them know what I was doing, because one of the goals with this for me was to bring it back into the *Vanity Fair* fold. And they were very welcoming. *Vanity Fair* has such a strong brand, and I felt like the Italian version had moved away from that.

Simplifying typefaces, establishing a limited color palette, and "letting the photography be the star" make for a more coherent design.

Smaller apps for mobile, that are well designed and don't crash, are part of the learning process of what to do next for media brands.

At Spin, you were the brand creative director and did a beautiful job creating experiences that honored each medium—from the bigger pages and heavier paper stock of the magazine to the usability of the website.

We spent a lot of time getting a strategy together before we made our first move. I think one of the mistakes that a lot of publishers make is they just jump in and say, "Okay, we need to redesign the magazine, let's redesign the magazine. We need an app; let's get an app up as fast as possible. Let's reskin the website." But instead of doing that, we just took our time; we took about five to six months to think things through and get feedback from readers, to find out what our advertisers wanted, and what the clients wanted. And then we started to put each piece together as three separate things. The magazine needed to feel like a special product, something you can't do online. So we improved the paper stock, we made it a much bigger size, and then moved all the things that were urgent from the magazine onto the website, such as music reviews and live show reviews, things like that. With the changing of the content strategy— which is how any magazine publisher who wants to hone in and target their three specific audiences should be looking at the products—we decided to ask, "What works best for each platform?" and not try to duplicate what happens in the magazine online or in an iPad app.

What do you think makes an editorial or brand experience effective across media?

If you really break it down to just the basics, and cut out everything else, then you're really just delivering content in a branded way. I'm really fascinated by the work that brands do on their style guides. I also think individual, smaller, very targeted apps that are coming out for mobile, that are really well designed, and work, and don't crash, are all part of the learning process of what to do next for media brands. How can we learn from those kinds of experiences? •

Case Study:
The New Republic

WEBSITE: NEWREPUBLIC.COM

FREQUENCY: BIWEEKLY (PRINT, MOBILE), CONTINUOUSLY (WEB)

FORMATS: PRINT, WEB, MOBILE

LOCATION: WASHINGTON D.C.

EDITOR: FRANKIN FOER

CREATIVE DIRECTOR: DIRK BARNETT

PUBLISHER: CHRIS HUGHES

FOUNDED: 1914 (PRINT)

When Facebook cofounder Chris Hughes acquired Old Guard political and literary publication *The New Republic*, the then 29-year-old's actions surprised many in both the tech and journalism camps. By hitching his wagon to a 100-year-old D.C.–based publication, he acquired its reputable name but also much of its baggage. His mission, he said, was to "[hold] onto the heritage of the magazine while trying to make it more responsive to what people are interested in and how they read in 2013," as he told *The New York Times*. In his new role as publisher and editor in chief, Hughes focused on a digital-first strategy that wouldn't abandon print. He set up a satellite office in New York and hired its first-ever on-staff creative director, Dirk Barnett, formerly of *Newsweek* and *Maxim*.

In an interview that was published on NewRepublic.com, Barnett describes how the website redesign came first, with a responsive design by Hard Candy Shell, an interactive agency in New York (also behind websites for the *Wall Street Journal*, the *New York Observer*, *Newsweek*, and *Gawker*). Barnett joined the team midway and "finalized the typefaces"—Publico Headline, Publico Text, and Atlas Grotesk, as well as the logo designed in Antenna—to fit with their design. "And I was continually thinking about iPad design from the beginning, so there are a lot of details that, while they look phenomenal in print, really come to life in our new app." He also noted the influence of its legacy. "My first few trips to the *New Republic*'s D.C. offices were spent poring through back issues. There are definitely some new design details in the redesign that owe their inspiration to those old magazines."

The home page is distinctly uncluttered and bears nary a trace of its legacy (the complete archives going back to 1914 are accessible to subscribers through the EBSCOhost database). The header is spare, giving users just three content categories to choose from, while the footer features many more options for navigation. And rather than filling the front page with the entire contents of the site, there's one splash image for a feature story, with links to additional headlines.

Article pages feature beautiful full-width images with centered, readable text and plenty of white space around it. There's persistent navigation at the top of the page to remind users, as they scroll, of which article they're reading and how to get to the next story (next and previous articles are also noted at the bottom of the page). A nice user interface detail is how marginalia (similar to footnotes except that, here, they sit to the right of where you're reading) are represented on smaller screens by red asterisks to either tap or click for the full annotation. On the desktop version, the annotation in the margin is inobtrusive. Many cues exist in the design to indicate progression and keep the reader from feeling lost.

The design also integrates ad units that are noticeable but not too disruptive to the reading experience, and notations on the left of each article track how many more free articles you can read without subscription. (The site is metered, with eight free articles per month.)

The *New Republic*'s decluttered home page focuses the reader on four possible lead stories and four secondary ones. Even the top navigation offers just three choices plus a search field. Below, article pages feature full-width images, easy-to-read large text. Navigation and social features remain persistent as the reader moves down the page.

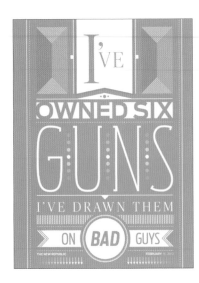

Cover (above) of the April 29, 2013, issue in print. From the same issue, the opening spread and beginning of the cover story on daycare. The bottom spread is from a regular section on Books & The Arts. **Opposite page:** Much of the same art direction and design of the printed magazine carries over to the iPad app (left and middle columns), while NewRepublic.com on the iPhone (right column) adjusts responsively to the format.

Jeffrey Zeldman

Founder and Executive Creative Director, Happy Cog

If your favorite websites work relatively seamlessly across browsers, that's because the programming adheres to the web standards established by the World Wide Web Consortium (W3C). Web standards emerged in the late 1990s as a way to make sure the web remained open and progressive, so competing browser makers—Microsoft and Netscape, at the time—couldn't dictate how web pages would be displayed on their proprietary software. Thanks in large part to the efforts of Jeffrey Zeldman, a cofounder of the Web Standards Project and author of the landmark book *Designing with Web Standards*, more websites are built semantically—using HTML5, CSS3, and JavaScript, as of this printing—and leaving less accessible programming languages such as Macromedia Flash by the wayside.

In addition to being a foremost advocate for the potential of the web, Zeldman is the founder of a trio of professional and educational resources for the online community, covering subjects from content strategy to mobile first and responsive web design. There's the web magazine, *A List Apart*; the slim, instructive book series A Book Apart; and the regional conferences An Event Apart. We reached out to Zeldman to ask his thoughts on content experiences across platforms.

In early 2013, you redesigned A List Apart, which has been evolving since 1998. Now the type size is nice and big! It was a pretty bold move to say, "we're doubling the type size, deal with it."
We're constantly redesigning and changing *A List Apart*. We're slowly rolling out features. We did a big brainstorming session, and [concepted what] was basically a million dollar project. The site doesn't really make money, so we scaled it back. We're losing a little money right now, but that's okay. We'd already increased the type size on An Event Apart and on my personal site. It really puts the content in your face. The idea on my site was that you'd have to sit back. Because I don't like doing this [leaning forward]. I had noticed that when I have a Kindle or an iPad, I'm relaxed. It's like you're working casually, much like

Show some empathy for the reader, love reading, and design accordingly.

you would be if you were thumbing through a magazine. And I noticed that you need a massage after working at your computer because you're leaning forward, squinting, and you're just always hunched forward. And I thought, wouldn't it be great if you could read as comfortably on a website as you could on our phone?

People buy these huge widescreen televisions, and they think they're going to be so awesome. But then they end up sitting so far back from them, that it's really the same as holding an iPhone at arm's length. It's really no different.

Do you subscribe to magazines?
Well, I think I don't want a magazine in my house now, now that I have the option. But giving you a 5-gigabyte download on your iPad doesn't really work for me. I still want the web experience of finding out socially from someone I trust that something is of interest, immediately accessing it on the web or through a device of some kind, and deciding for myself a couple paragraphs in if I want to keep reading it. At which point, depending on how much time I have, I actually sit and read it, or I save it for later when I may or may not actually read it.

But it seems like the web, because it's a scavenger hunt, point and click, it seems more about the hunt itself than about the acquisition. It seems like I often feel like I'm spending time finding the stuff that I think is cool.

Do you feel the web is a better platform for getting information out in the world than apps are?
I love apps. I would make an app if I had the right idea for it. I use them all the time. Most apps interact with the web at some point in their life, and that's really what it's about. I used to hate Instagram, but I love it now. Instagram was great if you were on Instagram on your phone, and you could see your friends' pictures and they could see yours. But if someone tweeted a link to their photo, it was a dead end. You'd go to a page that said, "You should download Instagram."

A List Apart website articles are all catalogued with a prominent number, are illustrated by Kevin Cornell, and feature large type for easy reading. And yes, the logo at the top of the page is meant to be cut off.
alistapart.com/article/the-web-aesthetic

And then you might see the photo, but you couldn't do anything. You couldn't even favorite it. You'd have to go looking for that person. You'd have to join. That process took twenty minutes, and then you'd have to see if you could find them and then hunt for their picture. The web is interconnected by its nature. Everything is connected, and everything is right there. I follow this thing, and it leads me to this thing. So that's what I love.

To the extent that apps seamlessly integrate with the web, they really work for me, and I love them. That's another reason I really like the Flickr app. It's just part of this process. Sometimes, I take a picture with my camera, and I do stuff to it on my computer, and then I upload it from my computer, and sometimes I take a picture with my phone, and I may process it with an app, and I send it to the web where people can comment on it. Either way, it ends up on the web.

E-books are a highly complex thing to get into. It's amazing how something so simple can get so complex.
It seems simple. Part of me always thought that websites should be about as simple as that. We get hired because we can make websites where stuff does all this, and we get hired because we can do that and still not get in the way of the reading experience or it can still be designed for the use case. But in my heart of hearts, I really love designer sites where the designer's a writer. Dean Allen did a great piece on *A List Apart* almost ten years ago called "Reading Designs." He was very prescient. To me, it was way ahead of its time, and it's very accurate. Design to be read.

If you don't read, you have no empathy for a reader. It's like designing the inside of a plane when you've never flown on one.
It looks cool, but it's not comfortable. I think in the '90s, there were a lot of young designers who came from the video game background or CD-ROMs and game design and weren't necessarily big readers. So they designed things as they would approach a first-person shooter. But that wasn't the right framework for understanding web content. For me, the idea that I could take different people's content and put it in the Readability format that I like, and read it and just enjoy it and enjoy the words meant, "Wow, designers need to be really careful and need to do a really good job." I used to give this talk where I would say, if we don't think about the reader, then people are going to use Instapaper and Readability. People aren't stupid. They're not passive. They're not consumers just helplessly waiting. It's not like they're watching a TV show they love and therefore they have to watch their commercial. People go away. So if you want them not to throw out all your work, and you don't want to be selling pencils in Grand Central, then you better show some empathy for the reader, develop some empathy for the reading experience, love reading, and design accordingly. •

Case Study:
It's Nice That

WEBSITE: ITSNICETHAT.COM
FREQUENCY: DAILY (WEB), QUARTERLY (PRINT), ANNUAL (BOOK)
FORMATS: PRINT, WEB, ANNUAL BOOK
LOCATION: LONDON
DIRECTORS: ALEX BEC AND WILL HUDSON
DEVELOPERS: WITH ASSOCIATES
FOUNDED: 2007

Codirectors Alex Bec and Will Hudson met as graphic design students at the University in Brighton, in England, and after working for others for a year, they decided to create their own type of creative company. Building on an idea that Hudson developed for a class, *It's Nice That* began as a blog for documenting the work of creative people and studios he admired ("Because I'm useless at remembering names," he says). That evolved into an essential daily editorial website for and about the creative community, as well as a print-lover's magazine and a completist's annual for the year's greatest hits. In March 2013, after eight semiannual issues, they replaced the weighty *It's Nice That* magazine with a slimmer quarterly, *Printed Pages*. Whereas the former shared a connection with the website, the latter features print-only content that isn't available elsewhere.

Will Hudson

Codirector, It's Nice That

Although trained as designers, Will Hudson and partner Alex Bec split their duties helming their creative enterprises. Bec leads INT Works, their commercial creative agency, while Hudson remains focused on their flagship publications and events. We spoke to Hudson about how each medium serves their stated goal of "championing creativity across the art and design world," through online and offline experiences.

What prompted you to start It's Nice That?
It was at a time when blogging had become so much more accessible. To build something was pretty straightforward, with no overhead really, and just a bit of hosting. So it just ran in the background of other work I was doing, until we got this opportunity to turn it into a business.

The magazine first started through doing the website, which was always free, so the magazine was an obvious opportunity to try to make some money. We kind of looked at it and said, "Yeah, we'd probably pay a tenner for that." The first issue we did 1,500, and it sold out within about four weeks and then we pushed the print run up to about 5,000, and it stayed there ever since.

Where did the name "It's Nice That" come from?
It's just bad English, but it's bad English that people say. When you say "What's nice about it is," you're not saying that it's the greatest thing in the world. It's what you say at a second glance or when you're just looking again at something.

What's been the relationship between your print and online platforms?
We post all this great stuff online that is viewed, has a lifespan of seven days, and then it's forgotten about. And print is an opportunity to pull back and go, "Look at this great stuff. We've reached out and found out a little bit more about it and put it into a little more context."

It's Nice That is primarily a website (left) but is also a book. The first annual edition (above) was published in late 2012 and showcased the best work from the site from the past year. *Printed Pages*, below, is a quarterly magazine that publishes exclusive content not found on the web.

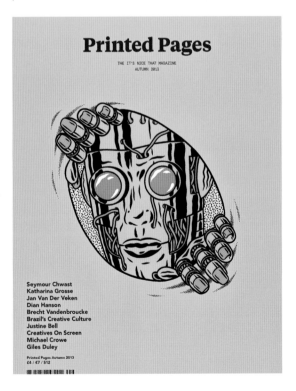

Various spreads from the *It's Nice That* 2012 annual. The publication showcases the best work shown on the website that year.

Like entertaining a boisterous puppy or cooking up a massive amount of fudge, there's something pleasantly exhausting about working at It's Nice That.

We've posted more than 2,500 articles over the past 12 months but we thought it was right and proper to revisit some of the most exciting and engaging projects we came across. We hope you enjoy reading it as much as we enjoyed putting it together.

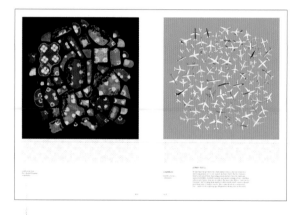

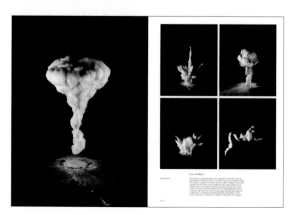

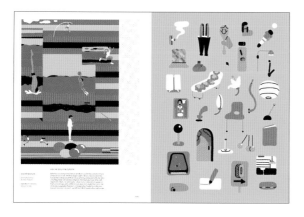

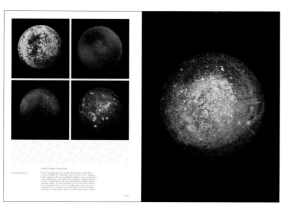

I think with both the magazine and what's online, we're trying to do something different. It's tough, but I think it's so important so that people know where they stand with you. And I think our big point of difference is the breadth of creative disciplines that we cover. Predominantly, we cover graphic design, illustration, photography, and art, but we also feature fashion, animation, sculpture—all these other things. And the magazine is sticking those things side by side and actually saying, "Look, there is a common thread here."

I love doing the magazine. I love the tangible nature of it and the things that print allows you to do that you can't do online. But if print doesn't work for us and what

we're trying to do, I'm not tied to it. I think there are a few people that, there's a bit of vanity involved in printing magazines, there's a kind of, I don't know, it elevates something as soon as you have a magazine. We have an audience of about 400,000 people a month online, and we'll sell 5,000 magazines. So it's that kind of balance of, we can publish content immediately and get a huge audience, or we can take a bit more time about it and craft something. So that's where we are at the moment.

What made you decide to publish an annual compendium of the site?
The way we used to approach the magazine was, we'd go through the website for the past six months and

go, "This is what we consider to be the most interesting stuff," and print it. Because of the volume of content that we're posting now—we do about nine articles a day—we wanted to experiment with putting out a nice, big hardback book and see whether our readers want that kind of thing. And they responded to it really well. We printed 1,500 and sold out just before Christmas. So it was available for a month on preorder and then just under a month after it launched.

But I think it's offering a good way for people to revisit content. No one will go onto itsnicethat.com today and go and look at what we were posting in March 2012. No one's going to go back to our archive and view it in that way. A book and even

Various spreads from *Printed Pages,* the quarterly magazine. The magazine features both longer-form written content and visual content that is not also available on the blog.

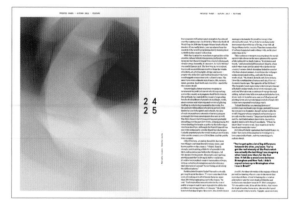

If print doesn't work for us, I'm not tied to it. There's a bit of vanity involved in printing magazines.

a magazine is something you stick on your shelf that you can revisit in three months or three years, and there's still something that you can take from it or something that triggers a thought process. We wanted to produce something that had real longevity. Hopefully, it will become a regular thing that we do every year toward the end of the year.

And so* Printed Pages *is a new approach to the magazine. Could you tell us about that?
We still believe there's this opportunity for print. With the new magazine and the name, *Printed Pages,* we really want to embrace "this is a magazine for print." With the big fashion magazines and a certain kind of design culture magazine, they're getting so big that you get lost in them for all the wrong reasons. You'll struggle to find something, or you'll read something and want to go back to it, and you can't remember where it is. So we want to strip that back and just make it dead easy to engage with each article. I think the smallest one is probably across six pages, three spreads, right up to eight spreads is the biggest article. So there's a nice journey through it, and you can engage in it and then put it down.

You're not currently doing a tablet version of it. Is that for any particular reason?
I think as soon as it becomes a behavioral thing that you spend time on your iPad reading digital publications, then that's when we need to get involved. But it's still such a commitment on the developing side. It's still not straightforward enough, in my opinion.

Creative Types On
The Silver
Screen — How
Hollywood Reflects
Our Industries

40
41

42
43

52
53

54
55

I started to be very
intrigued by how a painting
could maybe appear in
space, other than being
on a stretcher. I started to
reorganise my whole thinking
again about what painting
could do.

So have you always liked to read magazines?

To be totally honest, I'm one of those people who will buy magazines for the design, to kind of flip through and enjoy that part of it. I rarely read a magazine cover to cover. Some of these magazines are so big, it's such a commitment to go through them, and they just get heavier. And they're more difficult to lug around. You used to be able to stick a magazine in your bag and bring it out on the train or the bus. Some of these magazines you don't want to take anywhere.

What is your favorite aspect of producing so many kinds of editorial experiences?

I think it's the content surprise element. When things do better than you thought they would, or when an article gets picked up and suddenly a number of people are talking about it. Or to find out that some of the guys that we featured are doing illustrations for *The New York Times* within seven days of being featured on our site or that they've just been commissioned to do film work, or they've just been hired by a design firm— it's those things that we genuinely are facilitating. We are helping these people in their creative careers just through highlighting them on our website or in our magazine. And that's hugely satisfying. Yeah, I think that's probably one of the nicest things. •

Case Study:
The Awl: Weekend Companion

WEBSITE: THEAWL.COM/APP

FREQUENCY: WEEKLY

FORMATS: IOS APP (IPHONE AND IPAD)

LOCATION: NEW YORK

EDITORS: ALEX BALK, CHOIRE SICHA

CREATIVE DIRECTOR: CHOIRE SICHA

PUBLISHER: JOHN SHANKMAN

DEVELOPER: 29TH STREET PUBLISHING

OWNER: THE AWL NETWORK

FOUNDED: 2009 (WEB); 2012 (APP)

The first wave of iPad magazines from mainstream publications tried to replicate the print experience on the tablet, just with a few more bells and whistles, only to then discover that that approach didn't jibe with how people were actually using their devices. Just as print media has been looking for better ways to use the platform, online publishers have also sought an opportunity to create slower, more-focused reading experiences away from the frenetic 24/7 web. And both print and web folks are eager to sell their content through this nascent medium.

In late 2012, *The Awl*, a "daily web concern" founded by former *Gawker* editors Alex Balk and Choire Sicha, launched its first newsstand magazine app featuring a selection of five or six articles, repackaged around a theme and letter from the editor. The *Weekend Companion* app fulfills exactly the role its name describes— giving readers a friendlier reading experience with the content they might have missed on the blog, which posts at least fifteen articles daily and has a vast archive of long-form content going back to early 2009. Few readers could keep up with all of it. Not to mention the fact that the website experience is a fairly no-frills WordPress site, a design that's more efficient for engaging in the comments section than for uninterrupted reading. The *Weekend Companion* presents the text in clean, easy-to-read Garamond, with bylines set in Rockwell. Each cover is a template with a different color, a brief title, and the *Awl*'s logo at center.

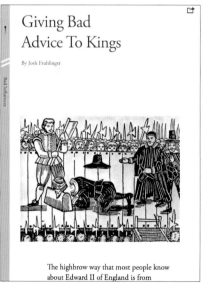

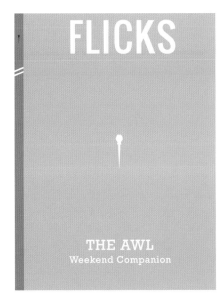

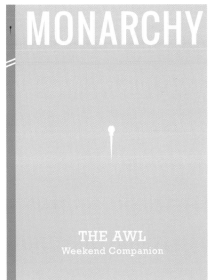

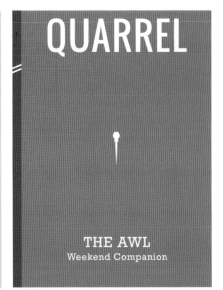

Covers for *The Awl Weekend Companion*, which have a standard design that's easy for its editors (nondesigners) to update each week with a one-word title and new color. Below, the opening page of the "Flicks" issue features an editor's note about the theme. The content flap is accessible with a swipe and acts as both a table of contents and navigational tool. **Opposite page:** Articles in clean, easy-to-read Garamond.

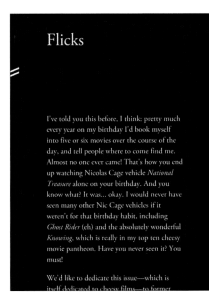

David Jacobs and Natalie Podrazik

Cofounders and Developers, 29th Street Publishing

29th Street Publishing is the technology company behind *The Awl Weekend Companion*, which is just one of the streamlined, minimal magazine-like mobile apps it has designed to provide bloggers and small publishers the means to easily package and sell their content by subscription. Built for Apple iOS, 29th Street's model stands in contrast with supersized magazine apps that take up significant amounts of storage space and emulate print. The platform is built on the premise that bloggers and online publishers are already producing excellent content, but not being paid for it. Readers who can't keep up on a daily basis can get a selection of the best stories in a weekly, curated bundle.

The company itself is formed on the holy trinity of design, content strategy, and development, each holding equal weight. Led by founding partners David Jacobs and Natalie Podrazik (developers), Blake Eskin (editorial director), and Tim Moore (designer, also interviewed here about his iPad magazine, *Letter to Jane*), their combined backgrounds in blog development and online editorial works to help authors and editors develop a strategy for choosing and presenting their content in app form; establishes a set of design standards unique to each publication, and then pushes those apps into the Apple iOS Newsstand, where they can be purchased as individual issues or by annual subscription allow-ing online publishers to make money through micropayments. This type of product development is what designer Craig Mod has dubbed "subcompact publishing"—small, stripped-down, easy-to-load, and easy-to-navigate apps. Its first app, *V as in Victor*, for sports writer Bill Vourvoulias, launched in August 2012 and was followed by apps for *The Awl* and music blogger Maura Johnston.

Podrazik and Jacobs met while working on blogging software at Six Apart, and have built their software business around creating tools and experiences that are pleasing for readers on the front end and authors on the back end. They spoke about why they're passionate about developing better serial editorial experiences that mobile readers will be willing to pay for.

What are the goals of the publications you work with, and how do these weekly apps satisfy them?
DJ: In the case of *The Awl*—it wasn't like [cofounders] Alex [Balk] and Choire [Sicha] spent their whole life wishing they could make a website. They're writers who love finding readers. This is just another way to do it. And I think there was frustration that their best work was going unread. Just skim the front page of the website, and you'll see at least twenty articles a day. And no one has time to read all of that.

We're living in this very narrow window in which the work experience for a lot of people is sitting around wasting time, browsing the internet—and I don't think it's really a place where critical thought can happen. People get excited and get emotional, and that's why you see the kind of dialogue you see on the internet. People get very responsive, but they're not very reflective. The *Awl* has content that demands to be reflected upon. The design of an article page is meant to arrange twenty-five to fifty elements, lots of little things on it such as images, bylines, teasers at the top, teasers at the bottom, ads, the whole sidebar. The *Awl* app is like, "Here's the thing you have to read this weekend." Some of the pieces may be years old, but it's all on a theme. So it's not just the six longest or the six most-read articles from that week. It's the state of mind of the editors.

NP: I think that, for a lot of the readers, it's "I wish I could read this; I don't have time." They'll find themselves marking articles to read later through other services. But, ultimately, there are also people who felt they wanted to support *The Awl*, and it was worth backing their subscription effort to read those great pieces in a different format. And the selection that Choire and Alex make every week is really fun. They're pulling the greatest and the new across a topic so it feels like, even if you are up to date with everything that's happening on the site, you still get surprises.

DJ: In the case of our app for *Little Star*, it's not like this is a digital-only, tablet edition of the website. The editor, Ann Kjellberg, has an artistic vision, which includes art criticism and painting. She does a book every year, an annual, so this is another outlet that she wanted to do.

How did you become interested in blogging?
DJ: I always liked zines and magazines. I was always a voracious reader. I started blogging in 1999, on a group blog. It was the right time. I was in college and into computer science,

People have always been frustrated by the experience of reading online.

and I was always trying things out right when they were available.

NP: I actually didn't know very much about blogging at all. But I thought it was the most fascinating thing possible for my computer science degree, in 2007. I could not think of a single other profession that talks to writers and fashion people and the news, science bloggers and politicians, and all the important media. I discovered what it was to be on the scene of media when working on blogging software, so I loved it.

DJ: Six Apart's mission, in a lot of ways, was to get people to communicate through blogs instead of trying to get someone else's story, like the PR person—blog what you want directly and get people to talk about it. At the time, that was not an obvious thing to say. People actually thought it was a little nuts.

But now, we take for granted that not only does every website have a blog but they also have Twitter accounts and Facebook pages. Blogging was really the first piece of social media marketing, a place where companies could have conversations directly with their customers. And that, in 2004 and 2005, when we'd go on sales calls, we'd have to explain to people what a blog was. "This is a little bit of software, it could run your website, it doesn't have to, but it's part of the website, and it's in reverse chronological order, and you set expectations, you try to update it on a fixed schedule so that people know. But you can update it whenever you want, if you have to."

How is the design of your apps different from what else is out there or being done with the Adobe Digital Publishing Suite?

DJ: DPS is actually a very specific, narrow definition product that there's very little you can do with at the end of the day. We want our apps to be dramatically different. You might be able to notice some of the visual vocabulary of the cabinets for the library and the flap for contents shared between apps. But someone wouldn't necessarily think *V as in Victor* came from the same designer who did the *One Story* app.

Ideally, it feels like it's one package because everything is considered: the content, the design, and the technology. Natalie doesn't build any features into the app or into the image or the console because she thinks it's a neat idea.

NP: Nothing is superfluous in what we build.

DJ: We're actually trying to bring content strategy back a little bit by tailoring the publishing experience for each magazine. But the core 99 percent of the code is shared, and it's the same, and we have a monthly schedule of upgrades we have to make. We fix bugs and find them and fix them and have other things so that it may be pushed back to the next month generally. But whenever we deploy a new magazine, it always gets the most recent code.

It's already hard enough to maintain a website when technology changes rapidly and reader expectations evolve with it. Do you ever find it maddening?

DJ: It's not new that it is difficult. People have always been frustrated with the experience of reading online. But before that, if you were one of the more prominent authors of zines that have a national audience, it was an enormous amount of work. You had to have a friend who worked at Kinko's or a friend who worked at *The New York Times* or somewhere with a really fancy Xerox machine. And then you had to fulfill these orders. Like, my zine was two dollars with a self-addressed, stamped envelope. There were a few distribution outlets where you'd get zines they sold on consignment. You could put a lot of work into it and be a good writer and have friends who are into what you're doing, but it's not like there was something that was there that was lost, and now we're trying to get it back. These tools have actually never existed before. So it's all a benefit. ●

Case Study:

Letter to Jane

WEBSITE: LETTERTOJANE.COM

FREQUENCY: WHEN POSSIBLE

FORMAT: IOS APP (ZINE FOR IPAD AND IPHONE)

LOCATION: NEW YORK

FOUNDER/DESIGNER: TIM MOORE

FOUNDED: 2010

When it launched in May 2010, *Letter to Jane* was one of the first independent iPad magazines in the app store. With a focus on cinematic photography and interviews with the people who make compelling images, the visual arts zine is the brainchild of one person: designer, author, and programmer Tim Moore.

Tim Moore

Founder and Designer, Letter to Jane

Tim Moore is an iPad native in the sense that from the moment he picked up the device, he knew he wanted to create for it. He is a self-taught designer and programmer who nearly studied physics but changed his major to photography and art history, earning dual bachelor's degrees from Oregon State University. His work on *Letter to Jane* led him from Portland to New York, where he is now a cofounder of 29th Street Publishing, developers and publishers of serial digital content for web and mobile. Now building editorial apps for clients, Moore has a unique perspective on the editorial design landscape.

How did Letter to Jane come about? Did you want to make a magazine?
When I graduated from school, I had spent the past four or five years writing and taking pictures. I needed a portfolio for my work to get a job, but I didn't really want to be a photographer, and I didn't know if I wanted to be a writer. I made a portfolio website, and I made a blog for it. But I thought, instead of making a portfolio, why don't I make a magazine as my portfolio? So I made *Letter to Jane*, the first issue, as a PDF, and I sent that out to people thinking, I'll get a job this way. I

didn't, but I had people who wanted to contribute to the next issue.

Then I thought, maybe I could legitimately make a magazine. With MagCloud, I made a print issue. That's how I learned that I'll never be able to do print. If I went to a printer, I would have to order paper in advance, and I'm not sure I'd ever be able to sell that many copies. If I'm selling them for thirteen dollars or fifteen dollars, and I'm getting maybe five dollars an issue profit, that's not sustainable. It's just me doing everything. I can't make it and sell it.

What was it that made you want to design for the iPad?
I didn't mean to make an iPad magazine. I tried everything first. I had a

SHADOWS

LETTER TO JANE

Shadows is the fourth issue of *Letter to Jane,* an iPad magazine by Tim Moore.

The table of contents and representative spreads show *Letter to Jane*'s ability to deliver a rich magazine experience without mimicking printed pages.

blog, but didn't like it. I tried print. I liked it, but I really liked the iPad.

When the iPad came out, I got it purely because I got a fairly good tax rebate that year. I wanted something to watch Netflix on, the simplest, most commercial thing you can think of. I started playing around with it and thought, "I really want my work on this." I really liked how I could view photos one at a time. It was very pure, like you're holding the image.

I heard this story about Alfred Stieglitz, how he always made his photography really small and handheld. He liked the small personal connection between the image and you. And it's true. When some people first see the iPad, they're like, "I don't get it; it's just a big iPod." But when you hold something, and you touch it, there's a connection you don't really get otherwise.

What was that learning curve like?
I had no idea how to code. I didn't even really know how to design. Through the first two issues, I taught myself how to design with some help from friends. Xcode, the development tool from Apple, was free to download. I already had a MacBook, and a developer license was ninety-nine dollars a year, which is a bargain for any artistic venture. So it was a really low barrier to just try it, using tutorials on YouTube. I think I quit twenty times because it was hard. Then I figured out one tutorial. Then I figured out another one. And I just kept at it.

How would you describe your approach to designing for the iPad?
I didn't come from a print background, so I instantly became different from everybody. They all had this print product and were trying to keep that page swiping or having multiple columns. Things I would never think about. I was just thinking, okay, I have one screen, how do I make that look good, and then go to the next screen. And they were thinking, we have all this content that has a hierarchy and departments and sections and categories. Their approach is so much more complicated, what they're trying to get on a device that I view as pure simplicity. I think the iPad's strength is that you can be very simple.

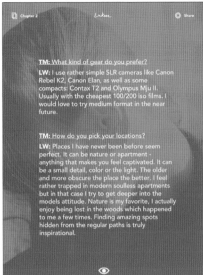

How do you design good editorial experiences?

How you make a good experience is how you design anything. If you make a poster for an event, you think about what the event is doing and try to translate that. You start with content. There's a big debate right now with iPad magazines—now people are like, magazines should be really small and streamlined, and these big, fancy iPad magazines are doing it wrong. The next *Letter to Jane* is going to be huge. It's got 1080p video, it's got hi-res images, the whole thing is about photography, it's about art. I'm not going to strip it down. I'm not going to make it small, because the content needs to be big. I know I'm going to get backlash. We let video games be

I assume that when people get confused, they're going to tap somewhere. So you have to make sure when you tap, something happens. When you swipe, something happens.

gigs because we want hi-res graphics—the content deserves it.

When you design for tablets, you really have to change your thinking. You're working with very little space. I think iPad magazine design has more in common with poster design. You're dealing with such limited space that you have to tell a story with a lot less. People don't factor this in, but you have a huge frame. It's really weird when you put a frame on your design.

The device itself adds a lot of weight to your design.

How do you know that you're doing it right?

I'm constantly swiping, swiping, swiping, even after we ship these apps. I read everything. With *Letter to Jane*, when I'm designing, I'll always hand over my iPad and not say anything; just, here, look at this. I see when people get stuck. I see when they get

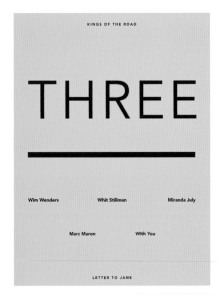

Screenshots from the fourth issue of *Letter to Jane*

confused. I assume that when people get confused, they're going to tap somewhere. So you have to make sure when you tap or swipe, something happens.

I don't feel it's wrong for people to be confused as long as it's easy to get an answer, because that's how you teach somebody a new experience. People think, the user should never be confused. Everything should be laid out. A button to read is here. A button to do this is there. But I think, you don't have a lot of space either. In print, you're working in 300 dpi, you can have smaller type. These are really low-res screens—even with the hi-res iPads, it's just doubling this. You're still working with less space than a book page.

I don't feel it's wrong for people to be confused as long as it's easy to get an answer, because that's how you teach somebody a new experience.

Loading instructions and a lot of UI/interaction stuff, you're giving away a third of your space and taking focus away from the content, just because you're afraid that some people might not get it.

I also look at analytics. If I see people opened the app, went so far, and got stuck at this point—I mean a lot of people—then I'd be a bad designer if I didn't address that.

At 29th Street Publishing, how do you advise clients on their apps?
I usually tell them, make an app only if you really want an app. I focused on iOS because at the time, it was really nice. It was only iPad, one screen. I could really mess around and try a lot of stuff. Now, even with iOS, I have to figure in six different configurations. And Android has like forty. It's still early, and no one really knows

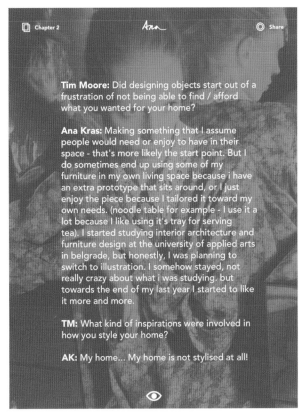

Tim Moore: Did designing objects start out of a frustration of not being able to find / afford what you wanted for your home?

Ana Kras: Making something that I assume people would need or enjoy to have in their space - that's more likely the start point. But I do sometimes end up using some of my furniture in my own living space because i have an extra prototype that sits around, or I just enjoy the piece because I tailored it toward my own needs. (noodle table for example - I use it a lot because I like using it's tray for serving tea). I started studying interior architecture and furniture design at the university of applied arts in belgrade, but honestly, I was planning to switch to illustration. I somehow stayed, not really crazy about what i was studying. but towards the end of my last year I started to like it more and more.

TM: What kind of inspirations were involved in how you style your home?

AK: My home... My home is not stylised at all!

what size to do things on. There's widescreen, there's super-widescreen tablets, there's just all these different sizes—and widescreen tablets are horrible to read on, it's just like a piece of paper folded in half. I like the smaller tablets because it feels more like a zine experience.

How do you design for a landscape that's always changing?
People are always going to read. We may have shorter attention spans, but we're not stupid. People can comprehend more. They might not have the attention spans, but they are never going to stop wanting to look at good content. •

Case Study: Paper

WEBSITE: PAPERMAG.COM

FREQUENCY: CONTINUOUSLY (WEB), BIMONTHLY (PRINT)

FORMAT: PRINT, WEB

LOCATION: NEW YORK

DESIGN DIRECTOR: ANDREA FELLA

EDITORS/PUBLISHERS: KIM HASTREITER AND DAVID HERSHKOVITS

FOUNDED: 1984

It's not easy to carry a name like *Paper* in an increasingly digital culture. Despite its medium-specific title, *Paper* is more than just a print publication—in fact, the magazine now represents a small but still significant fraction of Kim Hastreiter and David Hershkovits' publishing and event-planning business. Artist–stylist Hastreiter and writer–editor Hershkovits met at downtown New York digest *SoHo News* (where *The New York Times* street-style photographer Bill Cunningham got his start, too) and started *Paper* when *SoHo News* folded three decades ago. They didn't know much about publishing, but they knew the right people at the vibrant intersection of art, fashion, and music. Since launching the first issue in 1984, the magazine has redesigned numerous times, but has always reflected their enthusiasm for discovering and sharing new talent.

Celebrities feature prominently in their pages but not in a sensational Perez Hilton sort of way (*Paper*'s own gossip maven/editorial director Mr. Mickey Boardman could teach the younger blogger a thing or two about the genre). Rather, the people *Paper* celebrates are often unconventionally beautiful and unusually talented in their respective fields. *Paper*'s design also has a way of treating its subjects with respect without seeming fawning, using photographers whose work isn't especially slick or overly stylized. Designer Andrea Fella makes a point of using hand lettering and other analog techniques to give the design an honest, authentic and tactile feel.

Various covers of *Paper* magazine show how the logo adapts to the photography, rather than the other way around.

Andrea Fella
Design Director, Paper Magazine

The genuine and smart, yet still unabashed, voice of *Paper* is due primarily to Kim Hastreiter and David Hershkovits' own originality and that of its contributors. It's also transmitted in ways large and small through Andrea Fella's singular and somewhat irreverent creative vision. With a body of work from *I.D.* (the former U.S. design magazine), *The New York Times Magazine*, and *Nylon*, Fella joined *Paper* in 2009, the year of its twenty-fifth anniversary, when she redesigned the magazine in its entirety. We spoke to Fella about her trajectory and working with the *Paper* brand across media, starting with print.

What and where did you study in school? Did you always want to be a designer?
No, I had just applied to one school, the University of Michigan, and got in, but I had no idea what I was going to study. Luckily, the school had just started an independent concentration program where you could propose your own major, so I called mine "Design of Culture" and argued all my classes were taken with that idea in mind and that it would be useful for a variety of careers.

I got a psychology professor and an art history professor to back me up, and it got accepted. I did sneak a few graphic design classes in there at the end, though, thinking they might come in handy.

When I graduated, I moved to LA, where my father [designer Ed Fella] was teaching up at CalArts, and I had worked out there the previous summer. Lorraine Wilde [of ReVerb, now Green Dragon Office] needed some production help, and back then, it was still the old "paste-up mechanical" kind that I had learned as a kid. You would wax sheets of repro type and paste them down on key-lined boards. Then to correct something, you would have to carefully cut it out, replace it, align it, and so on. I actually

photographed by autumn de wilde
styled by **shirley kurata**

Hair by Yui/theexagency.com using Paul Mitchell
Makeup by Jolee Douglas/theexagency.com using Make Up Forever
Models:
Producer:
Stylist's Assistant:
Fashion Coordinator:
Interns: **Catering:** Heirloom
Shot at The Studio in Los Angeles
Dress by Mulberry
Vintage necklace from
The Way We Wore

the N E W New Look

really enjoyed that detailed, hands-on kind of work. And Lorraine was an amazing designer to be able to learn from. Everything was very considered and thought through. A font had to say something about the time period it came out of and be used in a meaningful way. Nothing was ever just "put that here, let's see what it looks like," but it was much more about, "What's it saying?"

I worked with her on a book for Thom Mayne of Morphosis for over a year. We did this interesting thing with the type where we'd change the font in mid-letter form. We were using computers by then, and it was really quite difficult and time consuming with the early software that was available at the time. So it felt like a huge accomplishment when the book finally came out. But then I realized that only a very small audience would ever see it, and would they even notice the typography we had worked so hard on? Also at that time, the studio was getting much bigger projects that required a lot of proposals and pitching—work that never sees the light of day—and I definitely was feeling unsure if graphic design was for me.

After that, you moved to New York and became an art director at I.D. ***magazine. How did magazine design compare with what you'd been doing before?***
One thing I loved was the immediacy. So my frustration about some of these projects that either didn't happen or took a year to produce was quelled. Suddenly, you have a magazine to design, and it comes out in a few weeks, and then you're on to the next one, and for me that was really satisfying. Whatever you did, it went quickly but also you could do better next time. You could let go a little, make choices that in retrospect you wouldn't do again. It's something that may be read and thrown out, or maybe you'd do something worthy of keeping. I also got to work with Tony Arefin, who became an art director at *I.D.* at the same time. He had never studied design formally either, so I think the two of us were freer to experiment and make design fun. At the time, the goal of the magazine was to reach out to a much larger audience than the design world.

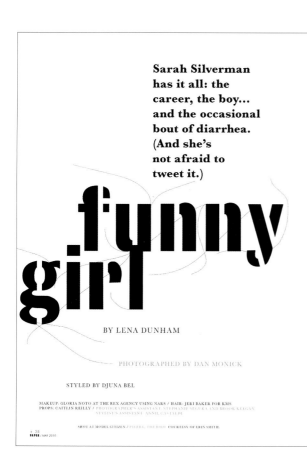

Sarah Silverman has it all: the career, the boy... and the occasional bout of diarrhea. (And she's not afraid to tweet it.)

funny girl

BY LENA DUNHAM

PHOTOGRAPHED BY DAN MONICK

STYLED BY DJUNA BEL

MAKEUP: GLORIA NOTO AT THE REX AGENCY USING NARS / HAIR: JERI BAKER FOR KMS
PROPS: CAITLIN REILLY / PHOTOGRAPHER'S ASSISTANT STEPHANIE SEGURA AND BROOK KELGAN
STYLIST'S ASSISTANT ANNIL CASTALDI

SHOT AT MODEL CITIZEN / PIERRE, THE BIRD COURTESY OF ERIN SMITH.

PAPER / MAY 2010

From there, you went to The New York Times Magazine *for four and a half years, going from a bimonthly to a weekly.*

Yes, that was another great experience for me. At *I.D.*, I really had to churn out a lot on my own, and there was no photo or production department to help and no one ever really saying, "No, try this again," or "That doesn't work." There was just no time for that. So to then go to a very different environment at the *Times* was a really good education for me.

Yet it was really weird because it was almost slower, even though it was a weekly. I thought I'd go there, and it'd be crazy and hectic, and it was, but there were seven designers, so I usually had just one piece of the issue each week. I went from design-

It's something that may be read and thrown out, or maybe you'd do something worthy of keeping.

ing covers and every story inside to "here's your spread for the week."

The *Times*' way of designing is also very much about the content: You read the pieces first and figure out which photos in which sequence really tell the story you want. It takes a lot of reworking and rethinking to get it right and satisfy all the parties involved. It's a huge effort, but it's really good because you keep learning along the way and seeing all these different points of view. But also the words and the photos

are definitely prioritized, so the design had to be strong and support those things. There was no design for design's sake there; it all had to be justified.

You eventually left to practice on your own, but it was too much about running a business and not enough designing, which led you to Nylon.

I was worried at first that I wasn't right for *Nylon*, because I always kind of hated the idea of fashion or fashion magazines. But the original

In the wake of so much going digital, I wanted that tactile feeling of out on the street and of paper itself.

idea for the magazine was more about real people, which did interest me. I just didn't like the look of slick studio shoots and wanted to push for more of a documentary style where people are actually engaged in something other than looking bored. I had this book of Billy Name photos that inspired me to think there was a way to make it work. Also, I realized very soon that studio shoots give you all this room to play. Often at *I.D.* or the *Times*, it was this struggle of how to arrange these rectangles that you can't crop into or really do anything to because they are showing someone's work or shot by some famous photographer. But when it's a fashion shoot, you get to crop, cut, color, rearrange. The freedom was so different for me and lent itself to doing a lot more typographically as well. And it was mostly young up-and-coming photographers who really wanted to shoot and be in print more than they wanted to be paid a lot of money. They got to do their thing without any heavy art direction, and then I got to do mine, and we all felt satisfied.

You've been with Paper *since 2009, and you redesigned the work that had been done by Peter Buchanan-Smith, who did a very drastic redesign in 2003. It had been a super-busy design, and he made it far more structured, clean, and minimal. Did you bring some of that original chaos back in? The new* Paper *logo, for example, is unusual in that its letter arrangement changes and moves around from cover to cover.*

I started thinking about it being called "paper" and still being a tactile object in the wake of so much going digital. I wanted that tactile feeling of out on the street and of paper

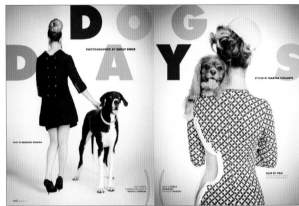

itself, so when I came across these brown paper stencils in a lumber yard, I immediately bought them and scanned them in and started experimenting. At *Nylon*, designing the covers was my least favorite thing to do, because we had to put so much type on the photo and work around the huge logo. Inevitably you couldn't pick the best photo—you had to pick the one that worked best under those constraints, and that bothered me. I wanted to make the *Paper* logo flexible so the photo could take priority and the logo could move around it. I figured the stencils had a strong enough identity on their own so that even as they change position each issue, you still recognize it as *Paper*. And they move around on a grid system of golden rectangles along with

the bar code and cover lines, so we don't have to spend days designing the cover for each issue. I just know myself, and I will fuss endlessly with things unless I give myself borders and boundaries.

Did some of this approach spill over to the website?
Yes and no. I first redesigned the website a couple years ago, but once the programs came out where you could track a user's every movement, we realized people weren't quite using it the way we thought they would. It was no longer the case where everyone would see the home page because instead, they were getting direct links to content through Facebook or Twitter. So then we had to rethink the whole system again

and just finished the new redesign a few months ago.

It's really interesting to be able to watch how people are using the website, but it can also limit your vision because the design then has to cater to the moves people are making. You need the page views so you can't control their path as much as it controls you. But it's also amazing to be able to get that kind of feedback you never get from print.

Paper is still a print magazine, even though so much of the business is digital or experiential, with events. Why is the physical artifact still so important?
This is definitely a question everyone in publishing has to ask. Is it worth the money to print this? Or could

dress by erin fetherston, hat by bernstock speirs for erin fetherston, gloves by addrm and shoes by marni.

hey nicki

you're so fine, you blow our minds.

hey nicki

hey nicki

photographed by howard huang

Adam Levine has spent the better part of a decade peeling off his clothes in public. Whether the Maroon 5 frontman is rolling around in bed with a model for a music video or stripping naked for a Vogue cover—the population at large has seen every part of Levine's tattooed physique, save his fur-covered manhead.

this just in

The Lonely Island guys have it their way on their hilarious new record, proving once again why they're the Internet's biggest stars. By Hobey Echlin

PHOTOGRAPHED BY **autumn de wilde**
STYLED BY **shirley kurata**

It's the story you're sharing, and it's a personal story. It's always about people.

it just exist online or as an app? Besides ourselves, it's the contributors and the subjects of our stories who really want it. A photographer doesn't want to shoot a huge fashion piece that'll only exist online. An actor or musician wants to be on the cover of an actual magazine. And we aren't in a position to be able to pay much to all our contributors, so getting to see their words and photos in print is the payback. It's their showcase, they want a portfolio piece.

The advertisers still want print, too. It seems the future for advertising is knowing your specific information and targeting you directly, so that seems to point toward apps.

What about the trend of publications creating branded content for companies?
Yes, that's a reality now, and I actually like doing it because I am an editorial designer and need a story to work off of. I don't think I'd be good at advertising because having to make up some idea to sell liquor or whatever doesn't move me, and I couldn't do it. But if someone comes to us to actually create and design something with real content, then it makes sense to me. Or having a great idea and needing

a sponsor to make it possible also makes sense.

What does editorial design mean to you?
For me, it's the story that you're sharing, and it's a personal story. It's always about people. The design ideas often come out of the individual people and how I can best tell their story to the readers. Sometimes, the story is not that compelling, so you need to pull it out of the photos. The editing is really crucial. Sometimes, you have 100 pictures or even 1,000, so how you edit those can tell different stories. It's about the pacing and pairing. What starts it, what ends it, what comes in the middle. And you have to figure out other ways of creating the story for different

platforms. You're no longer working in spreads, so you lose the image juxtaposition and often the typographic interaction as well.

When the iPad came out, everyone rushed to release their magazine app without even knowing how it worked. And it sounds like Paper *almost did that too, but then held back and focused on the magazine and website.*
A lot of magazines originally just took pages that they had done and made PDFs and added some interactive elements. They took that route because they don't want to let go of what they'd worked so hard to achieve in the print version. But I also don't think that works so well. So, instead, we actually went through the whole process of designing and programming a "party snaps" app [with 29th Street Publishing], and it had some great things going on, but then it got put on hold, and we haven't gotten back to it.

An app could give us a regular venue for outtakes from shoots, which would be great because you end up having to edit out so much in print. Because a lot of these things can also exist on the website, though, it's difficult to figure out how all our content would divide up or overlap. Would things appear in one place first and then go to another? Do people care if they see something first? None of us quite know, so we're all trying to figure it out at the same time. •

Case Study: Gather

WEBSITE: GATHERJOURNAL.COM

FREQUENCY: BIANNUAL

FORMAT: PRINT

LOCATION: NEW YORK

CREATIVE DIRECTOR: MICHELE OUTLAND

EDITOR: FIORELLA VALDESOLO

OWNER: GATHER MEDIA LLC

PRINT CIRCULATION: 6,000

FOUNDED: 2012

People have strong opinions about what they eat. Despite the fact that it's one subject that will always be of interest—our lives depend upon it—many beloved food magazines have expired in recent times. In their place, the web offers countless food blogs, and iPad apps such as Epicurious serve up instant access to tens of thousands of recipes, all indexed and searchable with reviews from other uses. Sites such as Smitten Kitchen and Food52 have taken their best recipes and published cookbooks. As satisfying as they are, it wasn't until food zines started to return (a handful of good ones such as *Cook's Illustrated* never went away) that we realized what had been missing: a recurring curatorial point of view and tasteful food photography, among other things. One publication filling that void is *Gather Journal*, a

beautiful, semiannual publication that organizes recipes around a narrative concept such as food inspired by classic summer movies (the *Jaws* seafood "chum" cocktail is one example). The editorial is smart without taking itself too seriously, and the design is simply delicious.

Covers and spreads from *Gather Journal*, which takes the subject of food and cooking and turns it into high-art storytelling, with special attention to sensual photography you can practically smell and taste.

Michele Outland

Creative Director and Cofounder, Gather Journal

Michele Outland met her editorial collaborator Fiorella Valdesolo while working together at *Nylon* magazine. The designer, who grew up in Golden, Colorado, has art directed extensively in the New York publishing world, for titles including *New York*, *The New York Times Magazine*, *Martha Stewart Living*, and the original *Domino* for Condé Nast. We asked her a few questions about the inspiration for *Gather*, "a recipe-driven food magazine for anyone who enjoys cooking and the experience of sharing meals with friends and family."

How did you become interested in editorial design?
I've always loved magazines. When I was doing my first design internship in Denver, they had a book on Neville Brody, who was the art director of the British fashion and culture magazine *The Face*. It showed the custom fonts he designed and the layouts of the magazine. I was obsessed.

What does the term "editorial design" mean to you?
Being able to communicate an effective "story" with type, image/illustration, and design preferably in the format of a two-page spread.

You've worked on some incredible magazines. What has been your career trajectory?
My first job in New York City was at *Martha Stewart Living* magazine. It was a great and educational first entrée into the editorial design world of New York that I'm so grateful to have had. From there, I went on to work for and be part of the beginnings of several magazines (namely *Everyday Food* and *Domino*), which have also been incredible learning experiences.

What made you and Fiorella decide to start your own magazine?
After we left *Nylon*, we both went freelance and had been discussing doing some sort of print magazine

together for several years. We both have a shared love of food, and that sort of focused our ideas down to what is now *Gather Journal*.

Gather *is primarily a print publication, but since it's only out twice a year, have you considered doing more online or in an app?*
We'd like to keep print the main focus, but we have a blog on our site, and we will soon be adding recipes from previous issues to the site. We are looking to do a recipe app in the future. We want to provide a variety of access points for people to get to our recipes to cook from, but we still think that there's such a wonderful experience from sitting down with a printed issue that you can't replicate

quite the same way in the digital realm. I think it's a pretty exciting time in independent publishing, and especially for independent food publishing.

How does designing a food publication differ from other types of editorial design?
It doesn't differ too greatly. Most editorial design is taking content and organizing it in the best way possible to tell the editorial story. First and foremost, we're a food magazine, and we want people to cook from it. So we want to make sure that the user experience is utilitarian and clear—thus, each recipe facing its corresponding picture.

What skills or qualities do you think makes someone a good editorial designer?
For me, I'm a bit of a stickler for typography. It's something I look for or notice right away. Having a great foundation in type understanding and design is a strong point for me.

What do you like most about being an editorial designer?
Seeing *Gather Journal* in print is an experience I can't get over. It's thrilling and satisfying. •

FALLEN APEROL CHOCOLATE CAKE

If there's a dessert for all seasons, let this be a winter meal's swan song. Delicately cracked like a sheet of ice and coated in a snowy dusting of fallen sugar this Aperol-tinged chocolate cake is as delightfully imperfect and unpredictable as the months it personifies.

Serves: 8 to 10

12 oz bittersweet chocolate
(we like 60%), chopped

1¼ sticks (5 oz) unsalted butter,
cut into pieces

3 Tbsp Aperol or brandy

1 tsp vanilla

¼ tsp salt

6 large eggs, separated

⅔ cup plus 1 Tbsp sugar

Confectioners sugar for dusting

1. Preheat oven to 350°F. Butter and flour a 9-inch springform pan.

2. Melt chocolate and butter in a large heatproof bowl set over a pan of barely simmering water, stirring until completely smooth. Remove from heat then stir in Aperol, vanilla, and salt. Cool 5 minutes. Whisk together yolks and ⅓ cup sugar until sugar dissolves then whisk into chocolate and cool to room temperature.

3. Beat whites with a pinch of salt using an electric mixer at medium speed until they just hold soft peaks, then, while continuing to beat, gradually add remaining ⅓ cup plus 1 Tbsp sugar. Beat on medium high until whites are glossy and just hold stiff peaks. Whisk about ⅓ of whites into chocolate, then using a spatula, gently fold in remaining whites just until evenly combined. Pour into pan.

4. Bake until top just feels dry and starts to crack, about 30 minutes. A toothpick inserted into the center should come out barely sticky but not wet. Cake will fall somewhat as it cools. Let the cake cool in pan to warm or room temperature. Remove ring from pan and dust top generously with confectioners sugar.

CHOCOLATE ENCOUNTERS

I once shared a park bench with Bill Murray. It's true. We chatted about the weather and a shared love of Davy Crockett. It was wondrous and heart stopping, now carefully preserved in my mind. Much like every chocolatey rendezvous. Always brief. Always magical. Each encounter with chocolate in your life is connected, layers building one on top of another, creating subconscious monuments that you'll carry along with you until the next darkened dessert crosses your plate. The moment it hits your lips the ghosts of chocolate past parade through your mind; the quadruple chocolate cake you made for your 10th birthday, the gooey brownies your mom bakes for every family gathering, and those bewitching little truffles from the corner bakery that you pop into your mouth three at a time on your way home from work. Each heart-stirring one will linger on, just as real encounters—particularly those of the Bill Murray variety—always do. EMILY KASTNER

WALNUTS, CHEESE & OLIVES

The Beautiful Decay

PHOTOGRAPHS BY GRANT CORNETT

CONCEPT '14

COTTON CANDY,
A
Sea
Change

A virtual cloud of sugary confection.
A diaphanous pile of sticky sweetness. An outsized saccharine bouffant.
Whether you call it cotton candy, candyfloss, spun candy or
fairyfloss, the light-as-air delight is, quite simply, the edible embodiment
of pure whimsy. First introduced at the 1904 World's Fair it has been
enchanting kids and adults alike at carnivals ever since; just watching the
machine spin and melt sugar, and the paper cone rolling around
grabbing its flossy remains is almost mesmerizing. Downy to the touch,
it has a tacky residue that lingers on the fingertips long after
it's passed your lips. When cotton candy traditionally comes in
contact with water it shrinks and hardens with displeasure.
A reaction that makes our cotton candy-built sea creatures only
the stuff of pure fantasy. And that's just fine with us.

Photographs by Gary Gold Cotton candy creatures by Crystal Hanehan

OCTOPUS
Striking in appearance—a bulbous head, eight arms—and intelligence; they are the smartest of the invertebrates.

SEAHORSE
Otherworldly, equine-like creatures with most unusual mating habits: monogamous for life with males bearing the offspring.

NARWHAL
The unicorn of the sea, the male's long spiral tusk is actually one of its two teeth.

STARTERS

The parade of small-bites teased your palate, now it's time to tantalize it with something more substantial. Baby octopus fried to a featherweight crisp, slimly shaved asparagus threaded with a sunny egg yolk, and a bracingly clean take on gazpacho, each abides (deliciously) by the floaty standard.

PHOTOGRAPHS BY Joseph De Leo FOOD STYLING BY Maggie Ruggiero

Justin Thomas Kay

Creative director, Doubleday & Cartwright

Justin Thomas Kay hails from Wisconsin, the land of paper mills, and was raised by parents in the printing industry. He studied communication design at the Milwaukee Institute of Art and Design, and in his decade-long career to date, he has been an art director for culture magazines *Complex* and *Mass Appeal*, was the creative director of music magazine *The Fader*, and has also worked on mass-market titles such as *Car and Driver* and *Teen Vogue*. Now, he works with Brooklyn-based studio Doubleday & Cartwright, helping them conceive and design custom editorial publications, print and digital, for brands.

It seems like you've been working in some capacity of editorial design for your whole life. What led you to choosing this field?
My mom, for almost her entire career, worked for a company called Quad Graphics that prints all the Condé Nast magazines. It was a small family-owned business, and now they're arguably one of the biggest printers in the world. Paper milled in northern Wisconsin is literally trucked down there, and that's what *Vogue* is printed on. So from super early on, I had exposure to the idea of making magazines as work. Growing up, I was around graphic design, but never really understood what it was. That came later.

My dad worked for a different printing company that used to print a lot of the Marvel hardcover books. He was able to bring home press rejects, so I had every possible volume of every Marvel hardcover book growing up, which was pretty amazing. I was obsessed with the idea of drawing comics. I initially went to school for illustration in Milwaukee.

At a certain point, I realized I was actually not a very good illustrator. But I loved composing. I made the switch over to graphic design at the suggestion of a few teachers. And the minute I switched to graphic design, I wanted to do layout. I spent pretty much all of college trying to figure out magazines as a format. I love to do short-form editorial.

And serial in nature?
Totally. The idea of magazines being a one-off object, but also part of a larger series—that was always super interesting to me.

After a series of bad jobs that just got me to New York City, I got my first job, at *Complex*, which is the first magazine I ever worked for. The creative director was Steven Baillie, and I worked most closely with the art director James Casey, who now does *Swallow*, the food magazine. I was at *Complex* for about two years. It was really small then. And it's funny to think about this now, but they didn't even have a website, which is absurd because now the Complex Media Network is massive, and they can have this pretty magazine that doesn't really need to succeed or fail.

From there, what did you do?
Eventually, I ended up working for Helicopter, the studio run by Ethan Trask and Josh Liberson. They had worked with Deborah Needleman on the initial design of *Domino* magazine. Working for them was my first experience in designing larger commercial magazines through redesigns. Josh and Ethan taught me how editorial functions in a conversational way. They were into the collaborative spirit behind their work—collaborating with clients, working with them to produce something lasting, rather than just embellishing something and then passing it off. I got to think about, how do we refresh something like *Car and*

As long as there are creative people who desire to make great things, there's going to be a place for that in editorial.

Driver, which was one of my first projects, and then we did a redesign of *Jane* magazine, where I was working with Fairchild for about six months.

A lot of the magazines that we worked on, however, no longer exist. *Domino* shut down; *Jane* shut down three issues after we did the redesign, which was a bummer because we spent so much time on it. So I started getting a little tweaked out at that point. I started to lose a little bit of faith. I grew up being around magazines. But this was 2007, before magazines started picking up steam again and actually understanding how to utilize the internet. It was before social media existed, which is crazy to think.

Why do you think you haven't done more work with mainstream magazines?

The step between freelance senior designer and in-house art director is a massive gap at a lot of these magazines, and they make use of this rotating cast of people who can come in and just execute layouts. And I was always much more into the idea of collaborating and building than being a freelance layout guy.

There were a tough couple of years in there where I freelanced, and I ended up at *New York* magazine briefly. It's funny because I feel like I was there forever, but in retrospect, I was only there for five months. That was an action-packed five months! Props to the people that can keep that up. It was working with Chris Dixon in conjunction with Adam Moss, and Jody Quon, the photo editor. It was amazing watching the genius at work at that place. And that really taught me how to move fast, making quick decisions and understanding that you're also going to be making another issue in a week. So if it's not the perfect layout, the world will move on, that's fine. But the fatigue of the weekly, I wasn't cut out for it.

My friend was the editor of *The Fader,* and they were looking for a new creative director. I ended up going over there for two years, and that was my first time having a hand in all of the different ways the brand was communicating. Not only was I able to produce a big, beautiful, glossy magazine—on nice paper with not so many words and huge photographs, so that was a lot of fun—but they really just gave me the keys to make the magazine how I wanted it to look. And we did a website redesign. I hadn't been involved in a full-360 project like that before. It was a small enough brand where I could do everything from the magazine to the website to event design for shows. That gave me this idea of how the editorial point of view really breaks down into all these moving parts.

Tell us about the work you're doing these days.

After *The Fader*, I had this opportunity to work for Doubleday & Cartwright. They have an in-house magazine, *Victory Journal*, sort of a sub-brand of the studio—which is interesting. We are a full-service creative agency with a strong focus on storytelling. So whether it's making an animation or a garment program or a printed publication or a branding project, we really work in storytelling, with a heavy editorial voice. I wanted to work with people and build products, and really utilize this idea of editorial to speak to people in a platform-agnostic way.

Why do you think editorial appeals so much to brands?

The idea of editorial—custom publications and web experiences and the boutique-y magazine sort of thing—is a very hot item right now. Whether or not brands actually understand how to harness it, they want to be a part of it. That's what's interesting about the supposed "death of the magazine" paradigm. No matter what, people are still a little starstruck by it, and they still want to be a part of this artifact or the idea of editorial. There's something about the texture of that conversation that I think can't really be achieved by very many other things. These brands want the genuine authenticity of that conversation. It's easy to create the look, but it's hard to understand how that genuine conversation is created.

What keeps you excited about the future of editorial design?

What gets me excited is when I see people pull off, in a truly beautiful way, the texture of type and image on the internet. It doesn't happen often, but when that happens, I feel good about the future of it in a digital sense. And I think that there are a lot of ways that it gets convoluted and overcomplicated.

What's naturally going to happen now is, who are the viable brands? What are the stable properties that people trust? The world of editorial still excites me because of stable brands such as *Vogue*—people love *Vogue*. As long as there are brands and creative people who desire to make great things, there's going to be a place for that in editorial. I don't know what that's going to be. I mean, it's easy to say that there's always going to be a printed thing. But given the fact that I got my first email address 15 years ago, and it's funny to think that for half my life, email basically didn't exist, it's hard to anticipate what the hell's going to happen. Who knows? Maybe in a couple of years, we're going to need all the trees that are left to clean out the air on the planet, and they're going to have to make magazines illegal. I have no idea. But I think that conversation, no matter what, is going to be there somehow. •

Case Study:
Apartamento

WEBSITE: APARTAMENTOMAGAZINE.COM

FREQUENCY: QUARTERLY

FORMAT: PRINT

LOCATION: BARCELONA

COFOUNDER AND CREATIVE DIRECTOR:
NACHO ALEGRE

COFOUNDER AND ART DIRECTOR:
OMAR SOSA

EDITOR IN CHIEF: MARCO VELARDI

FOUNDED: 2008

Apartamento is a biannual journal-size magazine about how creative people around the world really live. Its "about" statement declares: "A real living space is made from living, not decorating." The result is something seemingly intimate and authentic, and flipping through its uncoated pages is tantamount to stepping inside for a visit. Founded by Nacho Alegre and Omar Sosa in 2008, *Apartamento* takes readers into the live/work spaces of its subjects ranging from German illustrator Tomi Ungerer to actor and style icon Chloë Sevigny, and cult interior designer Jim Walrod. The magazine also includes a special coloring book insert, *Kinder*, created by artists such as Andy Rementer and Geoff McFetridge.

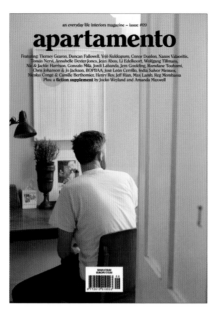

Covers of *Apartamento*. **Opposite page:**
The photography captures people's homes as they really are: lived-in, messy, real.

You live in LA at the moment. How long have you lived in your current home?
I've lived here now for eight years, which is shocking. I can't believe it.

You're quite the gypsy, aren't you?
Yeah. I mean even though my base is here I am a bit like a gypsy; we travel a lot.

Is that the longest time you've ever spent in one place?
Well, no. I was living kind of in Europe for about 20 years, [and] because I've got children I always have a home base. I had one main

I didn't pay him and I didn't charge him rent, you know what I mean? That was the dynamic. I'm always having lots of people and friends over. I have, like, a commune thing going on in my home. I just have one of those houses where people don't want to leave. Currently a friend and his three children are living with me. It's fantastic!

Do you like to cook?
Well, I like cooking but because I have so many people at my house it became better if I just had someone else do the cooking. We sometimes cook as a group. We seem to always be in the

home station, but I travel a lot. Whenever we can, I get out of here. My family has a house in St Barts and we spend a lot of time there too, with cousins and friends.

How would you describe your home in LA?
I have a very nurturing personality and I'm all about family and home. So I have a home where there are always lots of people who come and go. I always seem to have someone living with us – different people who are going through different things in their lives... They give back [though]. I had a chef living with me for a while and he would help me out. He would do a lot of cooking and stuff, I mean

kitchen. We don't really have meals in our house —we don't have a sit down dinner ever— but there's always this community going on. There are always people in the kitchen; there's always food. Everyone in my family's very active - we're always doing something. You know it's nice to sit down and have a meal, but we just don't do that in the normal traditional way other people do. It's a kind of buffet style we have like a buffet thing going. So it's a bit different.

What does your house look like?
I have a Spanish style house. I have six bedrooms – so a lot of bedrooms. I have just like a really nice kind of, homey house.

apartamento · Tierney Gearon

Omar Sosa

Cofounder and Art Director, Apartamento

Omar Sosa studied graphic design at EINA School in Barcelona. After graduating, he formed a studio with Albert Folch, mostly taking on editorial projects. He left in 2009 in order to focus on *Apartamento* and his own design clients. Now he divides his time between Barcelona and Milan, where he also art directs a design magazine for *Corriere della Sera*. Sosa told us about *Apartamento*'s approach to making a shelter magazine that focuses on its inhabitants.

Why did you and Nacho start Apartamento?
Nacho and I were quite fascinated by each other's work before we first met, and when we did, we started thinking of making something together because we both were working for magazines and both very interested in interiors. We both were moving to our first houses, and we found almost all interior publications quite repetitive and boring, and none that really suited our style, so we decided to make our own ideal magazine, a small publication about friends' homes that after one year of work and research became the first issue of *Apartamento*.

Apartamento *didn't invent the 6" × 9" (152.4 mm × 228.6 mm) journal size, but it was one the first small publishers to revive the format. How did you first decide to make your magazine this size?*
I could say it was matter of style, but the truth is that we didn't have much money to spend in the beginning, so we decided to make it as affordable as possible, which turned out to be this format. Then, afterward, we noticed it was the perfect size for making it more intimate and perfect for reading long texts.

Apartamento *is print only. Do you intend to keep it that way?*
I think we all love paper and its language, so making an online version

One of the many fun things about *Apartamento* is its spines, which look especially beautiful when grouped on a bookshelf. Starting with the fourth spine from left, *Apartamento #4* uses a classic composition book pattern; *Apartamento #5* uses a generic crocodile skin pattern; *Apartamento #6*, a pattern by Carl Johan de Geer; *Apartamento #7*, a security-envelope pattern courtesy of Joseph King; *Apartamento #9*, a pattern by Matt Leines; *Apartamento #8*, a pattern by Nathalie Du Pasquier; and *Apartamento #10*, a pattern by Tauba Auerbach. Below is a spread by Andy Rementer from *Kinder*, a kids' supplement.

A good education on classic typography makes you able to understand the best way to break the rules.

The stories and images always seem so genuine and personal. How does the design help communicate that authenticity?
There's no special formula or guideline of what is in or out. I think we just decide depending on our feelings and interests at the given moment. We may drop out a good story once in a while, and publish a less interesting one, but if that's what's right at the moment, that keeps it authentic and not dependent on what people say, or reflecting current trends or what advertisers want.

of it just makes no sense for us at this moment. We would love to find a way to develop the world of *Apartamento* digitally without repeating what we have on paper.

We love the Kinder illustrated section. How did that come about? What made you decide to make a coloring book section for kids?
None of us has kids yet, besides Varda, our COO assistant, but we love them, and we love how homes look when children live there. And illustration is just something we love, and we think coloring books are so fun, so it's as much for those who love illustration as for children. Also we want our magazine to be used, not just read and put back on the shelf.

In what ways have you most needed to adapt or evolve as a designer?
As a designer, I think you always need to evolve. Lately, I've been switching more toward pure art direction rather than design, though I still enjoy designing and being able to spend time on little details.

Are there any editorial design principles that are universal, regardless of media format or platform?
I think typography stands in the center of any editorial design. I'm happy

I had a good education in classic typography because this makes you able to understand the best way to break the rules.

What do you like most about being an editorial designer?

I wanted to be an industrial designer, but I just didn't have enough patience to do all the prototyping and then waiting years to see your product on the market, if it ever even happens. Making books allows you to play with materials, size, and weight—you are creating a product in addition to the pure graphic design on the inside.

What is the hardest thing about being an editorial designer?

It's a very time-consuming job. I mean, some people think that making a book or a magazine is just putting some pictures and text together and using nice typography. But anyone who has made a book knows that even the simplest one takes so much time, and that's not always well paid.

What skills are required for designers on your team?

Good knowledge of typography, some editorial design training, and a lot of curiosity.

How do you approach the idea of redesigning?

I don't like to keep changing the design all the time. It usually takes me a long time to come up with a design that I like and I feel comfortable with, so I prefer to keep changing small things that improve the design and just refreshes it a little bit on each issue. But my designs are very simple, making the content the focus, so by changing the content, you are also changing the design somehow. •

Case Study: Anorak

WEBSITE: ANORAKMAGAZINE.COM

FREQUENCY: FIVE TIMES A YEAR

FORMAT: PRINT

LOCATION: LONDON

EDITOR: CATHY OLMEDILLAS

CREATIVE DIRECTOR/DESIGNER: CATHY OLMEDILLAS

PUBLISHER: THE ANORAK PRESS

YEAR FOUNDED: 2006

The word *anorak* began as an Inuit term for protective, weatherproof outwear. Somewhere down the line, due to the garment's ubiquity among trainspotters, it got appropriated into British slang to mean a hobbyist or nerd. Founder Cathy Olmedillas reclaimed the disparaging label for her publication subtitled "The Happy Mag for Kids." The predominantly illustrated print-only magazine of stories, games, and activities for "boys and girls ages 6 to 12" follows in the tiny footprints of United Kingdom children's magazine *Playhouse* as well as American ones such as *Highlights* and often can seem like it's as much for design-aware parents as it is for their offspring. Although he is no longer on the masthead, the magazine's highly graphic look and feel were initially established by Rob Lowe of design studio Supermundane, creative director for the first twenty-two issues, and is now being carried on by a different designer each issue.

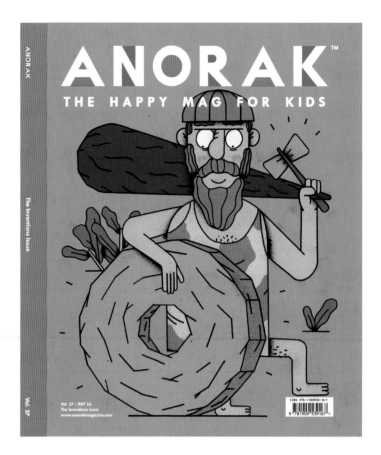

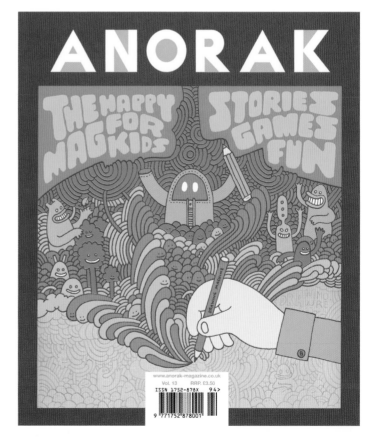

A stack of Anoraks. **Opposite page:** *Covers of* Anorak's Inventions *issue (top) and the* Drawing *issue*

Cathy Olmedillas
Editor, Anorak

How did the idea for Anorak *come about?*
I had been working in magazine publishing for about ten years when I became a mother. I realized that the kids' magazine market was homogenous and hypercommercial and wanted to launch a fun magazine that I could read with my son.

Anorak has a website, but more for e-commerce and company information. Do you feel Anorak *is best suited to being a print experience? What are your thoughts about screen versus paper reading for children?*

Anorak is very proud to be a real magazine, with real paper and real ink. It is at the heart of our commitment to provide kids with a calm, immersive, fun piece of culture, away from screen culture. Never say never, but I am happy for *Anorak* to stay a physical object for now. When I launched *Anorak*, seven years ago, iPhones didn't exist, so it never entered my mind that *Anorak* should be anything else but a paper magazine. Since then, I think kids have many opportunities to enjoy culture on a screen, and sometimes they need a break from it.

The apps you've developed have been for learning games rather than content. Have you considered how touchscreen devices could further Anorak's *content experiences on a serial basis?*
I have considered it. I think touchscreen devices are great, but they have very different functions and benefits to a paper product, so I would always want to do something bespoke for that medium.

You work with some amazing illustrators. What is the process like? Do you start with the illustrator and come up with the ideas together, or do you have the ideas that the illustrator then creates?
The ideas come first, and then I commission the illustrator whose style I feel would fit the feature best. I am very lucky because I receive a lot of fabulous portfolios every day, so I am spoiled for choice. Illustration

All I want to create is something that will keep kids entertained, feed their imagination, and tap into their natural curiosity.

really has come a long way since we launched—there is a lot of great talent out there.

What are some of the key factors to consider when designing an editorial publication for children?
Make it fun, unpredictable, and imaginative. All I want to create is something that will keep kids entertained, feed their imagination, and tap into

their natural curiosity. I don't care much for things such as age group or font size or legibility, and I hate rules!

Do you test with young readers to see what they like and don't like?
Nope, I just connect with the 8-year-old me, and somehow it seems to work! I am a mum, so if there is a story or a subject I am not 100 percent sure about, I will ask my son what he thinks. But it is very rare. I sometimes go to schools to do workshops, and it always enchants me to see how kids interact with the magazine. I think generally they love its anarchic content and the fact that it doesn't take itself too seriously.

How do you select themes for each issue? One recent issue is Writing.

With literacy skills varying so much from age to age, how do you make the subject engaging for kids at all levels?
I always pick the themes about one year in advance, and I try to mix so-called educational subjects with just plain fun subjects. They loosely follow the national curriculum because I do get inspired by some of my son's subjects at school. So, for example, our themes include Fear, Animals, Food, Jungle, and Friendship. I think you can find wonder and fun in anything, even the mundane, and that's what I try to encourage in children. With Writing, I wanted to demonstrate how we take it for granted, and that in fact, it's an amazing thing to be able to write, and it is magical. I also explore how writing has influenced

our history, and there is even a lesson in writing Russian.

Has your own childhood had an influence on the magazine?

I was born in France to a Spanish father and an Italian mother, but I have lived in London for twenty-one years. My father used to work as an engineer, so he favored what he called "proper subjects" such as math and science, which I wasn't very good at. My mother was a stay-at-home mum who is a brilliant knitter and crafter (and I am not). I spent my childhood with my nose in a book or writing in my diary, so I suppose being a writer was always in me, but I really had no idea I would end up running and writing my own magazine. I still can't believe it.

What do you look for in an editorial designer?

I look for someone who is going to be confident enough not to be shackled by rules. And not to let the fact that kids are our readers make them design a page differently. Kids are far savvier than we give them credit for. ●

Case Study: WAX

WEBSITE: READWAX.COM

FREQUENCY: BIANNUAL

FORMAT: PRINT

LOCATION: BROOKLYN, NEW YORK

FOUNDERS/CREATIVE DIRECTORS:
DAVID YUN, AERIEL BROWN, ZAK KLAUCK

YEAR FOUNDED: 2011

WAX is a magazine for urban surfers, a niche that perhaps you never knew existed and hadn't considered reading about. That's just part of the delight of discovering this biannual that has the intimate feeling of a zine but the high aesthetic values of a fine art journal. Whether or not you're part of the community it speaks to or are simply drawn to the physical beauty of its pages, *WAX* makes use of a watery palette in a clean, crisp minimalist design that evokes the loose, organic qualities of the life aquatic. It all began as an idea floating between designers, art lovers, and surfing buddies David Yun, Aeriel Brown, and Zak Klauck.

After coming up with the design and editorial concept, they ran a successful Kickstarter campaign and crowdfunded their first issue, "Dialogues," spring/summer 2012, which sold out of its initial 1,000-copy print run. A second issue, titled "Structures," came out in fall/winter 2012 and followed a structured three-signature format. The first section, "Speaking," features interviews, set in LK Futura, a font customized by Swiss designer Larissa Kasper; the middle section, "Looking," features fashion and photo stories, printed in vibrant color on a glossy paper stock; while the third section, "Writing," features nonfiction narratives in a large, readable serif. Like any zine, the publication has been a labor of love, one that has largely been funded by the team itself (Yun says they are working on a financial plan so the magazine will be self-sustaining). Despite the challenges of independent publishing, the *WAX* crew is riding it out.

Marble pattern by Kristian Henson for *WAX* issue #2.

David Yun

Cofounder and Cocreative Director, WAX Magazine

How many people work on Wax *and what do they do?*
WAX primarily consists of three partners who share almost all creative and administrative responsibilities: Aeriel, Zak, and me. There is so much overlap that it's hard to pin down roles, but in general, Aeriel handles the writing, I do creative direction, and Zak works on design. We also have some amazing help along the way: Luke Stettner is a contributing photo editor, Chris Rypkema assists us with design, and Matthew Anderson helps with social media and marketing. In addition, we frequently collaborate with several artists and surfers including Will Adler, Rob Kulisek, Carmen Winant, Jeremy Liebman, Mikey DeTemple, and Tyler Breuer.

How did you come up with the idea for a New York–based surfing magazine?
We first thought of *WAX*, fittingly, while lying on the beach between sessions. We were inspired by the range of creative people we were meeting in the water and wanted to tell their stories and help shape the growing surf community in New York City. At the time, we didn't have a name or an exact concept for the magazine, but we knew that there was an opportunity for a surf magazine to focus on urban environments around the world, and to focus more on the creative lives of artists who surf rather than on the sport of surfing itself (big airs and such).

Why did you decide to not list yourselves as editors in the masthead?
This relates back to the three of us and our roles being very fluid and overlapping. We see this project as a creative venture that generates a wide range of content. So being just editors seemed like a limiting title, and in some ways, creative direction

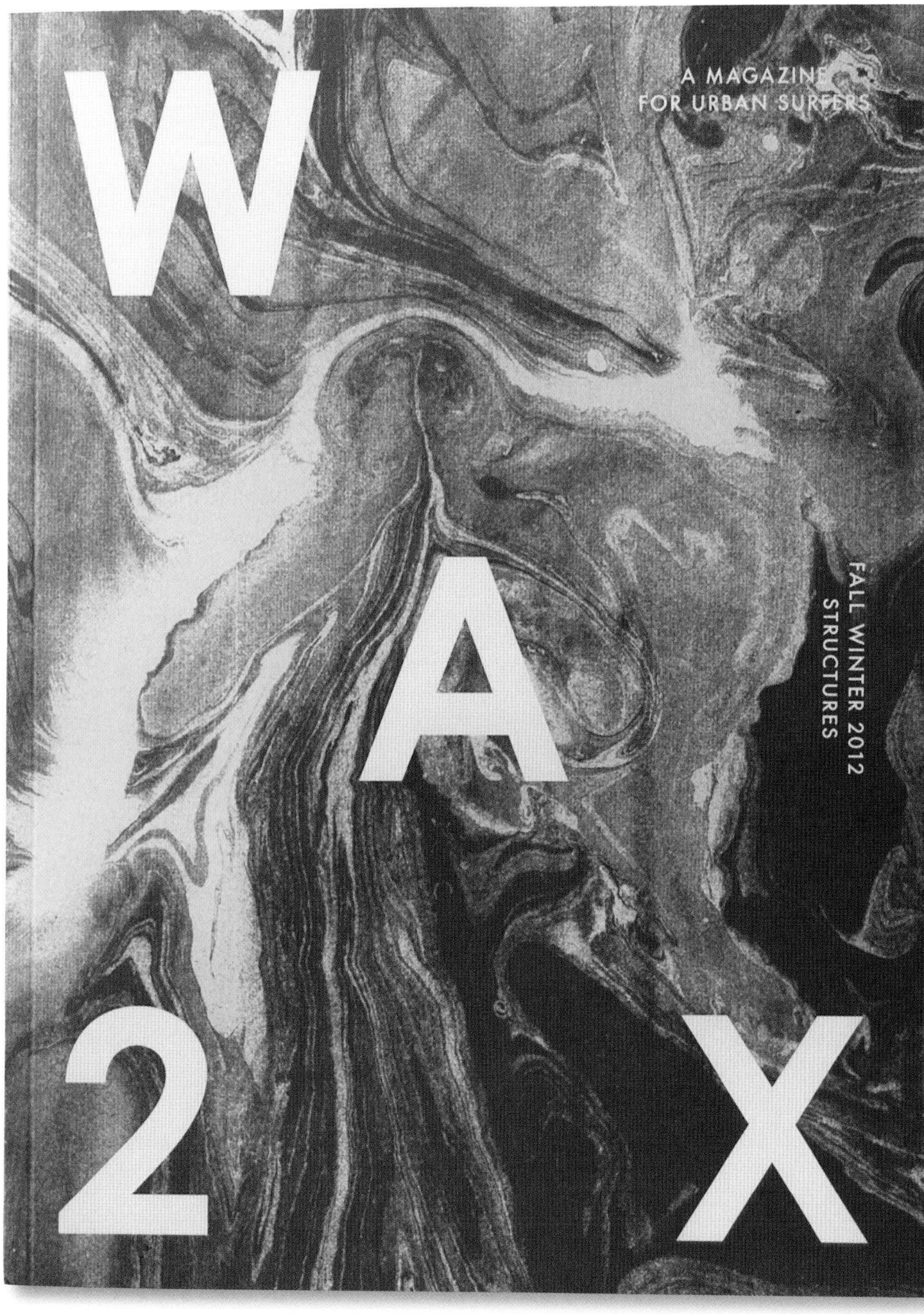
W
A MAGAZINE
FOR URBAN SURFERS
FALL WINTER 2012
STRUCTURES
A
2
X

An essay in *WAX* #2 in the "Looking" section printed on glossy paper (above) and a longer-form piece in the "Writing" section printed on uncoated paper (opposite page).

can encompass so many roles, editing being one of them.

How did you go about the design of the magazine? Is it different when you are also editing the magazine?

The approach to designing our own magazine is different in the simultaneity of design and editorial thinking that goes into each move. While this process at times makes for difficult decision making (over-thinking everything), there is also opportunity for design and editorial issues to be resolved at the same time, and for the two to have a more reflexive relationship. This is the kind of thinking that goes into any kind of design we do, whether it's for a client or for ourselves, but with the magazine,

there's an immediacy to the design and editorial decisions.

In terms of our general approach, we wanted the look of the magazine to be situated far away from any surf magazines we had seen and closer to the visual language of art, fashion, and design publications. We wanted the design to approach the content in a bold and intentional way, giving space to long-form photo and text-based essays. Through our use of artist-generated patterns throughout each issue, we introduced an opportunity for strong visual change from issue to issue. We are still exploring ways to evolve the typography and are planning to make subtle changes in each issue that will gradually evolve the typographic feel of the magazine over time.

Why did you decide to make a print magazine?

Zak and I are both trained in design, and Aeriel has a background in magazines, and through that, all three of us have a real love and appreciation for printed matter. There is something particularly rewarding, in our minds, about making an object versus making something that lives in the digital form. Creating something printed and bound also seemed to fit the kind of stories we wanted to tell and the way we wanted to tell them. It's very hard, for example, to get people to invest in a 3,000-word article on their computers. A printed piece slows the reader down, which can be a nice experience.

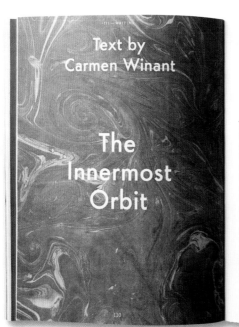

Text by
Carmen Winant

The Innermost Orbit

This is a story about the immediate relationship between our bodies and our spinning planet, as well as the proximate ties between the sea and the sky. Through the examination of a peculiar, sub-surface wave — the Rossby Wave — it will focus on the properties of balance, movement, dynamism and unrivaled stamina. If I have done my job well, reading this will remind you of the closeness of far apart things, the doggedness of time and the ever-abiding mysteries of nature. It might also remind you of why so many children aspire to be astronauts or marine biologists, two disciplines that present the unique possibility of waging adventure into an uncharted void. Though most of them will take on more practical careers when of age, it's an innate curiosity that informs this story all the same. Who, at any point in their lives, wouldn't want to go where maps cannot follow or lead?

***

How do you see editorial design as having changed in the past decade?
Change in editorial design has been driven by a few factors that have also changed the landscape of design in general. The financial crisis has so acutely affected the publishing industry that publishers have had to basically rethink their approach and are still in the process of doing that. Mainstream publishing can no longer follow a simple ad-driven model, and now all editorial content seems to be driven by marketing partnerships and branded relationships.

On the other hand, there has been an incredible explosion of small print publishing driving new journals and magazines, many of which are edited by designers. This puts design completely in the hands of designers, which is a fascinating trend to witness. Self-publishing by designers of course has its own history, which essentially traces back to the roots of printed matter in the fifteenth century and follows a lineage through Eric Gill, the Dada era, Lubalin in the 1970s, and others. But it's incredible to be a part of a current resurgence of designer-driven publishing.

More and more designers see self-publishing as an opportunity for authorship that can support a studio practice, not financially, but in terms of opportunity for a purity of voice (visual, verbal, design). So beyond the content, if a designer has something they want to try to experiment with—typographically, photographi-

> *More and more designers see self-publishing as an opportunity for authorship that can support a studio practice.*

cally—it gives them an opportunity and platform to do that. So the result is an exuberant, but probably mixed, bag: You get an outpouring of design, some of which lacks the skill and hand of a good editor, and some of which rises to the top because of its pure approach.

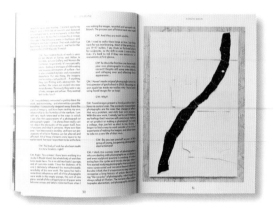

What do you read? Have your reading habits changed in the past five years?

We're inspired by a wide range of books and magazines. For the most part, if a magazine is both printed and available on an e-reader/tablet, the three of us will still read the printed version. This is different for text-driven books. Aeriel reads long-form pieces and books almost exclusively via e-reader, often toggling between books. Beyond using tablet/phone/e-readers for fiction and many long-form essays, our reading habits haven't changed much in the past five years.

What does it take to be able to do design well for editorial content?

Good design for editorial content is the same as good design for anything: a strong concept and strategy that can be applied consistently from the cover to the art direction, down to the editorial voice. It's also important that design decisions don't get weakened by editorial decisions, and vice versa, which is why it's essential for designers and editors to have good communication skills and express their intent early in the process. And of course designers also need a sensitivity to story and sequence, having an understanding of the message of each piece and translating that to a sequence and layout that supports the given message. ●

Resources

To be an editorial designer today means being prepared to learn continuously and relentlessly. The sheer number of resources available is staggering, so we've listed a few trusty ones. For more resources and links, see our website, **editorialexperience.com**.

Typography

Book Typography: A Designer's Manual by Michael Mitchell and Susan Wightman
This comprehensive reference for typography also addesses the entire design, editing, and production process as a whole.

The Form of the Book by Jan Tschichold
This book, published in 1997, is a heavily principled guide of essays on typography.

Fontsinuse.com
This "independent archive of typography" is community-populated, but its contributors posts fascinating type stories on the blog.

Web design

Designing with Web Standards by Jeffrey Zeldman
This book is the gold standard for understanding the role of design and the designer on the web. **zeldman.com/dwws**

Mobile First by Luke Wroblewski
This short polemic makes the case for accessible design across platforms. **lukew.com/resources/mobile_first.asp**

Alistapart.com
Articles by working professionals across the field and essential reading for anyone making websites.

Content Strategy for Mobile by Karen McGrane
Kristina Halvorson, Colleen Jones, and Erin Kissane are all must-read authors on the subject of content strategy, but Karen McGrane's *Content Strategy for Mobile* is a quick yet essential guide for anyone publishing serial content online. How your content loads on readers' smartphone and tablet browsers is only going to become more crucial. Not all readers will buy your app, but anyone curious about what you're doing will come to your website. **abookapart.com/products/content-strategy-for-mobile**

Contents
Contents is an online magazine "at the intersection of content strategy, online publishing, and new-school editorial work." Edited by Erin Kissane (author of *The Elements of Content Strategy*), the site features smart reads such as Paul Ford's "10 Time-frames" (**contentsmagazine.com/articles/10-timeframes**) and "Inside The Silent History," an interview with Eli Horowitz about his iOS serial novel (**contentsmagazine.com/articles/inside-the-silent-history**).

Boxesandarrows.com
Boxes and Arrows is one of the longest-running peer-written online journals for information architecture and interaction design.

UXarchive.com
The UX archive saves screenshots of user flows for a range of tasks on the iPhone. When we suggested adding "Reading" as one of the tasks, cofounder Arthur Bodelec (also one of the creators of the news reader Feedly) happily obliged. Compare how different apps design the reading experience and note the changes in iOS versions.

"The Web Is a Customer Service Medium" by Paul Ford
You might think you already understand the web and what users want, but Paul Ford sums it up perfectly: "The web is not, despite the desires of so many, a publishing medium. The web is a customer service medium." Might as well read everything on ftrain.com while you're there, too. **ftrain.com/wwic.html**

Prototyping

Flinto
flinto.com
Software for iOS app prototyping.

Laker Compendium
lakercompendium.com
HTML and CSS-based tools for publishing to tablets and smartphones.

OmniGraffle
omnigroup.com/omnigraffle
The industry standard for wireframing, diagramming, and documenting for interactive products. The pro version is worth it if you do this work on a regular basis.

Balsamiq
balsamiq.com
Similar to OmniGraffle but less costly, with a great community for sharing.

Journalism

These sites report on developments in journalism from a design and technology perspective.

The Nieman Foundation at Harvard
niemanlab.org

**Poynter Institute School
for Journalism**
poynter.org

Columbia Journalism Review
CJR.org

Newseum
This museum for news posts the daily front pages of newspapers around the world.
newseum.org

Magazine and News Design

Magculture.com
MagCulture is a blog by Jeremy Leslie and is a "resource for anyone interested in editorial design." Jeremy is also the author of *The Modern Magazine: Visual Journalism in the Digital Era*, which is a deep dive into the contemporary magazine.

Coverjunkie.com
Coverjunkie is a "celebration of creative covers and their ace designers," selected by Jaap Biemens, an art director based in Amsterdam.

Newmanology.tumblr.com
Veteran creative director Robert Newman's blog compiles "magazine, newspaper, book, and LP covers, posters, illustration, and other graphic visual joy" from the past and present.

SPD.org
The blog of the Society of Publication Designers is a great resource for finding what's new and what's newly redesigned on newsstands.

Designing News: Changing the World of Editorial Design and Information Graphics
by Francesco Franchi
The gifted art director for *IL* (Intelligence in Lifestyle), a monthly magazine bundled with the Italian newspaper *Il Sole 24 ORE,* presents a beautiful, detailed look at the state of information design in journalism.
francescofranchi.com/designingnews

Tech

Source.opennews.org
Knight-Mozilla OpenNews is a project "designed to amplify the impact of journalism code and the community of developers, designers, journalists, and editors who make it." Read here about the team that built "Snow Fall" at *The New York Times*.

Wilson Miner, "When We Build"
This talk given at the 2011 Build Conference addresses the opportunity and responsibility of building new digital tools and how each of the things we make creates a new environment. **vimeo.com/34017777** (note: his list of resources is useful too: **wm4.wilsonminer.com/build2011**)

Glossary

Alt text

Unlike an image caption, which can be creative in how it describes the content of an image, alt text is meta data for accessibility purposes and needs to say what's happening in it so that screen readers can relay that to uses with vision impairment.

Analytics

Analytics are a tool for measuring user interactions in programmed environments such as websites and software applications (apps). Analytics can be used to improve products, as a way of seeing where users click, tap, or swipe, and then modifying accordingly. They're also crucial for finding out if a product is meeting business goals. Google Analytics is currently the most common platform.

Annual

Published once a year.

Art

In this context, "art" means commissioned illustration and photography. In some cases, as with a photo essay or information graphic, the art is the content. In all other cases, the art either pulls in the reader or demonstrates something in the content that the reader would like to see.

Article post

An article post may be long or short, and should have a headline, byline, teaser or summary, body, and it might also contain other graphic or multimedia elements and links.

Bespoke or custom typefaces

Commissioned typeface design that is intended for a specific publication and for a specific purpose.

Biannual

Published twice a year.

Bimonthly

Published every two months.

Body

The body copy is the content of the article itself, the substance that all other elements serve to support.

Byline

The byline of an article or other post indicates the top billing of who created it ("who it's by"). It's generally for the author of the story and the commissioned photographer and/or illustrator. The style of how it's presented may vary per publication and even per story.

Caption

A caption describes the content of an image in a thoughtful way. When done well, captions illuminate something not obvious in the image or present commentary that echoes sentiments in the accompanying story. Captions need to be clearly connected to the images they are associated with, so as not to be confused with body copy.

Circulation

This refers to how many copies of a periodical reach the marketplace, mainly to help advertisers determine how best to target their desired audiences. Publishers may print a certain number of issues, but circulation is based on the number of readers actually reached. Audit organizations exist to calculate this, and they've started to figure out how the tablet version and tweets factor into the notion of reach. It's still a fairly inaccurate science, but one that affects the bottom line for any ad-funded media company.

Comments

Feedback from readers takes the form of comments, which may appear down the page from an article or, on newer platforms such as Medium, in a sidebar alongside the text. Some publishers such as *Popular Science* have decided to remove commenting from their sites because of the challenges of moderating them and verifying their accuracy; others, such as *Gawker*, have empowered their communities with more advanced commenting tools, making comments as much of a draw as the story.

Content management system (CMS)

A content management system or CMS is the crucial back-end tool of every multipage editorial website. It's a software application that allows editors to create, maintain, organize, and publish content on web pages. Many large publishers use a custom CMS to handle the breadth of their content (text, graphics, video, etc.), the volume of editors, and production flow. As of this writing, WordPress is one of the most popularly used platforms for editorial websites.

Content strategy

As defined by Kristina Halvorson, author of *Content Strategy for the Web*: "Content strategy plans for the creation, publication, and governance of useful, usable content." It's a complex job, but put simply, the content strategist identifies what kind of a content a site produces, the audience(s) it's meant to serve, how it will be delivered over time, and how it will be consumed over time.

Copy

Copy is essentially words, but can have several meanings, depending on the context. Writers submit text that's called copy after it's been edited. The article text that goes in between <body> tags in your HTML document is called body copy. Copy can sometimes refer to language that's constructed for the purpose of selling or informing. "Read related articles" is dull but informative copy, for example.

Credit

A credit line, like in a movie, tells readers where an image comes from (the rights holder). These should be subtle but still findable, often set in all caps or even sideways (alongside the image or in the gutter) to distinguish from other short pieces of text.

Date stamp

A date stamp communicates when a piece of content was published on the web. It's a small but not insignificant piece of information that may include simply the date or date and time (for frequent news publishers of timely info that may also be updated).

Desktop

This refers to a personal computer that hasn't been designed for mobility and usually stays in one place in either a home or office environment. Screen dimensions (in pixels) vary depending on the monitor, but may range from 1024 × 768 (standard dimension) to 1920 × 1080 (high-definition) and up.

Discovery

The act of discovery is connected with the user experience. The design of a home page, for instance, determines what's important by making it easily discoverable. A search field is the most basic tool for discovery but puts all responsibility on the user. If you want users to notice something, make sure it's easy for them to find it.

Folio

A folio is a printed page number, and may be accompanied by the name of the publication, its date, a kicker, section name, article name, or author name. The purpose of a folio is to allow a reader to find an article referenced in a table of contents or a citation in another publication.

General interest

The opposite of niche, these titles cover a wide range of topics, to serve the broadest possible readership. The editorial mix might include culture, arts, opinion, news, technology, and politics, but usually with a more specific brand personality or bent—such as "women's interest" (think *O The Oprah Magazine*) or regional (*Texas Monthly, New York*).

Headline or Hed

The headline is almost always the largest element presented on an article page. It's the big heading at the top of an article in a magazine or newspaper, and the <h1> heading in your CSS, and should be written in whatever is the house style of the site or publication. In print, it might be artfully constructed to play off a photograph, but for the web it should probably be direct enough that it's understandable by search engines and clear enough to tweet it.

Hierarchy

Hierarchy is an organizational structure that lets the reader know what's most important. This ranking of importance is conveyed through the arrangement in space and scale of text and images.

House style

A house style is a way of writing and presenting information consistently so that, over time, it identifiably belongs to a publication.

Information graphic

Data that may be complicated or difficult for the average reader to understand may be edited and presented as an information graphic. Infographics (for short) are "data visualizations that present complex information quickly and clearly. Think of maps, signs, and charts used by statisticians or computer scientists: Wherever you have deep data presented in visual shorthand, you've got an infographic." (Source: Visual.ly)

Kicker

A short tag that helps the reader understand the context of what comes next. It might indicate a subject category (such as "arts" or "music") or type of writing (such as "opinion" or "essay").

Lead-in or Lede

The lead-in or lede introduces a story to further entice the reader to commit to reading the article. Strong writing is the best way to distinguish a lede, but a visual boost helps. The lede is not another subhead but is part of the body text and should be obvious as such.

Long-form

This term refers not just to the word count of an article (although, technically, it's considered by many to mean 2,000 or more words) but also the quality of the content. Long-form became part of the lexicon after years of believing the web was only good for short blog posts for limited attention spans. Advances in web type, bookmarking/reading tools such as Readability and Instapaper, and recommendation services such as Longform, made in-depth, well-researched and skillfully written stories desirable again.

Metadata

The data within the data contained in your web pages is called metadata. It's part of the any well marked-up document and may include author name, the story title, publication date, description, and keywords.

Moderation

Moderation means that an editor or community of editors is making choices about what's acceptable in the comments section of a website. Terms for how these decisions are made should be clearly stated. But a site that has comments and doesn't use any moderation is going to find a lack of constructive dialogue and a whole lot of spam.

Navigation

Navigation is how users find their way or how your interface's design steers them through your site or application. In general, the site or app's architecture is far more complex than the navigation lets on. The navigation is there not to show everyone everything but to facilitate productive and joyful experiences.

Open Web

The Open Web is the entire basis on which the internet is conceived and developed. Advocated by the W3 (World Wide Web) Consortium,

a series of royalty-free, non-proprietary technologies underpin everything we make online. HTML (Hypertext Markup Language) is the publishing language to produce pages or documents; DOM (Document Object Model) is the application programming interface (API) that dictates the logical structure of documents and the way a document is accessed and manipulated; and CSS (Cascading Style Sheet) is the language for formatting the document content. See:

w3.org/wiki/Open_Web_Platform

Photo essay

A photo essay tells a story through a series of images that is selected, arranged, and edited in relationship to each other, the same way that a succession of well-crafted sentences form a coherent thought.

Production value

This refers to everything from the investment in storytelling assets (writing, photography, graphics, video, etc.) to the way it's distributed to an audience. A perfect-bound luxury magazine printed on heavy paper stock with gorgeously produced photography and custom type might be described as having high production values, while a laser-printed, one-color zine probably has low production values.

Pull quote

A graphic element that uses an excerpt of the article to grab the reader's attention and entice the reader to dive into the article. Pull quotes should be styled differently from the body copy or captions, and are typically a larger type size.

Quarterly

A publication that comes out four times per year, or every three months, or per season.

Responsive design

A strategy and structure for creating websites where the same HTML and CSS code displays differently after detecting the window width, "responding" with a layout that is optimized for the device that normally displays at that width.

Rhythm

The pattern and pacing by which someone reads is rhythm.

RSS feed

RSS stands for Rich Site Summary, but is more popularly known as Really Simple Syndication. Article pages that adhere to good web standards provide XML data that RSS readers (engines) can easily grab and pull into a feed, which users can subscribe to through a service such as Flipboard or Feedly. The data given to an RSS feed could be limited to simply a headline and summary or it might also include a thumbnail image, byline, and even the full article text. Publishers decide how much or how little they want to share with readers before they have to visit the site to read more.

Share tools

Share tools used to be limited to an "email a friend" button (a little envelope icon, maybe) but have evolved to include an array of social media platforms. Articles with share tools encourage sharing behaviors, so publishers have to decide where their readers will want to be (Facebook, and Twitter were the most popular as of this printing).

Short-form

This refers to quick reads that are easy to digest in two minutes or less, and usually timely. Most blog posts are short form. Short-form content might also be more visual than text-driven. Tumblr, for instance, was designed to be a microblogging platform, a place for sharing just a GIF or a link or maybe a few hundred words.

Style guide

An established set of standards for writing or designing content that is enforced across all of a media company's output by a copy editor or design director, respectively. This relates to details large, small, and micro, such as how to style links or ways to indicate the end of a story, or whether or not to use a serial comma (a comma separating each part of a series, like the ones we just used after the words "small" and "story").

Subhead or Dek

A subhead can be a phrase below a headline, a few sentences, or even a question. Its purpose is to clarify and contextualize the headline so that the reader knows whether to invest in the body of the article or move on.

Subscription tools

Buttons on article pages (and home pages) that encourage readers to add a site's RSS feed to their preferred feed reader. Not having the tools visible doesn't prevent someone from adding the link to their feed reader, but having them there does encourage subscription. This is free and not to be confused with the premium subscription services for, say, receiving a year's worth of issues or for full site access.

Tag

Tags, metadata, and keywords are almost always present behind the scenes for a properly coded site, helping with both search and accessibility. A tag is a non-hierarchical term or phrase assigned to a piece of information and that helps to draw related content together.

Taxonomy

The system of classifying the data structure of a website is its taxonomy. This is a hierarchical model that defines categories and subcategories and ultimately influences how all content is organized on the back end.

Teaser

Usually but not always accompanied by a headline and thumbnail image, a teaser quickly tells readers what a piece of content is about or creates enough interest to make someone click and read more.

Trim size

Printed pages are trimmed to make sure all pages are equally sized. This is why pages produced for printing are prepared with bleed areas of as much as a quarter inch to ensure no important information is cut off in the printing process.

About the Authors

PHOTO: DAN MUSICK

Juliette Cezzar is the director of the BFA Communication Design and BFA Design & Technology programs at Parsons the New School for Design in New York City. She established her small studio, e.a.d., in 2005. While books anchor the practice, her work has spanned a variety of media for clients such as the Metropolitan Museum of Art, *RES* magazine, the Museum of Modern Art, VH1, *The New York Times*, Eleven Madison Park, and Columbia University's Graduate School of Architecture, Art, and Planning. She is also the author–designer of four books: *Office Mayhem* (Abrams), *Paper Pilot*, *Paper Captain*, and *Paper Astronaut* (Universe/Rizzoli). She holds a B.Arch. from Virginia Tech and an MFA in graphic design from Yale University.

Sue Apfelbaum is an independent Brooklyn-based writer, editor, and content strategist whose primary interests center on design, art, music, and film. She is the former editorial director for AIGA, the professional association for design, and prior to that was an editor for *RES*, a bimonthly magazine for digital creators. She writes about design for *Communication Arts*, *Surface*, Red Bull Music Academy, and Adobe, and works on editorial and content strategy for the website of the Jewish Museum. Sue studied English and anthropology at the University of Vermont and user experience design at General Assembly in New York.

Acknowledgments

We are especially grateful to everyone who took time away from their busy production schedules to meet with us, or email or Skype with us, give us feedback on our writing, and share their knowledge about editorial, web, and product design. Beyond their generosity with their time for the book, the world is a better place for reading because of their dedication and persistence when it comes to their work. Our sincerest thanks go out to Jeanette Abbink, Thomas Alberty, Tom Bodkin, Alex Breuer, Mandy Brown, Stella Bugbee, Blake Eskin, Andrea Fella, Paul Ford, Eli Horowitz, Will Hudson, David Jacobs, Chris Johanesen, Justin Thomas Kay, Josh Klenert, Grace Lee, Andrew Losowsky, Tim Moore, Renda Morton, Steve Motzenbecker, Cathy Olmedillas, Michele Outland, Devin Pedzwater, Natalie Podrazik, Sam Potts, Robert Priest, Michael Renaud, Derrick Schultz, David Sleight, Omar Sosa, Richard Turley, Khoi Vinh, Krissi Xenakis, David Yun, Jeffrey Zeldman, and Jeremy Zilar.

Burak Nehbit and Camille Gervais were invaluable for their research assistance.

Damien Correll is our hero for making the artwork on our cover.

Index